Lesbian Mothers

Anthropology of Contemporary Issues

A SERIES EDITED BY
ROGER SANJEK

A list of titles in the series appears at the end of the book.

Lesbian Mothers

Accounts of Gender in American Culture

Ellen Lewin

Cornell University Press   *Ithaca and London*

First published 1993 by Cornell University Press.

International Standard Book Number (cloth) 0-8014-2857-2
International Standard Book Number (paper) 0-8014-8099-X
Library of Congress Catalog Card Number 92-54977
Printed in the United States of America
*Librarians: Library of Congress cataloging information
appears on the last page of the book.*

♾ The paper used in this publication meets the minimum requirements of
the American National Standard for Permanence of Paper for Printed
Library Materials Z39.48–1984.

For Beaumont and Rosie,
who stayed with me as long as they could,
and for Liz, who brought me to a new beginning.

Contents

Acknowledgments

This project has involved many people along the way—too many to acknowledge by name here. The exploratory discussions I had on this topic with Harriet Whitehead were followed by more formal conversations with Susan Griffin, Shirley Johnson, Marcia Kallen, and Ina Jane Wundrum. Their advice was essential to the first formulations of a research design, as were the comments and suggestions of therapists, attorneys, researchers, and community service providers whom I talked with early on. Among those who contributed in this way are Alice Abarbanel, Roberta Achtenberg, Susan Bender, Ricki Boden, Barbara Bryant, Christa Donaldson, Renee Epstein, Marilyn Fabe, Ann Garrett, Sherry Glucoft, Margo Hagaman, Carol Hastie, Donna Hitchens, Sheila Israel, Carol Jausch, Katy King, Camille LeGrand, Jill Lippett, Phyllis Lyon, Janice Macombers, Del Martin, Sandra Meyers, Mary Morgan, Byron Nestor, Pat Norman, Saralie Pennington, Cheri Pies, Barbara Price, Sue Saperstein, Donna Scott, John Sikorski, the late Fay Stender, Sarita Waite, Norma Wikler, and Yvette Williams. A meeting early in the project with Mary Jo Risher and Ann Foreman clarified my understanding of the long-term impact of custody litigation on lesbian mothers' lives.

Most vital to the completion of this very lengthy project were the 135 mothers who opened up their lives to me, taking hours to share their experiences and their feelings with little indication of how these confidences would be employed. I cannot acknowledge them by name, but I hope they will find something in this volume that will compensate them for the time they devoted to telling me about themselves.

The work of Terrie A. Lyons as research associate was fundamental to the successful design of the study and collection of data. I have benefited enormously from conversations with her about the interpretation of the findings and was constantly challenged by the clinical perspective she brought to her understanding of the mothers' lives and decisions.

Colleagues and staff at the University of California, San Francisco, and at other Bay Area institutions made tremendous contributions to this project. Victoria Peguillan and Sheryl Ruzek contributed to the preparation of the original proposal, along with staff members at Scientific Analysis Corporation in San Francisco. Betty Kalis was invaluable to the project as a consultant during the preparation of the interview schedule. Beverly Cubbage, Barbara Jordan, and Andrea Temkin had the major responsibility for the transcription of the interviews, aided by other staff from the Medical Anthropology Program and the University clerical pool.

As the project continued, Linnea Klee and Judith Barker served very ably as research assistants. Alan Bostrom trained project staff in the use of SPSS. Margaret Clark, Carol McClain, Ann W. Merrill, Virginia Olesen, and Harry F. Todd, Jr., provided advice and encouragement.

When I began this project, other research efforts in related areas were beginning as well. There was a tremendous amount of sharing among those of us who were undertaking this work, and our interactions were remarkably free of competitive feelings. Those whose collegiality I especially appreciated were Beverly Hoeffer, Mary Hotvedt, Martha Kirkpatrick, Jane Mandel, and Daniel Ostrow.

The preparation of this book in its final form owes an immeasurable debt to those colleagues and friends who spent many hours reading, evaluating, and criticizing the various drafts of the manuscript. I thank especially Mary Anglin, Melinda Cuthbert, Julie Hemker, Lois Helmbold, Kathleen Jones, Esther Newton, and Wendy Sarvasy for the important contributions they made to this work. I also thank Earl Klee for his useful suggestions in regard to Chapter 9.

An earlier version of Chapter 8 appeared in *Uncertain Terms: Negotiating Gender in American Culture*, edited by Faye Ginsburg and Anna

Tsing; their insightful comments while I was preparing that paper were enormously helpful to me as I returned to the larger project of this book. I thank them and Beacon Press for permission to use the material here. I also presented portions of the book at a Wenner-Gren symposium on the politics of reproduction in November 1991. The critiques of all the symposium participants, but especially those of Rosalind Pollack Petchesky and Shellee Colen, and of the organizers, Rayna Rapp and Faye Ginsburg, were central to the thinking I have done since then in trying to understand what I have accomplished in this project and what I need to do next. Carole Browner read the penultimate version of the manuscript with great care. She has known me so long that she knows what I mean to say when even I'm not sure, so she was often able to help me unravel my most wayward sentences. Most particularly, I acknowledge the meticulous comments Kath Weston offered on the entire manuscript in its final stages; her eye for detail and her clear understanding of what I was really trying to achieve prevented me from losing track of my own objectives. As series editor, Roger Sanjek has been consistently supportive, offering incisive comments even as he must have wondered whether I was ever going to finish. Peter Agree, of Cornell University Press, has been cheerful and encouraging throughout the preparation of the book and I am grateful for his patience.

This project could never have been completed without the support of the National Institute of Mental Health (Grant MH-30980) and the Rockefeller Foundation Gender Roles Program. Also essential to its completion have been the support and encouragement of valued friends: Dennis DeBiase, Mary L. Hackney, Ann W. Merrill, Esther Newton, the late Barbara Rosenblum, and Helene Wenzel. I thank them for their confidence in me and their willingness to challenge me during my many bouts of anxiety and self-doubt. Most particularly, I owe a boundless debt to Liz Goodman, whose resilience has never wavered and whose ability to shore up my sagging spirits has been without limits.

ELLEN LEWIN

San Francisco, California

Prologue

Whenever people learn that most of my work concerns mothers and mother-
hood, they have one predictable question: Am I a mother? Learning
that I'm not leads to further questions. If my interest in mothers does
not come from personal experience, then surely I must be drawn to
study mothers either because I'm trying to decide whether to become
one or (increasingly the assumption as I have advanced in age) because
my research focus represents a way to compensate for losing my
chance to be a mother. When I reveal my devotion to teaching and the
pleasure I take in working with young people, these same inquisitors
are convinced that they have located yet more evidence that I need to
resolve my nonmaternal state. My students (and very likely my many
cats, as well) are obvious child surrogates.

But a desire to be a mother is not what drives my work. I have
never wished to be a mother and have little firsthand experience with
small children. My feelings about motherhood when I began to study
it were not unlike those of any other anthropologist encountering a
strange and temporarily opaque local custom.

An incident that occurred while I was conducting fieldwork with
Latina immigrants in San Francisco illustrates the abyss that I perceived
between myself and women who were mothers. I was visiting with
one of my informants, a young mother of three, recently arrived from
Mexico. Several of her relatives were gathered in her home, all women
in their twenties (as I was at the time) and all mothers. For most of the
afternoon, the five mothers and I conversed in the kitchen while their
seventeen children, all under the age of five, played in the next room.
From the noises I could hear, I could only assume that the children were

systematically destroying every item of furniture in the room, but not before spilling Cokes and scattering food in every direction. As the afternoon wore on, I found it increasingly difficult to concentrate on anything besides the terrible headache I was getting. The women appeared to enjoy the tumult, and energetically competed with each other over whose child was most rambunctious. When not discussing their children, they directed their attention to their concerns about me and the fact that I had no children. How did I cope with the loneliness? How would I deal with the isolation I would undoubtedly face as I grew older? Who would take care of me in later years? While I was totally overwhelmed by the immediate assault these children mounted against my sanity, the women's focus was on the ways those same children connected them to the world and eventually would grow to perform many essential roles for them.

This story is not unusual. Mothers everywhere learn to cope calmly with the interruptions and noise their children produce. But what struck me at the time was that the meaning of motherhood for these Latina women was not at all the same as what I felt about it. Like them, I was a woman, but unlike them, I did not build my expectations for the future around motherhood. My interest in studying mothers was sparked then not by my resemblance to these women but by my acute sense of difference from them. For the Latinas, motherhood provided a connection—though an indirect one at best—to their economic future. Motherhood might mean many other things to me, but I knew it would never mean this.

My work with Latina immigrants convinced me that looking at motherhood as a strategy would be a productive way to examine motherhood in other populations as well. How would the strategies differ for women with different economic constraints and with different beliefs about the inevitability of motherhood? I knew a number of lesbian mothers through my involvement in the lesbian community. How would women who were not expected to be mothers make sense of their maternal situations? What kinds of strategies would they construct to deal with the problems they faced, and how would they view the future?

At the time I began to consider writing a research proposal on lesbian mothers, I was engaged in a personal struggle over the kind of career I would have as an anthropologist. In 1969, midway through my career in graduate school, feminism emerged as a force in my life. More than any of my previous political commitments, the women's movement came not only to shape my "personal" life but to define my academic interests. As a result, my progress in graduate school and in my early professional years became increasingly tied to the development of an anthropology of women.[1]

Like others involved in the development of the new feminist academic specializations, I felt I should generate knowledge that would help to eradicate sexism and patriarchal domination; I scrutinized each prospective research project for its potential applicability to what seemed to be the central problems facing women out in the world. Further, as a lesbian, I felt a special obligation to focus my energies on a "lesbian project"; at the same time, I was concerned, not without reason, that my fledgling career might prove to be a casualty of this kind of commitment.

Studying lesbian mothers seemed to meet all the criteria I had for turning my research into a meaningful social contribution, and for devising a way to maintain an explicitly feminist, and possibly lesbian feminist, agenda in my work. There was an obvious need to generate knowledge about this highly stigmatized population, first, to make its existence visible, and second, to help dispel the stereotypes that prevailed in custody challenges and that could be considered responsible for injustices in the resolution of these cases. I felt that this work not only would be the next logical step in my career but would turn it toward purposes nobler than mere scholarship.

But when I first began planning the research, I found myself being rather secretive about what I was up to. I had landed a minor research position, my first job after completing graduate school, and when I first tentatively mentioned my new interests to a senior colleague, I got the distinct impression that my topic created some discomfort. Convinced that I could not possibly conduct such unconventional research in a regular university department, I began working on a grant proposal with the development office of a private research organization known for sponsoring a range of sometimes radical research projects.

While I was still developing the preliminary version of my proposal, I moved to a different department at my university for a year of postdoctoral training. A senior colleague there, not coincidentally a lesbian, showed great interest in my work, and immediately offered me the resources of her department along with the opportunity to be the principal investigator (PI) on the grant, should it be funded. This was a significant offer, since junior researchers in my position often had to content themselves with subordinate status on their own projects, while senior faculty members served as PIs, sometimes enhancing their reputations with work done by the younger researchers. The offer also carried with it, at least at that time, the possibility of a future academic affiliation, since other faculty there had tended to be offered appointments only after serving an apprenticeship of sorts during several years of "grant-hustling." With this offer in hand, I extricated my project from the private research organization and began to prepare a final revision of my proposal.

My senior colleague, now my mentor, also advised me about how to apply for a grant. She demystified the process of approaching funding agencies, advised me about those I should target and how to get assistance from agency staff, and recommended that I think about doing a project far larger and more ambitious than the one I had originally contemplated.

Her encouragement, and that of other colleagues, made me feel that I had come of age as a scholar. I was thirty years old, one year out of graduate school, and very self-conscious about being a lesbian in a professional environment. My ideas not only were being taken seriously but were being received enthusiastically by an audience of seasoned researchers. A department research seminar took up my sampling design; various colleagues offered suggestions and amendments, and no one suggested that this topic was too hot to handle or a threat to the respectability of the department. Although I never discussed my personal stake in a topic concerning lesbians, it seemed clear to me that my colleagues understood that I was a lesbian researcher working on a lesbian topic, and that they found nothing wrong with that. The mere fact that the project could be developed as a conventional research grant proposal meant that not only the study but I myself had become legitimate.

I now understand that the exigencies of applying for, and later receiving, federal research funds had a powerful effect on the shape of the research I did on lesbian mothers. I applied to the National Institute of Mental Health (NIMH) during a time when the Institute was regularly supporting controversial social research. My application was considered by a committee at the NIMH charged with supporting research on something loosely labeled "social problems." This funding pattern depended on a broad construction of "mental health" as including the ordinary round of social behavior, particularly with reference to populations at risk for some kind of discrimination or economic deprivation.[2]

Scholars on the review committee were known to be primarily sociologists, social psychologists, and psychiatrists; their preference was for highly quantified hypothesis-testing designs, with standardized research instruments producing data amenable to statistical manipulation. It was clear that proposals for small-scale ethnographic studies of communities, the sort of thing I had been trained to do, would not fare well in this environment. As I became committed to actually getting the project funded, I accommodated the notion that I would have to do a large comparative study and so would have to include a control group of heterosexual mothers.

After some consultation by phone, I submitted a preliminary proposal to a senior staff member of the Institute. He showed great interest in me and my project, offering to assist me with the logistics of grant writing and with the sensitive politics of submitting a "gay" proposal to a federal agency. At the time, it never occurred to me that this intensive coaching might go beyond the usual requirements of his position, but months later, when we happened to meet, I realized that he was gay too. Among his suggestions was the advice that I change the title of the proposal so that the "L-word" would not appear in either the title or the abstract. His concern was that Senator William Proxmire or one of his minions, then on the lookout for federally funded research that could be ridiculed with the notorious Golden Fleece Award, would be less likely to notice the proposal if its title were sufficiently bland. The title became "Single Mothers: Adaptive Strategies."

I offer this account of the genesis of the project that became this book less in a confessional spirit than out of a commitment to the notion that scholarship is never simply an intellectual enterprise. I began thinking about studying lesbian mothers in 1975, submitted a proposal in 1976, carried out research in 1977 to 1981, and have struggled since then to transform an investigation done at a particular historical and personal moment into a work that would speak to a changing world and reflect my changing voice.

The years it has taken me to produce this book are also years during which uncertain employment and competing obligations battled with my desire to share the worlds of lesbian mothers with the public. Two cross-country moves, a period of employment as a typist, self-doubt, and constant reevaluation of the meaning of the project fed into what appeared to be a pattern of procrastination. But I now understand that I could not have finished any sooner. Not only did I have to wait for intellectual currents to offer me a way to jettison the positivistic stance promoted by the federal grant structure, but I could not complete this book before the "L-word" had moved toward becoming a complex and highly differentiated concept. With the growth of the new field of lesbian and gay studies, the need for secrecy and subterfuge is slipping into history, and while I know that our struggles are not over, it now seems that a promising future lies ahead.

Lesbian Mothers

I

Looking for Lesbian Motherhood

In December 1975, in Dallas, Texas, a lesbian mother named Mary Jo Risher lost custody of her nine-year-old son after her older, teenaged son gave testimony against her before a jury. I learned about the case when the *San Francisco Chronicle* picked up the story; the paper's front page ran a close-up photograph of the mother's reaction when she heard the verdict. Her face was twisted in agony and the picture was absolutely heart-wrenching.

By the time I saw this picture, I had come to know another lesbian mother fairly well. She was a generation older than I, and she had lost custody of all three of her children in the early 1950s after her former husband called the police to report that she was sleeping with a woman. The police burst in, arrested both my friend and her partner, and removed the children to foster care, where they remained for several years. Only after the death of her former husband was she able to regain custody, and this only after managing to convince the court that the lesbian episode had represented a "phase" that had now ended.

This was the context within which I began the research that has led to this book. At the time I began this work, in 1977, lesbian mothers and their families were not commonly discussed when the topic of the "changing American family" was raised. Most of my colleagues were confused when they learned of my intention to investigate lesbian mothers. Where would I find such people? How could a lesbian be a mother, they asked; wasn't that a contradiction in terms?[1]

The years since I began this work have been a time of transition for the particular population I worked with and for gay and lesbian people in general. Scholarship on gay and lesbian issues has emerged and begun to receive academic recognition, contributing to the evolution of my intellectual and personal perspectives on these issues.[2] They have been years during which homosexuality gained a public face— and an increasingly respectable one, at that—and lesbian motherhood has become a far more visible phenomenon.

During this period, public concern with gender, motherhood, and sexual orientation has changed. Feminism has given way, it seems, to the pluralism of "postfeminism";[3] at the same time, in the wake of the Reagan years, much popular discourse appears to be concerned with the rediscovery of so-called traditional values.[4] During the years I was working on this project, the feminist critique of marriage and the family as sources of patriarchal domination appears to have collapsed, to be replaced by a more civil-rights-oriented emphasis on access to the economic and social privileges associated with these institutions.[5]

This shift has also involved a heightened awareness and celebration of what are taken to be the unique psychological and spiritual attributes of mothers, a shift intrinsic to a growing acceptance of a "cultural feminist"[6] stance in the wider lesbian community[7] and which has been influenced by the publication of books on motherhood with a lesbian-feminist slant.[8] Homosexuality also has moved more squarely into public consciousness and may, depending on one's reading of current trends, be becoming more acceptable to the general population;[9] at the very least, its increasing visibility has meant that lesbian mothers are far less obscure today than they were when I began my research.[10] Technology has become a relatively routine dimension of many women's reproductive lives, apparently expanding options and even permitting older and unmarried women—whether they be heterosexual or lesbian—more easily to contemplate not only motherhood but pregnancy and childbirth. The irony here is that while motherhood is culturally preferred and normalized, even for lesbians, mothers share with other women diminished economic options and low occupational status. At the same time that pronatalism has made a comeback, the society devotes few resources to child care, health care, education, housing, or other areas of vital concern to parents.[11]

This changing political climate, both in feminism and in the wider society, has had troubling consequences for my work. While my earliest concern was to validate the very existence of lesbian mothers and to show that they were "good enough" to keep their children, now my findings threaten to support a trend that seems to privilege motherhood over nonmotherhood, regardless of sexual orientation. The similarities between lesbian and heterosexual mothers which I document, when considered from this perspective, suggest that motherhood, even more clearly than sexual orientation, defines womanhood, thereby intensifying the already existing bifurcation of women into mothers and nonmothers.

My early effort to gain a rightful place for lesbian mothers in the feminist reexamination of the family was only one example of a growing concern with carving out a place for lesbians in the expanding literature on gender and the family. This was also a period characterized by continuing feminist academic concern (both in anthropology and in other disciplines) with describing the nature of women's oppression across cultural boundaries and thereby legitimizing "women" as a domain for research. If women are a "group," characterized by universal, defining features, then sex oppression might be understood better and eventually defeated.[12]

What establishing the legitimacy and reality of lesbian mothers seemed to mean in 1976, when I first began to think about this issue, was describing them and showing that they were not different from other mothers. What did I mean by "different"? Community concern at the time was centered on what seemed to be a growing number of custody cases, cases that lesbian mothers usually lost. The Mary Jo Risher case was only one of a number of highly publicized cases in which judges (or in the Risher case, a jury) assumed that lesbians could not, by definition, be adequate mothers, or, more seriously, that by definition they were likely to be "bad" mothers. Mothers in these cases either lost custody of their children or won custody under highly compromised conditions, often with the stipulation that they not live with their partners or not allow their children to have contact with them.[13]

The "Sandy and Madeleine case" provides a good example of the kinds of issues that tended to emerge in custody cases. Sandy and Madeleine were two mothers who met through their children's Sunday school. Both staunch fundamentalist Christians, they never thought that their relationship could be immoral, since "God had brought them together." In 1971 their ex-husbands joined together to try to obtain custody, going back to court repeatedly during the 1970s each time judges gave the mothers custody with various sorts of conditions. Sandy and Madeleine felt so sure that their family was wholesome and normal that they had a film made about themselves, *Sandy and Madeleine's Family,* originally to be used in court, but later going into general circulation in lesbian communities around the country.[14] The film emphasized the family's strong religious values, the importance the mothers gave to (particularly outdoor and athletic) activities with the children, and the warmth and nurturance of their relationships with their own and each other's children.

This film was only one of the indicators of the centrality of custody cases in the way the organized lesbian community approached motherhood at the time that I began thinking about these issues. For example, in a major popular collection of articles about the diversity of lesbian experience, *Our Right to Love,* only two out of some fifty articles deal with lesbian mothers.[15] One focuses on legal, and specifically on custody, problems,[16] while the other, written by a psychologist, takes up the question whether and how to come out to one's children, an issue that derives some of its importance from the implications it may have in custody disputes.[17]

Given these concerns, I felt my responsibility would be to demonstrate that lesbians were at least *ordinary* mothers, and therefore likely to be "as good as" heterosexual mothers in comparable social and economic circumstances. It seemed to me that the basis on which custody cases were argued needed to be challenged, that the focus should be on the ways in which lesbian mother families, like other families, met the basic and recurrent needs of their children, rather than on the mother's affectional preferences. This also meant to me that research needed to be more sociological and structural than psychological, shifting concern from how the mother's sexuality or the absence of a father would affect the children's development to the ways in which the daily lives of lesbian and heterosexual female-headed families would tend to coincide.

Popular Feminism and Feminist Scholarship:
Assumptions about Motherhood

Though the reasons for their conclusions varied, feminists of many backgrounds and theoretical orientations had tended to view motherhood as the source of the problem we all sought to address: why women are devalued, deprived, or oppressed in so many, if not all, of the world's societies. Some reasoned that women's reproductive specialization, and particularly their tendency to have primary responsibility for the care of children, determined the division of labor by sex, insofar as child care was incompatible with many economic roles dominated by men.[18] Other focused on the symbolic impact of motherhood, seeing it as the basis for women's "otherness" in all cultures.[19] Psychoanalytically inclined theorists called our attention to the intrapsychic level;[20] those more concerned with social structure looked at the ways in which motherhood defined women's concerns on the more private level, blocking their acquisition of the tools needed for manipulation of the public domain.[21] And many feminists, coming from less academic perspectives, also generated theories of women's oppression which focused on motherhood or reproduction as the "culprits" responsible for women's enslavement.[22] While most early feminist analyses linked the oppression of women to the social and cultural organization of reproduction, many later "cultural feminists" instead emphasized ways in which motherhood endowed women with distinct (and possibly superior) moral or spiritual capacities.[23]

All of these perspectives tend to conflate motherhood and womanhood, as though they were interchangeable, mutually defining, and as though the status of woman could be entirely understood with respect to the meaning of motherhood in a particular situation. In the early period of feminist theorizing, the assumption that women's oppression was universal was accompanied by the notion that women must be viewed as victims of cultures they did not devise. Male dominance, or patriarchy, was simply there (and probably always had been), and women had to live with its consequences, somehow finding a way to manage their devalued situations.

It seemed to me, however, that motherhood, rather than being a unitary phenomenon (a misapprehension further enforced by the single word we use to describe "mothers"), could also be viewed in a more dynamic fashion. I began to think of motherhood as a strategy for dealing with devalued status, at the same time that it might be one of the causes of that status, and I approached motherhood specifically as an economic strategy. My early work on lower-class Latina immigrants, for instance, indicated that they tended not to see motherhood as a choice. Nevertheless, once women were mothers, their ongoing strategies all began from the resources offered by motherhood, sometimes involving highly self-conscious manipulations of ties with children.[24]

Lesbian mothers, I reasoned, would differ from the Latina mothers in that they could not avoid being more purposeful and self-conscious about their situations as mothers. In particular, those who had had their children outside of marital situations—that is, the women who had become mothers through donor insemination or adoption—probably had entered into motherhood voluntarily, despite its supposed negative effects on future opportunity and access to the public domain. A central question, then, was why, if motherhood is the source of women's devalued status, do women become mothers? And why, more to the point, do women who perceive themselves as having other options, especially women who cannot become mothers by accident, purposefully propel themselves into this problematic situation?

At the time I began to plan my research, virtually nothing apart from limited clinical reports had appeared on lesbian motherhood in the scholarly literature,[25] though several psychological studies got under way about the same time I began. These few were all tightly controlled comparatives studies of children of lesbian mothers and matched samples of children from "father-absent homes," all of which isolated variables presumed to indicate emotional adjustment or "normal" sex-role learning.[26] What little I could find in popular sources mainly took the form of personal narratives appearing in feminist and gay media as well as in *Mom's Apple Pie,* the newsletter of the Lesbian Mothers National Defense Fund.[27] I also located numerous accounts of custody problems,[28] and a small body of more polemical writing about the place of motherhood in a future Lesbian Nation.[29] Discussions of motherhood appeared with some regularity in radical feminist/separatist publications such as *Off Our Backs* and *The Furies,* with debates frequently focusing on the "problem" of male children and on the need for more collective forms of child rearing.

Since there were so few scholarly works on lesbian mothers, I depended heavily on scholarly (and sometimes popular) writings on divorce, unwed mothers, matrifocality, and single mothers in poverty.[30] On the basis of reports of custody problems and anecdotal material on lesbian mothers in popular works, I anticipated a range of problems and issues likely to be significant for lesbian mothers. The literature on lesbianism available during this period either was silent on the subject of motherhood or mentioned it only briefly; far more attention was devoted to questions of etiology and debates about pathology, along with speculation about sexual behavior and psychological status,[31] though an important article by John Gagnon and William Simon placed great emphasis on pervasive similarities in the socialization and emotional experience of lesbians and heterosexual woman, thus indirectly suggesting that lesbians *could* be mothers.[32]

The research design I finally settled on, organized as a comparative study of single mothers and developed to meet the requirements of a federal funding agency, was grounded in a growing conviction that lesbian mothers were really "just" single mothers who faced some additional challenges. (The Appendix provides details on my research design and methods.) In other words, I could pursue my desire to demonstrate the lack of significant differences between lesbian mothers and others by framing lesbian mothers as "single mothers." Once lesbian mothers had been transformed into single mothers, a deviant but relatively benign category, I could more easily make my case for tolerance.

Framing lesbian mothers as single mothers was already a congenial perspective, I should add, in that it conformed to my underlying notion that women, regardless of situational variations, share fundamental common experiences, and that these experiences lead to, or somehow are implicated in, their predicament in patriarchal society. As Rayna Rapp has noted, "single mother" (like "working mother") is a symbol in transition, no longer designating the strictly stigmatized "unwed mother" or the remaining parent in a "broken home," but rather signifying the growing validation of a common American domestic arrangement.[33] My thinking was that lesbian mothers, insofar as they share with other single mothers particular material circumstances, most of which are related to the absence of an adult male from the domestic unit, also are likely to be subject to similar sorts of "oppression;" that is, low incomes, difficulty obtaining adequate housing and child care, feelings of being overwhelmed by responsibility for the children, low prestige in the community, and so forth. I did anticipate some differences as well, reasoning that lesbian mothers would be more vulnerable to custody litigation or threats of such litigation, and that lesbian mothers' access to traditional—that is, kin-based—systems of social support would be impaired.

What were the consequences of this strategy for the findings generated by the research? There can be little doubt that the final design of the project—comparative, framed in a quantitative mode, and ultimately tied to the notion that lesbian mothers could be best understood with reference to other (heterosexual) single mothers—had a significant impact on the conduct of the inquiry and on the kinds of results the research generated. Despite the fact that the focus on "single motherhood" as a unifying theme was primarily a strategy intended to make the study workable within the federal grant context, the terminology started to take on a life of its own as the study progressed. Single mothers began to seem like a bounded group, similar to an ethnic group or a tribe, rather than the reification of a label I had chosen to use for reasons of convenience. Questions framed from this standpoint made it seem the "lesbian" was something to be added to "single," the source of additional oppression, but not the source of fundamental difference.[34]

I knew from the beginning that "single mother" was not necessarily the way either lesbian or heterosexual mothers designated themselves—that is, not a "native category"—but reminded myself that the term was just shorthand for the general civil status of the mothers I was studying. From a purely legal point of view, they were "not married" to the fathers of their children, a fact that influenced, or sometimes even determined, their economic status, their position in the judicial system, and the nature of the daily dilemmas they faced as parents, particularly with respect to the problem of bearing the primary responsibility for the survival and well-being of their children.

Narrative and Identity

Starting with the goal of destigmatizing lesbian mothers, of proving that they were just as worthy of custody of their children as nonlesbian mothers facing comparable material challenges, I was gratified to find that the narratives of both lesbian and nonlesbian mothers focused on very similar experiences in their roles as heads of their families. For example, despite my early expectations that lesbian mothers would tend to substitute friendship for kinship ties in constituting support networks, my interviews showed something very different. Lesbian mothers, no less than heterosexuals, regarded family members, particularly their parents, as the most reliable sources of support and as their most appropriate resources when times were hard.[35] This pattern did not seem to be seriously altered by the strains that the women's revelation of their lesbianism often imposed on family relationships. Though some of the women endured angry confrontations or periods when they and their relatives ceased communication, most commonly the passage of time seemed to make some sort of accommodation possible. Mothers I interviewed explained that their parents could not endure a permanent rupture, that while they often continued to raise objections to some aspect of their daughter's "lifestyle," they were able to find a basis for compromise. Family ties were simply too profound to be broken permanently, they explained, sounding much like heterosexual mothers who had disagreements of other sorts with their families.

Similarities between the accounts of lesbian and heterosexual mothers were not limited to their relationships with their families. Mothers in both groups also reported that they went to great lengths to encourage their children's relationships with their fathers, even with considerable provocation to the contrary; that they tended to seek out other single mothers, regardless of sexual orientation, as friends; that their friendships with people who were not parents became attenuated and fraught with mistrust over time; and that they expected relatively little support from sexual partners, whether they were women or men. Mothers who faced a custody battle or the threat of one mounted very similar strategies of avoidance and appeasement, whether the women were lesbian or not.

Similarly, the language lesbian mothers used to discuss what it meant to them to be mothers echoed that of heterosexual mothers. The association of being a mother with "goodness" was striking, as was pervasive imagery of motherhood superseding and overwhelming other sources of identity. The women spoke with equal intensity of their sense that motherhood formed the focus of their identities, both materially and spiritually, and that it gave value and significance to their lives.

The search for identity through motherhood was a quest that lesbians seemed to share with unmarried heterosexual women. Many mothers described themselves as having lived without a focus or worthwhile purpose until they had a child. They saw motherhood as having stimulated the emergence of creativity and industry, so that they now lived more productive, worthwhile lives. A few lesbian mothers used the word "single" to refer disparagingly not to women without partners but to women who had no children. They described such women as having significantly different (and less worthy) interests and goals, and spoke with some intensity of their motherhood as a more crucial determinant of their identities than their lesbianism, a more compelling indicator of loyalties and affiliations. Such usages alerted me to the need to examine motherhood not only as a practical condition but as a moral domain, one that enables mothers of all kinds to demand public recognition and to make claims to cultural, if not material, benefits.

But did this mean that something about being a single mother was a shared experience for both lesbian and heterosexual women? My growing understanding that these accounts would be best interpreted as having cultural, rather than descriptive, significance pointed to the problematic nature of the "single mother" label as a way to think about these women. Lesbian and heterosexual mothers framed their narratives similarly and selected particular experiences as meaningful and worth describing as instances of "being mothers." But strong feelings about the burdens associated with motherhood, combined with a focus on motherhood as the core of identity, tended to eclipse substantive differences in the routine life experiences of lesbian and heterosexual mothers, differences that often emerged indirectly. Further, information gleaned from interviews with others in informants' social networks sometimes yielded contradictory accounts of relationships and events. I began to consider the possibility that the narratives of lesbian and heterosexual mothers were similar not necessarily because the women's experiences were comparable but rather in spite of the fact that they may not have been.

From this perspective, it became clear that lesbian and heterosexual mothers, despite concrete differences in their daily experiences, use narratives to construct their experience as mothers, and by extension as women, from shared cultural elements. Their narratives are shaped by, among other things, concerns with achieving a satisfying individual identity, and particularly with demonstrating some measure of independence. They are heavily influenced by relatively conventional gender expectations centered on women's special vocation for nurturance and altruism and men's disinterest in parental responsibilities. They are further influenced by notions about the essential impact of motherhood on one's identity; more than other aspects of identity, motherhood is seen as being driven by elemental, probably biological, forces not readily controlled by the individual. These forces make mothers and nonmothers different in fundamental ways, and work to undermine desires they may have to understand and support each other. Finally, the narratives reveal a strong acceptance of the specialness of kinship as a source of support and continuity. While mothers often express frustration with particular dimensions of their relationships with blood relatives, they also demonstrate a commitment to transcend these difficulties, and thus to strengthen their bonds with their children.

Feminist Anthropology and the Search for Women's Experience

The shifts in my thinking paralleled changes in process in anthropology during the years I worked on this project, as ethnographers' concerns moved from an emphasis on positivistic description to an interest in the more relative, and explicitly negotiated, aspects of the production of ethnographic knowledge. Despite the recent preoccupation with postmodernist thought as the source of these changes,[36] the beginnings of this concern emerged earlier in social anthropology, in part as a reaction against the rigidity of structural models.[37] It might be argued, in fact, that these changes set the stage for the emergence of feminist anthropology in the mid-1970s.[38] Despite debates over other issues, feminist anthropology of all stripes came to be centrally concerned with the ways in which women's experience in male-dominated cultures amounted to more than what might be predicted from an inspection of the most formal level of organization. Early feminist ethnographers sought to direct our attention to how women themselves described their experience, often producing accounts that differed sharply from those produced earlier by male ethnographers.[39] These researchers were concerned both with investigating the informal level of sociocultural organization more thoroughly and with giving women a voice they had previously been denied.[40]

In this respect, feminist anthropology moved decisively in the same direction as feminist scholarship in other fields and popular feminist writing. On the one hand, the idea was that women's experience had been poorly documented because scholars failed even to ask questions about women; as the "other," women were not assumed to make significant contributions to culture, and hence it did not seem unreasonable to produce an ethnography that made virtually no mention of women's activities, or, when it did, confined such discussion to stereotypical domains of childbirth and marriage. Here the problem was that women's behavior was ignored.

On the other hand, feminist critics pointed out that even when anthropologists asked questions about women, they rarely sought women's own voices as the authoritative sources of information about them. The feminists' concern was not so much with what women did or were observed to do—such data could not help but be influenced by the observer's culturally determined expectations. Rather, the issue was more how to establish a context to listen to what women said about themselves, to discover how they framed their experience, what they made of their situations, quite apart from what any particular observer might claim.

The focus in anthropology on gathering women's own accounts of their experience is closely related, then, to a similar impulse in the wider domain of feminist scholarship to produce "feminist methodology."[41] And efforts to develop this methodology were inspired, in turn, by the process of collective understanding—consciousness raising—by which Second Wave feminism, particularly in its radical incarnation, built its analysis of patriarchy.[42] In practice, this meant that each woman would tell her "story" to other women belonging to her small group; each would listen to the story without interrupting. As the stories unfolded, patterns and convergences would emerge. The outcome of the process was a collective understanding of the ways in which Woman is constructed in culture. Of course, participants in this process, like anthropologists in the field, tended to take the accounts so collected more literally, or perhaps more concretely, than we might now consider appropriate, and this is where my method in the early stages of this project brought together my commitment to feminism and my 1960s training as an anthropologist: I thought I could know what women "did" on the basis of what they told me. This assumption provided a fundamental rationale for the organization of my data according to specific kinship and social domains (relations with relatives, children, friends, ex-husbands). Taking a point of view influenced by social network theory,[43] I saw people in each of these domains as resources that could be mobilized as needed and that would shape both the lesbian mother's perception of her location in an interactive web and her ability to cope with the various difficulties, both material and moral, she would be likely to encounter.

To some extent, feminist scholars now working to overturn the excesses of the earlier preoccupation with universal female subordination, principally represented by new critical writings by women of color, have made a similar error. These authors have attempted to extricate themselves from the hegemony of a single view of "woman" (what Gloria Anzaldúa has infelicitously called "whitefeminism"), highlighting the importance of cultural and historical variability in the shaping of women's experience and definition of themselves.[44] But here again the personal account becomes reified as literal truth, and the more subtle process of negotiation and self-definition tend to be lost.[45] If being a "woman" no longer determines the fate of a female person, then race or class in one view,[46] sexual orientation in another,[47] does the job instead, reducing women (or people) to straightforward representations of the claims they made in talking about themselves.

Some feminist scholarship, happily, has managed to merge the concern of feminist methodology with the primacy of experience with an understanding of the contingent and negotiated nature of narrative, leading to a singular grasp of the personal narrative as a reflection of a cultural process rather than as a videotape manqué or literal account of observable behavior. Women say what they do, or what they did, as a way of constructing key notions of self, and in the process go on to construct gender. More than hopelessly unmeasurable indicators of gender (or race, or class, or sexuality) as it affects opportunities or interactions, personal narratives offer us a chance to see how women *account for themselves,* make sense of their situations, and designate themselves in relation to others—how they, in fact, negotiate their identities in collaboration with or in opposition to prevailing cultural expectations.

Innovative work using the personal narrative in this way has already been done, often leading to ventures that break down traditional disciplinary boundaries.[48] Carolyn Steedman has pointed to the highly variable views of women's lives generated by shifts between the perspectives of mother and daughter, shifts that are not determined by class but that yet reflect the constantly changing impact of class on the views of the two protagonists, mother and daughter. Perhaps most important, the daughter/narrator in her volume is also the historian/analyst, so her construction of her own experience in relation to that of her mother moves along two axes simultaneously.[49] Similarly, Renato Rosaldo has shown that the hunting stories of the Ilongot of the Philippines not only are accounts of how particular hunts proceed but are occasions that help the hunters make particular kinds of cultural points. "Huntsmen in fact seek out experiences that can be told as stories. In other words, stories often shape, rather than simply reflect, human conduct."[50]

Faye Ginsburg has taken a similar approach to her study of activists on both sides of the abortion debate. Working in a small, relatively homogeneous community, Ginsburg collected accounts she calls "procreation stories" of women's maternal histories. She shows persuasively that both "pro-choice" and "pro-life" informants arrive at the particular commitments they have made on the basis of similar, if not substantially identical, cultural positions, framed largely in terms of views of nurturance and family generally shared throughout the community.[51] Women's politics, then, cannot be said to be derivative of distinct cultural positions, but rather unfolds as women's specific experiences interact with values they already accept.

Lesbian mothers are a good population for examining these kinds of ideas, in part because they seem to embody contradictions. On the one hand, insofar as lesbianism and motherhood seem to be culturally (if not biologically) incompatible, they transcend or challenge the ordinary organization of gender in American culture, which conflates "woman" and "mother" and defines lesbians as neither. In this sense, claiming the identity of lesbian mother may be construed as an instance of resistance to prevailing sexual politics.

But in becoming mothers, lesbians join heterosexual women in a particular organization of identity which partakes of mainstream gender ideology. The notion that motherhood (or womanhood, by extension) supersedes other dimensions of identity is espoused by both lesbian and heterosexual mothers. Lesbian mothers not only encounter the same material conditions as other mothers but demand access to the same cultural and symbolic resources available to nonlesbian mothers. This suggests that the resistance to conventional gender ideology implied by the oxymoronic status of the lesbian mother can be superseded or compromised by its resolution of the "problem" of lesbian identity. Though I do not argue that lesbians become mothers purposefully in order to regularize their status, as a direct response to stigma, I do contend that motherhood indirectly enables women (whether lesbian or heterosexual) to claim a specific location in the gender system.

The centrality of images of nurturance and altruism in mothers' narratives about the meaning of motherhood, for example, stands in stark contrast to the pervasive stereotypes of decadent, selfish, and above all nonprocreative behavior attributed to gay men, and by extension to lesbians. Similarly, the responsibilities associated with motherhood clearly contrast with the image of homosexuality as "arrested development" popularized by psychoanalytically oriented mental health professionals.[52]

One of the consequences, then, of both the material and symbolic predicament faced by lesbians (and by single heterosexual mothers) is that solutions to a range of problems generated by the traditional cultural/gender system are themselves embedded in that traditional system. The multilayered problems caused or complicated by financial limitations, the perceptions of oneself as isolated and at odds with the wider culture, and the struggle to establish a positive identity for oneself and for one's family are difficulties shared by all mothers whose circumstances are not conventional. The resources available to deal with these difficulties continue to be relationships with biological family, friendship ties with other mothers, and an elaboration of an ideology of consanguineal (blood) kinship. Resistance and complicity overlap and define each other, making it impossible to judge any particular strategy as one or the other.

These observations do not really change my view that lesbian mothers are not systematically different from other mothers who share some similar concrete problems. On one level, to be sure, all mothers in our society must operate under similar material conditions; all mothers confront a range of powerful structural constraints to which they must craft strategic responses. But these strategies are also articulated in a cultural context; they represent the operation of a shared cultural process, one that can be traced as easily in the accounts of the lesbians as in those of their heterosexual counterparts. Both lesbian and heterosexual mothers participate in the implementation of gender on the same basis, constructing their identities from mutually available elements and negotiating identity in ways shared with us all.

2

Becoming a Lesbian Mother

The "lesbian baby boom" and the increasing visibility of lesbians who become mothers through donor insemination or adoption constitute the most dramatic and provocative challenge to traditional notions both of the family and of the nonprocreative nature of homosexuality. The growing popularity of parenthood in the gay community has generated interest within the community itself (popular media, books, advice manuals, workshops, and public events), in the mainstream media, and in academic circles.[1]

While these developments capture our imaginations and challenge commonly held assumptions about lesbians, they tend to mask a less dramatic reality: that many, perhaps most of the children of lesbian mothers are still born in the context of a marriage. Some of the mothers were attracted to other women before their marriages, and in fact had established lesbian identity or behavior early in life. Others discovered their homosexuality later, either while they were still married or after their marriages had ended.[2]

Lesbian mothers who were married when their children were born (the "formerly married") went through two kinds of transitions on their way to their current situations. They began to see themselves as lesbian at some point—"came out," either to themselves alone or to other people in their lives—and they left their husbands. These two transitions did not necessarily occur simultaneously, though they sometimes did, and did not necessarily influence each other directly. At the same time that coming out has specific ramifications for lesbians not strictly comparable with the experience of heterosexual women, lesbian mothers who have been married share much of the experience of heterosexual single mothers—leaving a marriage, getting a divorce, and dealing with its legal, economic, and emotional ramifications.

"Coming Out" as a Process of Discovering One's "True" Self

It should probably surprise no one to learn that formerly married lesbian mothers' descriptions of their passage from a heterosexual lifestyle to lesbianism are couched in a heavily psychologized language of personal transformation. Our culture is centrally concerned with the individual and the formation of identity as a solitary quest;[3] and in the late 1970s, when I began to interview these women, the popularity of a wide range of personal growth psychologies and self-improvement movements may have had an impact on the mothers' perceptions.

These elements have been central as well to the women's movement as it emerged in the late 1960s and early 1970s, both in its liberal and radical and eventually in its more cultural incarnations.[4] The slogan "The personal is political" became interpretable in many instances as "The political is personal," suggesting that one's "lifestyle" and sense of oneself would reveal the extent of one's success in battle with the patriarchy. This political way of thinking about personal development comes through clearly in the accounts lesbian mothers give of the experiences of coming out and divorcing. Often, in fact, it is difficult to distinguish between the way mothers interpret these transitions in the larger system of gender as they conceptualize it and the particular feelings they experience. Experience and interpretation become confounded, influencing each another and finally becoming totally circular and indistinguishable. The process permits one to view oneself through a specific feminist lens at the same time that review of one's own life validates the wider interpretation. The process might be called "political autobiography."

The most explicit expression of this perspective appeared among mothers who described membership in a feminist consciousness-raising (CR) group as having had a direct impact on their paths into lesbianism. One such woman was Rebecca Collins,[5] who joined a women's group after she separated from her husband. Lesbianism was an unfamiliar and rather uncomfortable topic for her, and discussions of it in the group were the first she had ever heard. But as her thinking developed, she found she could discuss lesbianism without embarrassment.

I'd become much more my own person, for one thing. I was a lot more open to possibilities, I'd seen a lot more. And I'd been real frustrated in relationships with men. . . . [My marriage] was not a bad experience in comparison [with other heterosexual relationships I had], but it was nothing compared to a relationship with a woman.

It was Rebecca's CR group, and the changes it led to in her views of women, that made it possible for her, as she sees it, to consider a lesbian relationship. She began to see relationships between men and women as "inherently alienating," and came to value women more than she had done before.

I realized more and more that women were doing the interesting things in the world, feeling the interesting things. They were the interesting people to talk to. All of the conversations I had with men, they were empty, there was nothing going on. I realized more and more why I'd been so frustrated. I was putting all this energy into something that just wasn't there.

Rebecca met her lover, Sheila Ryan, at work. Their relationship developed out of a long friendship that began while Sheila was still involved with a previous lover. Rebecca views coming out as a total reversal of the direction her life had been taking until then.

I feel like it's just such a total change, and a reversal in such a positive, self-affirming sort of way. . . . I'd been so oriented to other people generally. Taking care of my family . . . and then . . . just always being involved with one man. It was like I never knew who I was, and never even allowed myself to think about it. . . . Coming out and being a lesbian has really turned all that around. I feel like I'm much stronger. I know myself much better. There are many more possibilities. I feel much closer in my relationships . . . in terms of friends.

Deborah Cohen's coming out was also accelerated by involvement in the women's movement, although she describes many of the key events as having been accidental. Deborah had married young, largely to facilitate her family's immigration to the United States. After the birth of her daughter when she was twenty-one, she became bored and lonely, "counting the hours of the day to end," but couldn't figure out how to extricate herself. A book club sent her Betty Friedan's *Feminine Mystique* and she began to realize that she wasn't the only woman who felt isolated and unhappy in what appeared to be a "good" marriage. After a series of experiences with human potential groups, Deborah and her husband agreed to separate. She then became involved with a series of male lovers, still not feeling very satisfied with her situation.

Shortly after her divorce, Deborah returned to college and there found herself registered for a women's studies course "by accident." The class was "full of lesbians," and Deborah decided without hesitation that she was a lesbian as well. Within three months she had met her first woman lover and broken up with her boyfriend.

For me, coming out was like going home in a way. It felt really good. I felt like I could breathe. I felt like I could have it all—I didn't have to have a best friend and then go home to this man. I also hated sex with men, and I didn't have to deal with that anymore. . . . Being with a man was so contradictory, because I'd get my emotional stuff from women and then keep trying to get it from a man and I couldn't. . . . Also, coming out for me is very much connected with getting my strength together as a woman and not needing to be the shadow of a man. . . . Coming out also meant . . . learning how to go out in the world and be a person and work.

Deborah's emphasis on the accidental elements that promoted her coming out support an underlying claim that being a lesbian is "natural," perhaps inevitable, needing only the right circumstances to reveal itself.

Such interpretations of the meaning of coming out were not limited to those lesbian mothers whose experiences were facilitated by membership in a CR group. Tanya Petroff, who remains on good terms with her former husband, found herself increasingly alienated from her marriage after the birth of her daughter.

I know that after my daughter was born I just had this big energy surge for doing things. I immediately went back to school full-time and I stopped catering to my husband. Like, I now had a real child to take care of so I didn't have to take care of a phony child.

Tanya's first relationship with a woman began shortly after the breakup of her marriage, though she was aware of often being perceived as a lesbian long before she was "officially" involved with women. Nonetheless, Tanya sees her coming out as having changed her in important ways.

It was like a whole world of possible behavior opened up to me that I couldn't even consider when I was having to consider pleasing men or having to survive through having a relationship through a man. It was kind of frightening on the one hand to say, well, I'm not having any more relationships with men, but it was also wonderfully creative in that, you know, it made me think about how was I going to survive. It was clear that I wasn't going to find another woman to support me, although there are lesbians that do that sort of thing. But that wasn't my idea of being a lesbian. So I just got all these wonderful feelings of my own power, my own possibility for survival, and of doing nontraditional work. That was one of the things that made it possible for me to do the work that I do now.

Her work is perhaps the most unusual thing about Tanya. After years of moving from one dead-end clerical job to another, never managing to do much more than pay for child care, she decided that the best way out of poverty would be to get into blue-collar work. A veteran of the military, she describes herself as having bluffed her way into her current position in an apprenticeship program for refinery operators. She is the only woman in a blue-collar job at the refinery, and having sustained months of verbal hostility each day on the job, she now says that her male co-workers are beginning to treat her with grudging respect. So far the job has made it possible for Tanya to make a down payment on a modest home (with the assistance of her former husband); she intends to keep this job at least until her financial situation will allow her to return to college full-time.

Paula Abrams, who now lives with her son and daughter in San Francisco, describes her coming-out experience in almost mystical terms. She believes that an adolescent "best friend" relationship had underlying lesbian content, that she has "always" been a lesbian though for a long time she was unaware of it. After her marriage

ended, she become more and more involved with women's organizations, came to read and think a lot about feminism, and reached the
intellectual conclusion that heterosexuality was learned or condi-
tioned behavior. Through her contacts in feminist organizations she
became acquainted with several lesbians, some of whom were mothers. She describes her first sexual relationship with a woman:

*It was really electrifying. . . . I thought, this is really it. It was real easy. There
was absolutely no turmoil, no guilt, no doubts. It seemed so natural, and so inevitable. It made so many things so clear.*

The beginning of the process that would allow her to achieve full
"personhood" came with her divorce; the second part came when she
became a lesbian.

I have a sense of rightness about myself that I never had before. I feel at peace.

Paula's elation was so spontaneous and unself-conscious, in fact,
that she decided to call her mother to tell her about it.

*I was so excited when I first fell in love with a woman that the first person I
could think of to call and tell was my mother. She was less excited, but the thing
about my mother was that she could understand how I could love a woman. What
she found difficult was how the world was going to look on that. . . . She just
made a big point out of how unhappy I was going to be because the world doesn't
accept that.*

Elaine Weinstein's passage into lesbianism, in contrast, occurred
while she was still married and led directly to the end of her marriage.
She became close friends and then lovers with a neighbor whose
children were about the same age as hers (five and seven at the time).
She told her husband about the relationship and he immediately
moved out. Though he promised that they would have an "amicable
divorce," he eventually started a custody suit that involved her in
lengthy litigation. Winning custody of her children required her to lie
about her relationship, but even after she secured custody, she has
continued to be extremely secretive about her lesbianism because of

her employment as a teacher. Despite these difficulties, she feels that becoming a lesbian has enabled her to grow personally in a way she values.

In one way, I've become more independent. But then again, I accept support more easily. It was almost impossible for me to accept support from men, but I can with women. . . . In a way, I'm stronger since I'm more able to accept support, if that makes any sense.

Martha Kennedy also came out as a lesbian while she was still married. She was already dissatisfied with her marriage when she and her husband moved to California from the East Coast. Shortly after they arrived, she started a business in the hope of establishing herself as economically independent. About the same time she began to read a lot about women and joined a bisexual rap group in which she met her first woman lover. Although discovery of this relationship led her husband to move out, he continued to come and go without warning, and she felt that she had to file for divorce in order to have some legal protection from his capricious behavior. Her relationship with her former husband has been somewhat stressful—his payment of child support is erratic and his behavior is antagonistic when he has been drinking—but she is managing well financially. She lives with her lover and her eleven-year-old son, runs a successful business, and feels that she has put the marriage behind her. About being a lesbian she says:

I feel like I'm living the life I should be living, or being the person that's most comfortable for me to be, whereas before I never felt like I was living the right life for me. It always felt like a shoe that didn't fit. I just feel real comfortable with my life, sort of like coming home.

For other women, coming out so eclipses marriage that divorce seems almost like an afterthought. Alma White, for example, had gone into the Navy right after she graduated from high school and became involved in her first lesbian relationship shortly afterward. But when the relationship was discovered, Alma was discharged, and she returned home to her mother in disgrace.

I had really enjoyed the involvement that I'd had with this woman but I also had a great deal of hurt over it. And also the experience of being discharged from the Navy was very painful and so I felt that any involvement with women could only lead to unhappiness . . . so I felt that getting married was the real thing to do.

But from the beginning of her ten-year marriage, Alma felt that something was "just really not right," and the feeling persisted even after her son was born. After about five years she resumed the relationship with the woman she had known in the Navy, but her lover soon withdrew from the relationship, not wanting to be the cause of a divorce. Nonetheless, Alma was not willing to give up lesbianism. She "discovered the bars" and met another woman with whom she had a three-year relationship, still while living with her husband. At this point Alma and her husband finally decided to divorce; the decision seems to have been prompted by his desire to remarry as much as by her situation. They had experimented earlier with various communal living arrangements, and even after the divorce and her husband's remarriage they continued to live in the same house for a time.

Alma sees being a lesbian as a definite advantage in life, particularly because it broadens the possibilities of friendship and gives her access to a kind of supportive community that straight women, especially divorced women, cannot experience. But mostly she thinks of coming out in terms of comfort, a sense of being in touch with her "real self."

[There was] some sort of tension in trying to maintain that facade that was going on in the marriage and so that tension was all gone and it was just a release, a relaxation, a sort of feeling of finding myself, of being at home with myself, you know. The first time I walked into a gay bar it was just like, wow! This is where I belong.

Not all the coming-out stories are free of anxiety or concern about stigma and discrimination. Winnie Moses, who lives with her lover and her two teenage sons in Marin County, says that ongoing tension between herself and her former husband has undermined the elation she feels at finally having found a good relationship. Winnie had a significant lesbian affair when she was seventeen or eighteen. She didn't see any way, however, not to move in a more conventional direction as she got older, particularly because she was eager to have children. She felt that she "had" to get married, and Philip seemed like a good choice: he was much older, did not object to her pursuing a career in social work, and made few sexual demands upon her. He had little interest in their two sons, and he made it clear that it children were tolerable only if he could be totally freed of responsibility for them. The loneliness of being a mother in these circumstances eventually propelled Winnie toward divorce and toward coming out again. Although she never discussed her lesbianism with Philip, he learned about her relationship with a woman from a friend of his who happened to be the teacher of one of their sons. He immediately threatened to institute a custody proceeding, though he made it clear that if he won custody of the boys he would place them in boarding school. He became obsessed with the idea that one of the boys had been displaying "effeminate" behavior, and began to scrutinize both children for signs that Winnie's lesbianism was damaging their development. Philip agreed not to go to court only when Winnie promised never to discuss her lesbianism with the children. Although she suspects that the two boys "know"—she doesn't see how they could not—she worries about the stigma of homosexuality among adolescents and sees this danger as another reason to avoid the topic with her sons. She has lived with her lover about six years, but the boys have never asked any questions about their relationship.

For other women, coming out involved a return to an earlier, more authentic sense of self. Harriet Newman, an artist who lives with her two daughters in a rural area north of San Francisco, fell in love with another woman during her first year at college. Everything was going well until her parents found out.

It was awful. They brought me home. They had gone into a box of letters, and had taken them to a lawyer. Fortunately, [my lover] was just three days short of turning twenty-one when they did this. They were hysterical. . . . It was as if your daughter was a heroin addict. Something in between sick and criminal, insane and criminal. They wanted to believe that it wasn't me, it was her. I would never do this. She had bewitched me or done something evil. Was forcing me. All kinds

of weird stuff they were trying to read into these letters. It was so bizarre. . . .
They were so pathetic to me, and I felt so guilty for bringing all this up in them.
I had to take care of them while they were doing me in. And enraged at the same
time. I couldn't believe that that kind of restraint was going to be put on my life.

This experience convinced Harriet that it would be safer "to be a regular person in the world." After graduating from college, she met a gay man who also wanted to lead a more conventional existence.

The main thing that made us decide to get married was that we very much wanted
to be part of the mainstream of life, instead of on the edges. We wanted to be sub-
stantial . . . part of the common experience.

According to Harriet, they had children almost impulsively, because she was "hit with a very big urge to have a baby." Once they had children, however, Harriet realized that she could not tolerate the marriage. Her husband was devoted to their daughters, but despite the fact that he was now a family man, he continued to live a rather erratic and marginal life, rarely holding a job and continuing to be involved with other men. Becoming a mother accentuated Harriet's growing sense that the marriage itself was artificial; in the same way that she experienced motherhood as the outcome of natural impulses, a return to lesbianism represented a restoration of her authentic self.

All of these accounts emphasize the *naturalness* of coming out. Each of the women feels that she has arrived home, has returned to a familiar place representative of her true inner self, and in the process has achieved a peace and serenity never before possible. Feelings of isolation and shame get little attention in these narratives. When they do surface, they tend to be discussed in two ways. First, a woman may have been experienced bad feelings about being a lesbian in her youth, when the pressure of peers and convention were more compelling, and in particular when her parents' disapproval could have serious consequences. But these feelings, she now believes, are not appropriate for a really mature adult. Second, negative feelings appear in connection with continuing interaction with former husbands and sometimes with family members. Here women express concern about obtaining money they are entitled to (such as child support) while also avoiding custody litigation or other forms of harassment by their former husbands. In this context, doubts about having made a deviant choice are externalized and appear as something that must be "managed" and circumvented, but not as part of the woman herself. Thus these coming-out narratives emphasize personal growth and increasing maturity and self-awareness; contradictions of these feelings have their origins in a hostile and fundamentally alien external environment.

Divorce as a Passage to Adulthood

Lesbians discuss the breakup of their marriages in very similar sorts of language, and their accounts reveal themselves to be culturally constructed in much the same way as the coming-out stories. Mothers speak of the end of their marriages as a period of heightened self-awareness, a time of personal development, and, in some cases, as facilitating a kind of growing up they had not been able to achieve before. While it is clear that a breakup and divorce often involve dislocation, guilt, and emotional turmoil on many levels, the end result appears to be assessed as a special kind of personal growth and evolution into full humanity. The key element appears to be the emphasis on independence and autonomy as qualities realized in the course of the breakup.

To some lesbian mothers, the most important result of ending the marriage is a new awareness of their competence and capability, a pride in being able to make major decisions on their own. The end of Harriet Newman's marriage, for example, provided her first opportunity to test her ability to meet important obligations.

In that first year after the marriage, it was terrifying to me to be with two babies out in the world alone. And that I could do it was hugely important to me. It was terribly important to me to know that I could do that.

Paula Abrams says she felt stifled in her marriage, even though her husband was a good person.

I just felt the need to get out—not even necessarily forever. But after eight years, I just felt totally stifled, and didn't know why. I really didn't know what was going on in myself. It was kind of a blind, foolhardy move, because I didn't have any plans for what I was going to do outside the marriage. I just wanted to get out.

During the months after their separation, Paula realized that her marriage was not really bad, but that marriage itself was what she wanted to be released from.

That was a real revelation to me, because I wasn't leaving this particular man, I was leaving marriage. I also realized I couldn't find a better man. To this day, I believe that if I had to find a man, that he would probably be the best one.

Paula's husband didn't want the separation to be final and Paula herself was not at all sure what she wanted. Her feelings alternated between euphoria and depression as she struggled to figure out what was "out there" for her. She wanted to return to the comfort of her relationship with her husband, yet something in her resisted.

And then I discovered that there really wasn't anybody out there that I had to be dependent on but me. That was a big discovery—that I was responsible for myself. And I was scared, but I was really determined to see what I could make of my life.

Claire Jackson, who lives with her nine-year-old daughter and her lover in an East Bay suburb, runs a clerical business out of her home. Her divorce was an extremely stressful experience, largely because her husband was involved in unethical business dealings that she was afraid might compromise her own financial security. Ending the marriage has led Claire to feel stronger and more sure of herself.

I learned to trust myself, to trust my instincts. I gave myself validity and identity. I live for myself, not as an extension of somebody else. I make my own decisions, I make my own life. I bought my own furniture, I set up my own house, I started my own business. Little by little I got more and more powerful. I felt a sense of self that I'd never felt before.

One of the advantages she sees in being divorced is that she no longer has to consider her husband's reaction when she makes a decision, but is free to determine what she wants to do.

Being a single mother, you're in control of your life. You're in control of your child's life. There is no one to answer to, there is no one to work around or with. You work out your life exactly as you want to work it out. It's really very simple. I know it gets complicated with all of the intricacies of daily living, but what it comes down to is total independence, as opposed to having to think and coordinate your life with another adult, who 99 percent of the time is into role playing. I see marriage as just filled with conflicts that are always having to be worked out.

For some women, the end of marriage means no longer having to take care of a husband, a burden they liken to child care. Carol Martin, a lesbian mother of two who lives in Oakland, equates the ending of her marriage with freedom from onerous obligations to her husband.

After he left I felt such relief, I can't say. You see these ads of people jumping up in the air with their arms in the air. That was really quite a burden. I didn't have to take care of him. I had made myself do that for so long. Fixing the meals and the laundry, and just so much that I had done for him. Much like a mother.

Carol makes clear the association the divorce has with growing up and with assuming the role of an autonomous adult for the first time in her life. Marriage in her view is an arrangement that stifles the individual, forcing women to be more concerned with their husbands' needs than with their own preferences and desires.

Oh, [being divorced has] allowed me to grow. I felt before that I was in a jar. There were a lot of things cooking around inside, but the lid was on. And now I feel I've had the opportunity to really think for myself, find out what I can do for myself, make the decision myself. . . . I am the head of the household. I can feel it. That feels good to me. I was the head of the household essentially when he was here, but there was a deference to him anyway. . . . I feel more grown up than I ever did.

Among the decisions she was able to make once she was no longer married was to become a lesbian, something she claims never to have considered before her divorce.

For Adele Marcus, a thirty-nine-year-old mother of five, coming out and divorce were inextricably bound together. Adele is a successful and highly paid attorney. Though she had been dissatisfied with her marriage for some time, becoming lovers with her best friend and then getting divorced still came as something of a surprise to her. She had known Nora Olson for a dozen years. The Marcuses and the Olsons and later their children were close friends. She was unable to explain the transition of the relationship with Nora. "I don't really understand it. It just happened." Nonetheless, becoming a lesbian and solidifying her commitment to Nora seemed to be the catalyst that was needed to end her marriage. On one level, becoming a lesbian seemed to have allowed Adele to articulate the problems that had dominated her marriage.

I feel very happy in the relationship I'm in now. It's very satisfying, and much more equal. The communication is much better. I don't think there's any way that I could give that up.

Once she was out of the marriage, she felt stronger and better able to determine the course her life would take—"much more in charge," as she explains, "of what happens to me now." This assessment is striking when one considers that she had a successful career in a male-dominated field and had long been able to coordinate her marital and maternal obligations with the demands of her profession.

These new feelings of autonomy are tied to her assessment of what it means to have become a lesbian. She draws the comparison not only with heterosexuality but with the entire structure of conventional married life. Once again the emphasis is on recovery of the self, on the achievement of personal gratification and authenticity.

I think it's helped me be more sure of myself, perhaps. I feel happier, I feel more confident, and like I have somebody who is there if I need them. A feeling of love and caring for her seems to be a lot different than the feelings of responsibility and drudgery that I had with my husband.

Bernice Nelson's account of her decision to be a lesbian and her divorce reveal some ways in which coming-out and divorce stories dovetail in their concern with self-realization. Now thirty-five, Bernice lives in an affluent suburb with her 7-year-old daughter and a housekeeper who works in exchange for a room. Although her income declined dramatically after her divorce, she has managed to continue to live in this area with income from child support and some family investments. Self-sufficiency is a central value for her, not only as she describes her exit from the marriage and her commitment to lesbianism but as she reveals her long-term plans for financial stability and personal satisfaction.

My goal is to become completely self-sufficient on every level. . . . I have it projected, and I guess by the time I'm forty or forty-five I'll be completely financially independent, in the sense that I'll never have to go out and get a job.

Bernice's sexual experiences with women began while she was in college. She found her attraction to women frightening and decided that she would have to marry and try to achieve what she considered a more normal sort of life. She married, but after her marriage resumed her involvement with women, and finally formed a serious relationship when she and her husband began a communal household with several other couples. She views her decision to end the marriage as a major step toward the kind of self-reliance that would have significant implications for the rest of her life. Bernice believes that ending her marriage helped her to accept her sexual preference for the first time, to convince herself that being gay did not represent some fundamental personal flaw. Bernice's lesbianism and her individuality are fundamentally linked.

I accepted that I'm alone and threw out the idea that I'll ever be dependent on a man again for anything. My focus became real career-oriented. . . . My whole focus . . . has changed, from a more childlike position of the need to find somebody to take care of me to learning how to take care of myself, to be independent and act independently.

Bernice's simultaneous formulation of a career plan and the emotional commitment to prosperity it entails fit into this larger picture.

So I've made a major shift away from a victimized position to a real creative, high-energy, centered kind of position. . . . The main thing has been my view of myself, seeing myself as alone . . . as needing to stand on my own two feet, as needing not to be dependent on other people. . . . Being a lesbian for me is being equal to somebody, not being superior or dependent. . . . Part of being equal is accepting that you're alone, and accepting that you're in charge of yourself and your life.

Ironically, Bernice's vision of autonomy also allows her to explain her reluctance to pursue back child support and other financial help from her former husband. Her self-esteem does not release her from experiencing intense anxiety about how public knowledge of her lesbianism could jeopardize her professional aspirations, result in custody litigation or other harassment from her former husband, or expose her daughter to ridicule and stigma. Along with pride and self-reliance, she feels a need for caution in letting people know that she is a lesbian; she feels very vulnerable to the intolerance of most people.

Similarly, the stress she places on "taking full responsibility" makes it possible for her to tolerate her lover's unwillingness to be a co-parent. Independence necessitates, as she indicates repeatedly, "being alone," if not literally, then in terms of the level of what one can safely expect from another adult, whether male or female. She says that she used to look for "partnership in relation to parenting" but now, having made a "transition" to independence, she doesn't expect her lover to assume consistent responsibility.

Lesbian and Heterosexual Divorce Stories Compared

Heterosexual women's accounts of their divorces overlap and converge with those of lesbians. Like lesbian mothers, heterosexual divorced women revel in their ability to handle difficult challenges, to pay the bills, to fix the car, to negotiate a busy schedule, while often feeling frustrated or overwhelmed by many of these same responsibilities. Lesbian and heterosexual mothers use similar language to describe these transitions, a language heavily endowed with terms associated with psychological growth. Heterosexual mothers' images of homecoming or of discovering a more authentic version of themselves sometimes give rise to the same kinds of euphoric expressions of victory we hear from lesbian mothers.

Some heterosexual mothers, like some lesbians, came to the end of their marriages through consciousness-raising groups and the discovery of a feminist world view. Ruth Levine, a thirty-five-year-old mother of three, was married while she was in college and had her first child while she was still a student. She now lives in Berkeley with two of her children, her male lover, and his children, and works as an editor. At the time she first got into a women's group, she was feeling very much the trapped housewife and was especially unhappy about her inability to have a satisfying professional life of the kind her husband enjoyed.

I became involved in a consciousness-raising group and it really was revolutionary for me to spend one evening a week with other women talking about myself and realizing that it wasn't that I was crazy or that I was sick, it was that I was experiencing something that other women were experiencing, that I was feeling tied down, that I was feeling . . . unable to express myself and become myself and it became more and more intolerable for me to stay in the marriage. [My husband] did not want to change and I did.

The actual impetus for ending the marriage was Ruth's short affair with another man. Her husband left and instituted divorce proceedings. He remarried two weeks after the divorce was final.

I was sort of beating my way out of what felt like a suffocating cocoon. . . . Finally he left and I felt on the one hand . . . enormously freed and on the other hand I didn't know what I was going to do with myself, how I was going to support myself. I'd never really worked. I didn't have any skills. I was totally unrealistic about life in the world.

Ruth had never held a full-time job and was bewildered at the prospect of finding her way into a profession. For nine years after her marriage ended she worked at a variety of jobs, barely managing on her earnings and modest child-support payments. She eventually returned to graduate school, and once her skills had become more solid, she worked her way into a promising job with a publisher. She talks with great animation about her work and what it means to her; now that her children are older, having fulfilling work is more important than ever before.

I felt like my life was over while I was married. I felt like I had given up. . . . Ending my marriage was a way of taking the bull by the horns . . . and saying that I dare risk being alive, I dare take the risk of really finding myself and finding what I really want, not what I think people want me to be or do. . . . It just opened me up in every way—professionally, personally, sexually, spiritually, as a mother. . . . I just feel like I'm a much richer, fuller person.

Discovering their own ability to accomplish stereotypical masculine tasks amazes some women and fills them with pride. Sylvia Carlton, a thirty-year-old mother of two, has been separated from her husband for two years. She attends school full-time and manages on a combination of rental income, child support, spousal support, and a small inheritance. She describes herself as having been very isolated and boxed in during the marriage, feelings that were intensified after her first child was born. Her husband resented the time and attention the children took; she feels that he saw the children as obstacles to the kind of life he wanted to live, one in which he would have constant romantic attention from his wife.

Sylvia frankly admits that her feelings about the end of the marriage are quite mixed, and that she frequently feels lonely and depressed.

Most of my depression, if I have any, comes from feeling that I will be alone the rest of my life. Not that I will not have men in my life, but that I won't be truly connected. . . . That feels sad. . . . I'm going to get older and less attractive, too, and then my options are going to be less.

But these feelings are increasingly superseded by joy in her new-found competence and strength.

I was feeling terribly, terribly depressed, and fearful. Lot of fear. That slowly and gradually changed to the knowledge of my own strength, and feeling self-satisfaction that I had never known in my life. Learning how to fix broken windows, and change the oil in my car, and take care of my son when . . . his chest was retracting and he was feeling like he couldn't breathe . . . then all of a sudden going back to bed and realizing I was alone—there was no one to hold me in my fear. Just feeling strange, because I had never been alone like that. To this day I have this strange feeling every once in a while—oh, I'm doing my life alone. . . . [But I am] very much stronger in practical kinds of things. . . . Last week my tenant shaved, and got all this hair in the sink. So I just got out my New York Times *how-to-repair-everything book, and my* you-don't-need-a-man-to-fix-it *book, and looked it up, and took the pipes apart in the bathroom and fixed the clog. I feel very strong, because I no longer think of plumbing or even electricity as something that you don't touch.*

Susan Beecher, who lives with her eight-year-old son and her male lover in Berkeley, describes the period immediately after her divorce as lonely and bewildering.

It was real lonely. I was part of nobody. In fact, it's interesting how much of my life had become an extension of this other person, and without this other person I was nothing. Really nothing. I had nothing to talk about.

But she now says that the end of her marriage was "the greatest thing that ever happened to me."

Independence . . . as an adult to have control over my own life. To make my own decisions, to not to have to ask anybody to do anything. To do whatever I want without having to consult. In terms of raising my child, to do it the way I see fit, and not to have to fight somebody else over that. My image of that is a flower that's tightened within itself. After the divorce, it opened up like— Have you ever seen a slow-motion [film] of a flower opening? That's what I felt like. My personality and my strength just really blossomed.

Images of divorce as a passage into adulthood come as readily from the lips of heterosexual women as from those of lesbians. Lynn Howard likened divorce to starting life over "in the kindergarten of life." Lorraine Marshall saw ending her marriage as the impetus for growing up.

I think I started growing up after I was about twenty-five [the year I divorced]. I think the years I was married were kind of underground years.

Shirley Baker, a financial analyst who lives with her two daughters in Berkeley, sees herself as having been tremendously awed and over-shadowed by her former husband, a college professor. Since her divorce,

I feel more independent. I feel more self-confident. I feel like I've grown up. In some ways, I look at my twenties as sort of an extended adolescence. I went from my nice, cozy home . . . to a fairly cozy environment in college, to a cozy marriage. All very protected. . . . I never lived alone. . . . I worked, but I never knew it was my life-support system.

Although Shirley is now in a relationship with a man who treats her like an equal, she still is reluctant to consider marriage to him, fearing it would shift her back to pleasing someone else rather than herself.

For Phyllis Siegel, whose divorce has brought the loss of a large income and an extremely affluent lifestyle, ending the marriage was "terrifying."

I had been that classic woman who allowed all those things to be done for me. I mean, I had never done the checks. [I was] a real infantalized person in a lot of ways. . . . My fears around breaking up the marriage had to do with all sorts of things about money, and technical things, and how would I manage. . . . His fears, of course, were around loneliness and all the areas in which I felt compe-tent. . . . When I'm feeling good about myself, I can look back and say, OK, I've come this far, I've done all these things. But I honestly have to say it's been like I've had to drag myself kicking and screaming into adulthood, into the real world.

But even women who were already active professionals during their marriages find that divorce has permitted them to rediscover their ability to be fully independent, competent adults. This was very much the case for Virginia Lowell, the thirty-nine-year-old mother of a teenage daughter. Virginia lives in a fashionable district of San Francisco with her daughter and works as an executive in a large corporation. Well educated and sophisticated, she worked throughout the years of her marriage, taking only a few months off after the birth of her daughter before returning to a pressured work environment. Even with the self-confidence and professionalism she radiated, however, Virginia was hesitant to strike out on her own after twelve years of marriage, even though her husband drank excessively, saw other women, and had occasionally been physically abusive. The impetus for leaving him was a major promotion that convinced her that she didn't need him for financial security.

I'm so happy I did it. . . . I think it's made me a new life. I've experienced and enjoyed life and pleasures and the feeling of independence and not having somebody hanging over my head, about to come down on me. I guess that's the greatest exhilaration, is the independence—there's not somebody going to be mad at you for doing something that's really OK to do. That's probably about the best part. I frankly just met and enjoyed people that I never would have been able to before, because I wasn't allowed. . . . I don't think I probably would have gone as far in my jobs. . . . It's a very recent change in my life, to realize that I'm going to, or that I want to, always work at some responsible job. Probably always support myself.

Some women's marriages increased their domestic and emotional burdens without bringing any sort of real cooperation or support. At the same time, the presence of a husband compromised the mother's adulthood by undermining her ability to operate as an autonomous person. Alice Molinari, who now lives with her three children in San Francisco and works as a secretary, divorced a husband whom she describes as pathologically jealous and controlling. One night he beat her savagely but the police refused to arrest him. Her parents urged her to return home to San Francisco to live with them, but it was another year before she finally left, largely because he threatened to get custody of the children and prevent her from seeing them. Once she made the decision to end the marriage, however, she knew she had done the right thing.

It just got to the point where I was glad to see him go. He never contributed anything when he was home. He was just another burden, another mouth to feed, more clothes to wash. He would just sit and take up space.

Alice's experience of being on her own centers on a new sense of adulthood and autonomy, undiluted by her responsibility for three children.

It's so nice to just decide for myself how I want to spend my time as an adult, and not have to constantly check in with another adult. . . . It's nice being in charge of my life.

The image of the husband as a burden is pervasive in the mothers' stories. Denise King expresses sadness over the end of a married life that provided many good memories, but still says that ending the marriage has been freeing.

It was heaven! I felt like I was turned loose. I didn't have to cook every night, for one thing. No more of this coming home from work and fixing some elaborate goddam meal. . . . It was amazing to realize I didn't have to spend all my life in the grocery store or the kitchen.

Along similar lines, Beverly Walton, who now lives with her nine-year-old son and seven-year-old daughter in an East Bay suburb, describes her marriage as "a disaster from the start."

Being married wasn't the fantasy ideal that I had had. Like in the movies and books—the prince comes and carries her off and it's happily every after. That wasn't the way it was. It was cooking dinner every night, and changing sheets, and trying to communicate with another person. . . . I was so concerned about pleasing him, doing what he wanted, I didn't have any confidence in myself to make a decision.

When they finally separated, Beverly was surprised that she experienced so little regret.

It was like somebody lifted a mountain off my shoulders. . . . It was like somebody had been standing on my back, and had suddenly gotten off. I felt free. So relieved. It was amazing. . . . I've done nothing but grow ever since then.

Beverly's view is strikingly similar to that of a formerly married lesbian mother, Rita García, who responded this way when I asked her to describe the difference between being a married mother and a single mother:

A married mother, from what I've seen, is a slave to the family, to the house. Even if she works, she has to go home and clean house while the husband sits down and watches TV. . . . [Married mothers] have to take care of everything for the children, everything for their husbands, and everything for themselves. And they always come last, OK? A single parent usually, just from my own experience, gives the children more freedom to think for themselves, gives them a little bit more independence, and she's not tied down to a family, to a house. My house is a mess. I could care less. I'll clean it tomorrow. If I had a husband, he'd want it clean now.

For many of the formerly married mothers, feeling fully adult is closely related to being able to manage financially or in the world of work. Now an administrator at a local college, Pearl Josephson, a heterosexual mother, has a fourteen-year-old son who was born when she was twenty. Her marriage ended some nine years ago when her husband moved in with another woman. At the time, she was very reluctant to end the marriage and was terrified by the prospect of trying to manage on her own.

After we were separated, the first big stroke came at work, when I finally got a raise, and I was sitting down figuring out my budget, and it occurred to me that I could really support myself and my child. That I didn't have to worry about child support. . . . I just felt really good that I could do it on my own. Then, it put more emphasis on career. . . . Caring more about getting ahead. . . . I guess sort of as the head of household, that was more important. Becoming independent in thousands of different ways. The hardest thing for me for many years was not having the second opinion. . . . It was very hard to get over not having it, and just say well, it's my money, I'll go and buy it if I want to.

Like lesbian mothers, heterosexual divorced mothers not uncommonly employ an almost mystical language of rebirth in describing their feelings about leaving their marriages. For Sandra Tiger, the mother of two sons who works as a house painter, the issue revolved around her sense of being a separate person.

I began to see that the role I had set up for myself, to love and support this man on his trip through life, just wasn't for me. I had my own unfolding to do. I didn't know what it was, but I started to sense that, that I wanted to be my own person.

Ursula Clinton expressed similar feelings. Now thirty-two years old, she lives with her son in a Peninsula suburb and works as a secretary. She sees herself as having been very dependent on her husband during the marriage; when he left her ("all of a sudden my whole life just blew up in my face"), she had not had a job in many years, and was so bewildered about how she would survive that she briefly considered suicide.

But during the four years since their separation, Ursula has found that she is capable of dealing with the legal system, getting a job and figuring out how to handle the kind of domestic emergencies she once depended on her husband to resolve. She now sees the divorce as a positive development in her life.

It made me a person again. . . . I was so dependent on [my husband]. I didn't do anything, I didn't make a move without his OK. As far as affecting my life, anyone that knew me when we were married, and knows me now, they know two different people. I'm a very independent person, I have to be. What choice do I have? . . . It's made me a person you can sit down and talk to, rather than a housewife who can't talk anything but house and kids. That was my world. The house and [my son]. It's opened a whole new world for me. . . . It's a terrible thing to say, but it's the best thing that could have happened to me.

Most dramatically, many heterosexual mothers, like the lesbian mothers described earlier, see the divorce as allowing them to achieve, perhaps miraculously, a transformation into a different and more meaningful personal identity. The old identity resembles that of a child, a less-than-adult person who cannot manage the kinds of challenges any adult should understand. As a married woman, she is not really an individual, certainly not autonomous, and hence not a real person.

Angela Marshall, a thirty-five-year-old heterosexual mother who lives with her two children in the East Bay, has been separated for eight years. The marriage was quite conventional and she describes her husband as expecting to be waited on when he came home from work. After her divorce, she went back to college, struggled through a series of dead-end jobs, and finally got a minor administrative position in a bank. She is considering furthering her professional prospects by going into an MBA program.

I'm a totally different person now than I was. I'm not submissive at all. It's taken me time to come around to this but I stand up for my own rights because I know at this point nobody else is going to. I try very hard not to rely on other people. Whenever I've tried to rely on other people, they've let me down, so basically I'm learning to be as independent as possible. . . . I have lonely times alone but basically I'm not as alone as when I was married because then you never thought you should be alone but even with him there I was alone.

Problems of Autonomy and Personhood

These convergences between lesbian mothers' coming-out stories and the divorce stories of both lesbians and heterosexual mothers point to a telling contradiction in American culture. Marriage is seen as a special kind of success for women, but it also imposes a loss of autonomy and personhood that threatens to compromise the individual's quest for accomplishment and individuality. As observers of American culture have noted since Alexis de Tocqueville described his impressions in the mid–nineteenth century, individuality and the related concept of privacy are such core dimensions of American culture that conditions or behavior that might be interpreted as dependency seem questionable if not shameful.[6] Though the diverse ethnic makeup of most American communities certainly undermines the power of this ideal, there is considerable evidence that Americans do value independence and individual assertiveness, and tend to view people who seem lacking in such qualities as inadequate or morally flawed. In a classic study of aging in America, for example, Margaret Clark and Barbara Anderson point to the consequences of the emphasis on "proud independence" for the changes typical of old age. "In America," they explain, "one must simply not admit that, when one grows old, one will need to lean more and more upon others. In America, *no adult* has any *right* to this."[7]

In a similar vein, Robert Bellah and his colleagues characterize the "mythic individualist" as having an ambiguous relation to the larger American society. One of the core images is that of the cowboy, idealized as completely autonomous, standing somehow outside of society while still serving it. Closely related to this concept of the free-standing individual is the notion that one must "find oneself." This quest rests on self-reliance. You must leave home and earn your way; you have to "'make something of yourself' through work. . . . Clearly, the meaning of one's life for most Americans is to become one's own person, almost to give birth to oneself. . . . Traditionally men, and today women as well, are supposed to show that in the occupational world they can stand on their own two feet and be self-supporting."[8]

But the face of the archtypical American individual is clearly masculine. Assertive behavior, along with displays of independence and individual ingenuity, is valued and expected in men but is viewed with suspicion in women.[9] Despite an avalanche of evidence that women increasingly serve as heads of households, have as compelling economic needs as men, and desire the gratification of occupational accomplishment, pervasive stereotypes continue to classify energetic women as unfeminine, selfish, and victimizers of men, and at worst as having robbed men of both their jobs and their self-esteem.[10]

Marriage poses particularly poignant contradictions for women. Popular lore continues to portray women as more eager to be married than men, yet women tend to represent their divorces as having been instigated by themselves.[11] Their claim supports the explanation of the current high divorce rate as having its genesis, in part, in women's increasing ability to manage without the financial support and legitimation afforded by marriage.[12]

But it isn't just that women can manage on their own financially (though not usually very well) and that their jobs make divorce possible. It would be a mistake to reduce these transformations to mere economic calculation. Marriage, which is supposed to define successful femaleness, also undermines successful adult humanness, and it is this contradiction that both lesbian and heterosexual women confront in divorce. This aspect of divorce seems paradoxical if we assume that marriage is unequivocally valued throughout our culture. The historian Glenda Riley argues, however, that the quest for individual fulfillment and for personal happiness has been associated with high divorce rates throughout American history.[13]

Lesbian mothers speak of coming out in a similar way. Despite the fact that being a lesbian continues to be stigmatized, women do not accentuate the numerous social disadvantages associated with being gay when they describe coming out; rather they claim to welcome their arrival in this new identity. They don't speak of changing; they don't lament their situations; their stories are about feeling whole in a way that they couldn't approach when they lived more respectable lives.

Though it could never be said that coming out and getting divorced are the same kind of experience—not the least because of the kind of stigma that accompanies assumption of a homosexual identity—the emotional experiences of these transitions are remarkably similar. Most notably, both coming out and divorce shift women's status downward in the eyes of the society as a whole, yet the women who experience them view them in many respects as steps up. At the core of both coming-out and divorce stories is the theme of increasing autonomy and competence, and both kinds of accounts tend to focus on discovery of one's "true" self. In these respects, as Kath Weston has observed, they constitute odysseys of self-discovery;[14] at the same time, they demonstrate a concern with achieving adulthood and autonomy which is a particular consequence of the infantilization that both marriage and heterosexuality can impose on women.

American gender ideology presents both lesbians and heterosexual women with the same underlying cultural problem. On the one hand, marriage and heterosexuality are held out as the normal resolution of personal development, the goals to which all women ought to aspire, particularly insofar as they enable one to achieve motherhood and with it, full adulthood.[15] On the other hand, these "correct" choices bring with them the shame of nonadulthood and dependency, thus nullifying the achievement they apparently facilitate. To be a wife and to be dependent on a man, either economically or emotionally or both, is to concede that a woman cannot stand on her own feet, that she must derive her status as a person from the achievements of another, that her connection with the wider world is always mediated by a man. To be divorced or to be a lesbian is to confront the world on one's own, to know that one's accomplishments are of one's own making, and to be fully adult and human.

3

"This Wonderful Decision"

Being a single mother is difficult, often very difficult. As the lesbian mothers who speak in these pages make clear, and as other research on single mothers documents abundantly, motherhood without a husband brings with it a range of problems. Single mothers, whether they are lesbian or heterosexual, are likely to face financial pressures, the stresses of bearing sole or primary responsibility for their children's welfare, problems in their efforts to manage time and energy, discrimination in housing, difficulties in finding adequate child care, and the varied stresses that derive from the need to orchestrate children's links with their fathers.[1] Though no reliable figures are available, a substantial number (and possibly the majority) of lesbian mothers seem to resemble single heterosexual mothers in the pathways that led them to their current situation: they had their children during a marriage or a long-erm heterosexual relationship and through various circumstances have made a transition to single/lesbian motherhood.

But increasing numbers of lesbian mothers present a very different picture. Like some heterosexual women who find themselves wondering what their lives will be worth if they never have children, more and more lesbians are deciding that conventional circumstances are not the only context in which a child can be born. They are having children on their own, becoming "intentional" single mothers. Though we have no way of knowing how many, or what proportion of lesbians are taking this path, we do know that the visibility of intentional motherhood among lesbians is increasing. Groups for lesbians considering parenthood are thriving in major cities; books and manuals have been written for women who want to become pregnant or adopt children;[2] documentary films have sought to present positive images of lesbian families;[3] and even the mainstream press is giving significant attention to the phenomenon of artificial insemination among lesbians.[4] Media treatment, not surprisingly, is superficial, tending toward either sensationalism or blandness.

But there can be little doubt that intentional motherhood through donor insemination or, less often, through adoption is becoming a common feature of life among lesbians. Gay media are making more frequent mention of children and family issues, and child care, once rarely even thought about in connection with lesbian or gay cultural and political events, has become a routine feature of such functions at least of those expected to draw women. San Francisco's lesbian and gay synagogue, for instance, has so many members with children that a religious school has been opened to provide several levels of instruction, including preparation for Bar and Bat Mitzvah. The coincidence of these developments with the AIDS epidemic and its devastating impact on the gay community in the San Francisco Bay Area cannot be ignored; synagogue members suggested to me that the enthusiasm for activities involving children now evidenced by the men in the congregation seems to parallel their weariness with disease and death.

The Link with Technology: Artificial/Donor Insemination

Artificial insemination has joined in vitro fertilization, embryo transfer, and sex predetermination among the "new" reproductive technologies commonly being talked about. But artificial insemination, the introduction of sperm into the vagina by means other than sexual intercourse, is in fact an ancient procedure. According to Jalna Hanmer, the earliest recorded mention of artificial insemination is in the Talmud, reflecting its practice in the third century A.D.[5] Originally applied to animal husbandry, as of course it still is today, it was first successfully applied to humans in 1790 by the Scottish anatomist and surgeon John Hunter.[6] For nearly a century only the husband's sperm was used (AIH, or artificial insemination by husband), but after experiments proved successful in 1884, artificial insemination by donor (AID) slowly came into use for wives of infertile men.[7] By

1979, AID conceptions were thought to account for between 6,000 and 10,000 births in the United States annually.[8]

Aside from mastery of the procedure itself, by which sperm is introduced into the vagina with a needleless syringe at a time calculated to correspond to the woman's ovulation, the ability to freeze sperm, perfected in 1949, created the basis for expanded use of artificial insemination, both in animals and in humans.[9] Some controversy has surrounded Herman Muller's suggestion that artificial insemination be used for eugenic purposes in humans; the infamous plan to store the sperm of Nobel Prize winners for this purpose is only the most publicized of such efforts.[10]

Less well reported is the lack of regulation governing the operation of existing sperm banks, which are under the control of physicians. Not only is medical screening of donors not consistent, but doctors appear to use their personal values as a way of deciding who may use their costly services.[11] As a result, unmarried women as well as low-income patients may not have the same access to artificial insemination afforded affluent married couples.[12] Meanwhile, debates over the paternal status of the donor and the legitimacy of the offspring continue to rage, inflamed by the application of the technology to so-called surrogate motherhood.[13]

Despite these obstacles, the low-tech nature of artificial insemination and the existence of alternatives to established sperm banks have permitted women to exercise some control over the procedure. At the same time that the women's health movement and self-help gynecology were changing women's views of their reproductive options, women were beginning to circulate information about how to achieve insemination outside the medical establishment.[14]

Adoption and Other Options

The right of lesbians and gay men to be adoptive or foster parents is highly contested, and so far efforts to establish the principle of equal treatment in this area have only occasionally been successful. Unmarried adults, even if there is no question about their sexual orientation, are not preferred as placements for children, particularly for the much-desired healthy Caucasian infants who seem to be in such short supply. Such people are likely to find themselves at the end of a long waiting list with little hope of even having a child placed with them. Their chances increase, of course, if they are willing to adopt so-called hard-to-place children—those who are older, are physically or mentally disabled, are of mixed racial backgrounds, or have not fared well in previous placements.[15] But only in a few areas of the country are agencies willing to consider the possibility that a lesbian or gay applicant might offer a suitable home for a child. Foster placements to lesbian and gay applicants have been increasing in recent years, however, particularly for teenagers who have been identified as homosexual.[16]

Lesbians and gay men who wish to adopt seem to do somewhat better when they make a private arrangement directly with the biological parent or parents, bypassing agency waiting lists. The adoption must still be approved by a state or private agency, but since the evaluation is carried out after the placement, a positive recommendation is more likely. Still in contention, however, is the status of the second parent. Since all states require that unmarried persons adopt only as single individuals, it is difficult to achieve legal recognition for a second parent, either at the time of the adoption or when a biological parent seeks to have the relationship between her partner and her child validated. Some adoptions of this type have been approved, nevertheless, though legal scholars generally doubt that many will follow.[17]

There is no way to gauge how often women undertake relationships with men in order to become pregnant; certainly instances in which men's personal qualities are secondary to women's primary reproductive goals may be far more common than is generally acknowledged. As we saw earlier, some formerly married mothers, both lesbian and heterosexual, tend to view their marriages as arrangements that permitted them to have children under culturally sanctioned circumstances. Not a few of these women, now that their marriages are over, go further and perceive single motherhood as having improved their situation in various ways. These women may see single motherhood as more desirable than motherhood in a marriage at the same time that they are constantly concerned with a range of financial and social problems exacerbated by their status as heads of households.

Though it appears that "intentional" mothers may still be in the minority among lesbian mothers, they are the most visible element of the so-called lesbian baby boom, or at least the one that attracts the most opprobrium. But these mothers afford us special insight into the underlying meaning of motherhood in the wider culture; as levels of social approval are stripped away, we are left with a view of the goals that lesbians and other unmarried women seek to achieve through motherhood and the strategies they employ in their attempts.

Why Do Women Want to Be Mothers?

Perhaps not surprisingly, intentional mothers are no more self-conscious about their reasons for wanting children than many other lesbian mothers. Indeed, some women have so long and intensely yearned for motherhood that questions about it are almost incomprehensible to them. These women's comments often reveal at the same time a feeling that the conventional context of parenthood—marriage—is undesirable or unattainable.

Michelle O'Neill, a lesbian whose one-year-old son was conceived through artificial insemination, puts it this way:

I've always loved children, particularly babies, ever since I was a very young child myself, and I always wanted to have children. My grandmother had [a big family] and it was a very positive thing in my family to have children.

Until Michelle learned that artificial insemination was possible and found a way to accomplish it outside the medical establishment, she believed that this valued goal would be denied her.

Similarly, Bonnie Pereira, who got involved with a man specifically in order to have a child, feels that motherhood, but not marriage, had always been a goal for her:

When I was real young, consciously I always knew I wanted to be a mother. I didn't know how I was going to go about it. . . . And as I grew older, I used to

*make comments like . . . that I was going to remain single and have a
child . . . That's what I said. That, of course, in those days especially, was taboo
to say. You always got married, you always had kids, but you did it in order. And
I just knew, just knew, I wasn't ever going to get married, I just felt that very
strongly.*

Camille Walsh had two children, a nine-year-old daughter and a
seven-year-old son, during relationships with two men. She sees
clearly that her major goal in getting involved in each of these relationships was to become a mother, and to do it on her own.

*I really wanted to have kids. That was clear. When I was a kid I did lots of baby-
sitting and really liked being around kids. I just felt like I wanted to raise
them. . . . And at the time I decided that I was ready it wasn't clear to anybody
else that they wanted to do that also. So I just got pregnant. There was enough element of doubt [about paternity] in it that [my daughter] became my child rather
than mine and somebody else's.*

For some women the desire to have a child is tied explicitly to a
desire to create or enhance a family. Joan Emerson, the mother of a
one-year-old daughter, explains:

*I think that I was really into a home-family situation. I wanted to enhance
that. . . . I still wanted that nucleus, that core of a family situation. Which are
children, I think.*

Some women perceive having a child as solidifying their links with
their natal families, allowing them to contribute to the ongoing development of the generations. Annabel Jessop, whose six-month-old
son was conceived through insemination, feels closer to her parents
and siblings since she has become a mother.

*I had a strong sense of family when I grew up and I like feeling like I have a
family.*

But many lesbian mothers once feared that their desire to have a
child was irreconcilable with their sexual orientation. Sarah Klein,

who now lives with her one-year-old daughter and her lover, found this conflict especially worrisome.

I've always wanted to have a child. In terms of being real tied up with being gay, it was one of the reasons that for a long time I was hesitant to call myself a lesbian. I thought that automatically assumed you had nothing to do with children. . . . I felt, well, if you don't say you're a lesbian you can still work with children, you can still have a kid, you can have relationships with men. But once I put this label on myself, [it would] all [be] over.

Some mothers, in contrast, claim not to remember wanting children when they were younger. Kathy Lindstrom had a child by artificial insemination when she was in her early thirties, but says she never really thought about having a child until she was twenty-seven or twenty-eight. The only explanation she can suggest for the timing of her interest is some sort of "hormonal change."

It just kind of came over me. It wasn't really conscious at first. It was just a need.

These comments echo those of Rose Allen, a heterosexual mother whose family background and personal history were quite erratic, and who came to a sudden decision to have a child during an acid trip. She was involved with a man at the time and set out deliberately to become pregnant despite his lack of interest in parenthood. When asked why she wanted to have a baby, she explains:

I just thought I needed one. . . . I guess it was the mother instinct. I don't know. It was just like I needed a child.

The term "need" as an explanation for the decision to have a child is particularly interesting when it is used by women whose situations appear to be at odds with conditions in which one would "normally" become a mother. Some heterosexual women, such as those who live particularly unconventional lives, share with lesbians a sense of being inappropriate aspirants for the status of mother. For these women, biologizing the process may serve to remove the stigma of having made a socially proscribed decision; if they couldn't help wanting to be mothers, then they can hardly be blamed for following their "natural" impulses. The claim that becoming a mother is the result of yielding to an involuntary biological urge bears a striking resemblance to arguments that homosexuality itself ought not to be stigmatized because it is the result of innate biological characteristics.[18]

The undefined need that other lesbian mothers are trying to meet appears to center on a desire to settle down, to achieve adulthood and to transcend the uncertainty of their lifestyles. Ruth Zimmerman, the mother of a five-year-old son, began a relationship with a man because he had qualities she thought would make him a "good" father, although the relationship ended not long after she became pregnant.

I definitely felt like I was marking time, waiting for something. I wasn't raised to be a career woman. I was raised to feel like I was grown up and finished growing up and living a regular normal life when I was married and had kids. And I knew that the married part wasn't going to happen. I feel like I've known that for a real long time.

The notion that having a child connotes adulthood, social responsibility, and a demonstration that one has "settled down" appears in the accounts of many women, echoing their accounts of divorce and coming out. This assumes particular importance for mothers who perceive their earlier lives to have been chaotic, lacking in purpose or direction. For example, Louise Green, a young counterculture lesbian who had her daughter, now eight months old, through artificial insemination, credits motherhood with making her a more reliable person.

I feel like I have a really huge responsibility and that I knew that I would and it's really grounded me and centered me a lot. I feel like I'm emotionally real together now. . . . I feel like I really like myself a lot now and I think I made a wonderful decision having her. I think it's turned my life into this really good thing.

Louise characterizes herself as a former hippie and describes her earlier life as rather disorganized. Since becoming a mother, she has stopped using drugs and alcohol and has come to place great importance on cleanliness, nutrition, and education. She has attempted a reconciliation with her family, with whom she had not been in contact for some years, and resumed the conventional given name that she had earlier replaced with a more fanciful appellation.

The search for meaning through motherhood is a quest that lesbians share with unmarried heterosexual women. The settling down that many women seek when they become mothers is linked with their notion of behavior appropriate to their age. These mothers describe themselves as having lived without a focus or worthwhile purpose until they had a child. Samantha Paulson, a heterosexual mother who lives alone with her seven-year-old daughter in an East Bay suburb, speaks eloquently of the way her child has changed her life.

Prior to [my daughter's] arrival my life was basically go to work, party after work . . . come home, sleep till noon, get up, go out to lunch, go to work, repeat the cycle. I had no hobbies. I . . . did nothing but the basic necessities for the apartment and spent very, very little time there. . . . And after having her, I was forced to stay at home—I wanted to stay at home—and I just started doing the little domestic-type things. . . . I think the first thing I did was a garden. And then I resumed going to the library, started getting books and reading, started doing little home repairs.

Samantha had her child during a rather unstable relationship with a man. She sees motherhood as having stimulated the emergence of latent creativity and industry; the implication is that she could not have generated these energies without an external impetus.

Similarly, having a baby permitted Rosalind Daniels, the heterosexual mother of a two-year-old daughter, to overcome a tendency to let the man she was involved with influence her major decisions. She had become pregnant once before, and at his urging had had an abortion. Her anger about the abortion when it wasn't what she really wanted led to a new resolution.

I just felt I can do it and I never again will get to that point of having a man control anything that is significant in my life and then it just evolved . . . that I wanted a baby and that I could do it on my own. . . . And, so I got pregnant. It was exactly the evolution that I had planned.

Achieving Goodness

What some women achieved by becoming a mother seems to be not just adulthood and responsibility but an identity as a "good" woman. Childhood is a time of innocence and discovery, and a woman can gain spiritual benefits by being close to a child and by her contribution to the child's growth and development. One lesbian mother said:

You get to have a lot of input in another human being's very formative years. That's real special to have that privilege of doing that, and you get to see them growing and developing and it's sort of like you put in the fertile soil and . . . hopefully what will happen is that they grow and blossom and become wonderful. . . . I think it's definitely the most important thing that people do . . . to build the next generation.

Another lesbian, Sarah Klein, put her feelings a bit differently:

I now feel there's something more important in my life. I'm much more in touch with my death. I know it's coming and I have to not fuck around as much as I used to in terms of doing some things I want to do before I die. . . . I have a chance to change humankind, in terms of a person who will see herself differently than anyone else.

Regina Carter, whose daughter is six, spoke of the meaning of motherhood this way:

My kid has given me more knowledge than any other experience in my life. She's taught me more than all the teachings I've ever learned as far as education, and I mean that as far as academic education, spiritual education [is concerned]. Taught me things that no other person, place, or thing could possibly teach me. And those are, you know, those things are without words.

Bonnie Pereira associates motherhood with honesty and worthiness.

I've become more at peace with me [since having my daughter]. She's given me added strength; she's made me—it's like looking in the mirror in many ways— she's made me see myself for who I am. She's definitely given me self-worth. I've become, I think, a more honest person.

Camille Walsh also emphasizes the basic honesty of children. Being near children allows the adult to let go of the corruption of life in the world.

Somehow [having a child] freed me. I don't really know how to explain it but it was like a freeing process for me. The stuff that everybody bottles up, you can let go of around kids. . . . It was like a reeducation. . . . It helps me a lot, I mean it helps me in everything I do. It helps me see the world better. It helps me feel other people better. It helps me, you know, understand what's happening with the people I work around and all these different things. . . . I'm not sure how I figured out that having kids was going to do that for me. Obviously it is a selfish motive, but my life felt really icy without them. I mean inside of me felt kind of devoid of emotion.

Motherhood, then, can bring a woman closer to basic truths, can make her more able to empathize with the feelings of others. Sarah Klein says that being a mother has made her more "accepting" of people who have made decisions different from hers, essentially has enabled her to achieve a level of tolerance that was unknown to her before she was a mother and was "a lot more judgmental."

These feelings are extremely powerful, particularly in such women as Christine Richmond, who experienced a kind of transformative altruism after the birth of her son, now three.

I think that probably the biggest thing is my ability to be closer to people, and my capacity for loving has increased and it has made it easier for me to live with somebody in a loving relationship and be happy to do that. . . . I just feel more rooted in that place, I don't feel so anxious about what's out there or what might be out there. That's maybe partially getting older, but I think it really has a lot to do with him.

On this level, motherhood provides the occasion for a woman to declare her commitment to a kind of authenticity, a naturalness. As we shall see later, becoming a mother also allows women to establish themselves in families. The creation of family ties proceeds both because the mother and her child constitute a new family and because having a child tends to bring her into closer alliance with her family of origin.

Being Ready: Age, Finances, Relationships

Age looms large in the accounts of many of intentional mothers. Often the importance of age in the decision to have a child is tied less to a concept of age-appropriate behavior than to a concern with the effect of advancing age on fertility and the health of the child.[19] Women who discuss their decisions in these terms tend to articulate a specific deadline—most commonly thirty-five—after which child-bearing is risky or somehow incongruous.[20]

Clarice Grant, a thirty-five-year-old lesbian whose six-month-old son was conceived through insemination, had considered having a child for many years but had not been motivated to take serious steps in this direction. Once she entered her thirties, however, she felt that she was getting to "the deadline zone of thirty-five, where you have to start worrying about Down's syndrome." This also proved to be a time in her life when other factors made motherhood a possibility. She had a job from which she could take a leave of absence, she had a long-term lover who could be expected to share parenting, and her lover's financial situation could provide for both of them without strain.

For similar reasons, Laura Bergeron made a concerted effort to find a donor for her third child when she began to edge toward forty.

I really did want to have a girl, and I was getting older. See, I had my first child at thirty-two, and I was feeling that I didn't really want to have children past the appropriate childbearing age. I had been doing too much reading about retardation and mongoloids and everything else . . . so I put some ads [for donors] in the paper.

Annabel Jessop voices similar concerns, explaining that they influenced her to go ahead with artificial insemination despite the fact that she would have preferred to wait until she was settled in a long-term relationship.

I decided that I wanted to have a kid, and that because I'm in my thirties, my time was limited. I look at it as a life choice. There's only so many things you can do in your life, and this is one of the things I wanted to do, and it was time to do it. Waiting wasn't going to do any good. Professionally, I was together, I was as stable as I was ever going to be financially, I had a little put away, and there was just no reason not to do it now.

Karen Bernstein, a heterosexual mother who also considered thirty-five her deadline for having a child, used similar language to explain the compromises involved in deciding to become pregnant when the opportunity presented itself.

The fantasy was that the lasting love of a man could happen and we'd have a child together. But the reality that I saw all around me was that love and lasting were mutually exclusive. All my friends who had gotten married in their early twenties were divorcing. All of them. . . . So anyway, the feeling was that that was it, that was my big chance. And if the perfect thing wasn't going to happen, then fuck it.

Whereas these women decided to have children even though they had not yet found stable relationships, others stress the importance of embarking on parenthood with the help of a supportive lover. These women tend not to view themselves as "single," but as living in situations comparable (or superior) to a heterosexual union in terms of stability and commitment. They describe the decision to become pregnant as having been made jointly, with strong consideration given to the benefits to be derived from having two caretakers and two incomes. Clarice Grant explains:

Looking around at the other couples that were in the birth class that we went to, she's more nurturing of a parent than any of the fathers seem to be, that I've seen around. She spends when she's home more time with him. Really wants to, I can kind of sit back and she takes over. . . . I really feel like it's coparenting.

Closely intertwined with other decision-making factors are prospective mothers' assessments of their financial situations and their ability to manage motherhood on their own. Subjective judgments of what constitutes a sufficient income or an adequate standard of living vary considerably, as does the extent to which mothers engage in concrete financial planning.

Evaluations of financial status can be inextricable from considerations having to do with age, career, or relationships. For both lesbian and heterosexual women who have reached a point of stability in their work, for example, timing tends to have to do with feeling that things are as good financially as they will ever be. Women in this situation usually derive some sense of security from having established themselves in careers; they believe that they will be able to regain their earning power easily once they return to work. After their children are born, however, they often find that they failed to anticipate all the expenses associated with motherhood or that their assessment of their ability to return to work was unrealistic.

Other women's financial stability derived from knowledge that they would be supported or assisted by friends, lovers, or family. One lesbian mother whose lover supports the family planned the birth with this support in mind; others receive regular assistance from their parents. Some mothers view welfare or some other form of public assistance as offering a regular, predictable, though (they hope) temporary source of income. Despite wide variations in the income on which mothers and their children actually live, women's evaluation of its adequacy has more to do with the solidity of their support systems than with the amount of money they actually have in hand each month. Those who have an intimate circle of supportive friends or relatives are most likely to perceive their economic situations as comfortable, regardless of their objective financial status.[21]

Many women view their incomes as merely making motherhood possible, in essence as not preventing it, rather than as necessarily providing them with an adequate standard of living. Lilly Parker, a lesbian who has a one-year-old daughter and derives her principal income from AFDC, expressed it this way:

I figured that I've been poor most of my life. Not that poor . . . I'd always managed somehow. And that with a child, I'd manage. Also, I figured that I could get AFDC for the first year of my baby's life . . . because then I wouldn't have to work a lot. . . . And I had a baby so that I could take care of the baby, not so that somebody else could take care of the baby. . . . I feel like AFDC is government-

subsidized— They won't give us good-quality child care and everything, so we all get AFDC instead. Although it's not what you'd call a fortune at all.

While Lilly talks in detail about the sparseness of her AFDC award, it is clear that she considers this a minor inconvenience, which she must endure in order to achieve the more important goal of motherhood. She shares her flat with two roommates, has a close and supportive relationship with a sister who lives nearby, and has received some tangible support from her family. She has not told them she is gay.

Finally, a few mothers view their financial situations as not only enabling but obliging them to have children. Julie Clark, who was left a substantial inheritance, was motivated to adopt a child in part because she herself had been adopted. She felt strongly that it would be selfish or not responsible to fail to share her good fortune with a homeless child. Her views coincide with those of a heterosexual adoptive mother in Marin County. She had adopted two minority adolescents some years earlier because she earned what she considered a good salary and felt that she shouldn't keep it all just for herself. Though these mothers don't go so far as to criticize women who don't extend themselves and their resources in this way, their decisions reflect the concern with selfishness or lack of responsibility among childless women to which other informants often refer.

How to Have a Baby: Choosing a Method

Once a lesbian has decided to have a baby, she has to figure out how to go about it. Heterosexual and occasional lesbian women in relationships with men may seem to have a ready solution at hand, but issues of later obligation may undermine its apparent simplicity. In some situations involving a relationship with a man, his future involvement as a father may be at issue, as may the durability of the relationship itself. All of these questions may become merged with the decision to have a child, making the matter of intentionality murky at best.

Though lesbians sometimes have intimate relationships with the men who father their children, this approach is not what most prefer. A sexual entanglement with a man not only may be personally unappealing but may raise potential problems of custody or control. At the same time, insemination by a physician may represent an unpleasant intrusion into one's private life; that is, a threat to one's autonomy. A lesbian may circumvent these problems by opting for insemination outside the medical establishment, but that route may have other unwanted consequences; in particular, she may not be able to shield her identity from the donor. Finally, adoption is always difficult for a single woman, and a lesbian is likely not to qualify for adoption at all if her sexual orientation is discovered.[22] All the intentional single mothers I interviewed had to negotiate a variety of priorities in deciding to become mothers and in choosing a way to realize that goal, but lesbians had to take their stigmatized status into consideration in devising a strategy.

Relationships with men

Some lesbian mothers I interviewed already had a relationship with a man at the time they decided to have a baby. Though some of these babies were welcome by-products of existing sexual relationships, other women turned to friends or casual acquaintances to become pregnant "the old-fashioned way."

But becoming involved with a man in an effort to conceive a child may not only lead to awkward entanglements but entail serious risks. Like formerly married women, "unwed" mothers who have ties to their child's father may find themselves either fending off attentions they consider excessive or having to compensate distressed children for their fathers' failure to show an interest in them. A few such fathers play their social role with enthusiasm, offering both time and financial support to their offspring, but most seem to feel no obligation and some even deny their role in the child's conception. Women rarely are financially or emotionally prepared to launch the kind of legal battle that must be waged to establish paternity and gain judicial recognition of the father's identity.

Before Laura Bergeron came out as a lesbian, she was in a long-term relationship with a man. As she moved into her early thirties, she decided that she wanted to have children even though her partner did not.

He had one child already by a previous marriage and there were a lot of problems around visiting the child and he just felt that he didn't want to go through that again in case we were to split. And also he didn't want to be financially responsible for bringing up any more children. . . . So we had a contract that it would be OK if I had a child as long as I was willing to be totally financially responsible, and I agreed to that.

During the time the relationship continued, this agreement remained firm; the father made no financial contribution directly to the children and provided no assistance whatsoever in their care. More recently, however, he has established a regular visiting relationship with the two boys and with the daughter Laura had through artificial insemination after she came out.

More commonly, such relationships collapse soon after the women become pregnant. If the male partners are truly unwilling collaborators in parenthood, they tend to extricate themselves from the relationship as soon as they can. Lesbians have mixed feelings about these developments. They want their children to feel some sort of connection to their "fathers," but at the same time they may feel relieved to be able to avoid interference or active hostility from these men. Beth Romano puts it this way:

I'm glad I did it that way, that I made no compromises. Just in practical matters now, there is no threat, I'm pretty free to do what I want, there is nobody saying, "I'm going to take your kid away." . . . I guess it's rather egomaniacal to say, "I produced this child by myself," but that's how I feel.

These remarks are echoed by heterosexual mothers who expected or hoped for more from the men who had impregnated them. Samantha Paulson said:

[My daughter's father] maintains very little [contact]. I think he'd like to but he feels guilty about not participating more in her growing up. So every three to six

*months he'll make an appearance or call, but nothing worthwhile. . . . I think
the only reason I've survived is because I expected nothing. He told me initially
he wasn't going to participate at all so I knew exactly what I was getting into
before she was born. . . . He let me know where he was coming from; he told me
he . . . might not even be able to stay around because he couldn't accept the
responsibility. So I knew I'd be a single parent. Although somewhere at the back
of my mind I thought, he doesn't really, he's not really meaning this, he'll come
around. I had some hopes, but I always knew that he wasn't willing to be a
father.*

Many heterosexual single mothers, like lesbians, move back and
forth between a strong desire to be independent, to manage motherhood on their own, and wistful sentiments about what might have
been. Many of these accounts differ little from those offered by formerly married mothers, regardless of sexual orientation, in which
they attempt to rationalize (with little apparent success) constant disappointments with their children's fathers by insisting on their commitment to independence and autonomy.

Ruth Zimmerman describes the long-term relationship with her
son's father before she became pregnant (and before she had come out
as a lesbian) and her efforts during her pregnancy to encourage his
involvement with the child. The father apparently couldn't decide
how to relate to the pregnancy, and finally she gave him an ulti-
matum: Either stay and be a father or leave altogether. He stayed but
continued to be indecisive until he was offered a job too far away to
make commuting feasible. The job enabled him to avoid a definitive
commitment. Over time, his professional obligations have gradually
moved him farther and farther from the Bay Area, although he has
continued to make regular financial contributions and to correspond
with Ruth.

More commonly, lesbians try to maintain some distance from the
child's father because of their concerns about possible threats to custody or to their maternal autonomy. Ruth, for example, harbors some
resentment about her former boyfriend's failure to be involved with
their son at the same time that she views his behavior as ultimately
beneficial to her. Because he has kept his distance for so long, she

reasons, it would not be in his interest to challenge her custody. His name does not appear on the birth certificate and to claim the child he would have to establish paternity in court and become liable for the costs of AFDC during the time his child was supported by public funds, both powerful disincentives.

Some mothers carefully omit the father's name from the child's birth certificate to prevent possible custody disputes.[23] Camille Walsh made this choice mainly because she did not trust her children's fathers:

[There is] some side of me that's very cautious and I thought if there was something on an official document that that might jeopardize my hold on [my children].

The fear of a challenge to their custody had led many lesbian mothers to distance themselves from the father and to take precautions against his discovery of their sexual orientation. Like formerly married women who have similar fears, women who have children on their own use whatever resources they have at hand to discourage their children's fathers from even considering litigation. Their strategies often are based on various ways of increasing distance from the father (and thereby decreasing his ability to scrutinize their lifestyles) as well as on more formal means to separate him from the family. Mothers reason that fathers who lack legal claims to children will not be motivated to pursue questionable custody litigation, but many of them still experience considerable anxiety about the possibility.

Some lesbian mothers, in contrast, make persistent efforts to bring the father into their children's lives. Sarah Klein conceived her daughter, now one year old, in a relationship with a man she had selected for qualities she felt would make him a good father. Although he makes no formal financial contribution, he has made a regular commitment to care for the child; the fact that he lives only a few blocks away from Sarah and her lover simplifies these arrangements. Sarah regards him as a parent and anticipates that he will play a vital role in the care of their daughter throughout her life. She apparently has no fear of his challenging her custody and in fact considers him a friend and has maintained a social relationship with him apart from the time he devotes to the child. The fact that they have continued these arrangements with minimal stress is intriguing in view of his initial resentment at being "used" for his sperm. Once Sarah became pregnant, she terminated her sexual relationship with him, and he reacted angrily.

He was really pissed off. It was a classic, you took my sperm, you lesbians, you all plotted against me. . . . It was sad, he was really hurt.

Clearly the consequences of selecting a man as an "inseminator" are unpredictable. Though such premeditated conceptions may seem to preclude future ties with the father (or donor), actual relationships range from quasi-joint-custody situations such as Sarah's to total estrangement.

Some women who want to become pregnant manipulate situations in which the man is willing, or even eager, to establish a more extensive commitment. Bonnie Pereira reports, for instance, that though she was a lesbian, she embarked on a relationship with Bob because she had decided it was time to have a child. He wanted to marry her, but though she was not averse to his having some connection with their offspring, she was not interested in any legal entanglements. Bob visited often when their daughter, Tina, was small, but his involvement gradually waned and eventually disappeared entirely. Because Bonnie felt that Tina wanted a connection with her father, she made what she considers major efforts to keep channels of communication open with him. These efforts have met with no success.

I have done what I can do: I have written, you know, and I have called and I've let him know where I've moved to and so forth and so on, and then I've made it very clear that he's never going to be turned away from here if he wants to see his daughter. He's made that decision himself, that he feels uncomfortable, I guess.

More commonly, lesbians tend to be extremely cautious in limiting their connections with the men they choose to father their children. Laura Bergeron made a written agreement with the father of her third child.

We just wrote down a few basic things, which for one, I would never claim him as a parent for any reason. And I would never apply for welfare and give his name for the father. I wouldn't use his name on the birth certificate. I wouldn't expect any moral or financial obligations that might come up later. In other words, he was just a sperm donor, except that we were doing it in person.

Because she does know the father, however, Laura sees herself as having avoided one of the serious problems presented by donor insemination: the child's future questions about her father's identity.

Other lesbians, however, and some heterosexual women as well, perceive a relationship with the child's father as a threat, mandating secrecy and caution. Lilly Parker, for example, consciously manipulates information about her daughter's conception in an effort to prevent friends from figuring out his identity. She never told the man that he fathered her child and has no interest in any contribution from him at all.

I don't want him to be only half-assed involved. I'd rather have no involvement at all. I don't feel like he is a father. I feel like he's a donor.

Lilly would like to have another child, but has decided to use artificial insemination if she does so to avoid the problems with secrecy she has had with her first child.

Donor insemination

Beyond concerns about the consequences of a relationship with a "father," some lesbians can feel nothing but distaste at the prospect of having sexual relations with a man in an effort to conceive a child. In fact, many of the women I interviewed explained that they had thought biological motherhood was not a realistic goal because they were not willing to consider heterosexual intercourse. For some of those who later discovered artificial insemination, motherhood had become a remote dream, the price to be paid for living in a way that was otherwise comfortable. Joan Emerson, who now has a nine-month-old daughter, explains how she came to choose artificial insemination.

There wasn't any decision. I didn't want to adopt, I wanted to have my own child. I didn't want to go out and pick up, I didn't want to have to sleep with a man to get her. So artificial insemination was the only way.

Maggie Walters, the mother of an eighteen-month-old daughter, had been familiar with the idea of artificial insemination since childhood and found the decision easy to make.

I hadn't never fucked anyway, so I wasn't going to do it for that. Plus, see, when I grew up, one of my best friends . . . had been conceived that way . . . and it wasn't like it was any big thing. . . . So it was just kind of interesting, but it wasn't any big deal.

To several mothers, either specific or vague concerns about custody made artificial insemination seem the only viable option. Joan Emerson explains:

I wanted the total responsibility of the child. . . . I guess I didn't want to take the chance of anybody trying to take her away from me.

Like many others, Joan chose to become pregnant through a medical facility, believing that this way of obtaining a donor would give her the fullest assurance of anonymity. Anonymity, however, is won at the cost of some personal control over conception, a central issue for some women.[24] These women tend to take a strong critical stance toward mainstream medical practices, particularly in regard to the increasing use of high-tech interventions in gynecological and obstetrical care; some of them are committed to various sorts of alternative or non-Western medicine.

The need to exert autonomy during the reproductive process was a central concern to Louise Green, for example. Further, because of her counterculture lifestyle, she felt so removed from mainstream medicine that she did not even consider that such resources would be available to her. Her approach was to ask men she met if they would like to be sperm donors until she found one who was willing. She was careful not to let this person know her full name and after conceiving she moved to another state. Even so, Louise still harbors considerable anxiety about the donor as a threat to custody, should he ever have the ability to trace her and make a claim.

Louise's nonmedical approach to conception met her spiritual needs as well. She carried out the procedure alone in her room.

I had all these candles lit . . . and it was real quiet and I had this nice music playing that I really liked, my tarot cards out. It was real nice, it was real peaceful.

After doing a vinegar douche (to help conceive a girl), Louise used a menstrual sponge to keep the semen from leaking out.

While I was lying there I was imagining . . . kind of like clouds . . . and from the cloud would . . . come like raindrops . . . [and] each one was a baby spirit. . . . It was like the perfect baby spirit was going to drop and . . . come inside me. And it did.

Louise became pregnant on her first attempt, believing that this occurred because of mystical forces. She intended to have her baby at home, where she would be able to create an agreeable spiritual environment, but after a protracted labor she was transferred to a hospital, where she had a long and difficult delivery. Despite the multiple medical interventions and considerable physical trauma she endured, she describes the birth of her daughter in mystical terms.

It was about the best thing I ever experienced. I was totally amazed. The labor was like I had died. . . . I had just died. The minute she came out, I was born again. It was like we'd just been born together.

Louise's story reminds us of the intrinsic, and often spiritual, values women associate with motherhood. By becoming a mother a woman may achieve not only adulthood, but a glimpse of the most ultimate and stirring truths.

Like lesbians who became pregnant through relationships with men, those who resort to donor insemination are fearful of future interference by the biological father. These anxieties may conflict with the desire that many of them feel to share their child with him. Some mothers wish they could have some sort of supportive connection with their child's genitor, and others focus more on what they imagine the child later may want to know about him.

Grace Garson used a gay male friend as a go-between to obtain a sperm donation, and gave no thought to possible problems when she was setting up these arrangements. Now she wishes there had been some way to record the donor's name in case her son may later want to trace his biological roots.

Michelle O'Neill has similar feelings:

When I did do the insemination, I deliberately did not want to know who the father was, I didn't ever want to meet him. I regret now that I did not have the name of the father put on file someplace so that if [my son] ever wants to know who the father is . . . I feel that it's his right to know.

Some mothers want to have more information about the donor but not enough to establish his identity. Kathy Lindstrom, for one, feels that it would be good to be able to tell her son about his ethnic background on the paternal side, and she suspects that he will have the same kinds of questions about his father that adopted children have about their biological parents. The underlying assumption here is clearly that "ethnic background" has something to do with biology or genetic heritage.

Maggie Walters expresses other kinds of misgivings about having a child without a known father. Her concern focuses on whether it is right to bring a child into the world with a lesbian mother and no father. This was the issue that she considered most carefully when she planned her pregnancy, and although she finally went ahead and was artificially inseminated, she still feels that the problem is unresolved.

The reactions of the families of the women who have children through artificial insemination sometimes confound their expectations. Most mothers report that after a period of confusion, the existence of a new grandchild came to overshadow the way the child had come into the world. Michelle O'Neill, who had grown up in a conservative Catholic family, feared that her mother would never accept her grandchild. When she told her mother that she was pregnant by artificial insemination, her mother was not only shocked but concerned that her daughter's "freaky" way of getting pregnant would be written up in medical journals. The actual birth seems to have eased these anxieties, however, and Michelle's mother has been consistently supportive, both emotionally and financially, since the child was born.

Though most mothers ultimately achieve some measure of acceptance by their parents, some families find out-of-wedlock pregnancy, especially by artificial insemination, simply too shocking to manage. Kathy Lindstrom's mother was very enthusiastic when her brother's wife had a baby, but she could not summon similar feelings when Kathy became pregnant. The pregnancy has apparently ended their relationship altogether. Although her mother lives in the state, she has made no effort to contact Kathy since the birth six months ago.

Since she's known I became gay, she's maintained a visiting relationship, but that's even broken off since I had the baby. . . . It's just something that goes unsaid. . . . I guess she couldn't approve of my method of having [a baby].

Adoption

Adoption is rarely an option for a lesbian, or for any other unmarried woman, for that matter. Of all the mothers I interviewed, only five had adopted their children—four lesbians and one heterosexual. Three had found their children through public agencies and two through private adoptions.

The patterns associated with these adoptions all resemble those we might expect if we looked more generally at adoptions among single adults. The three mothers who adopted through agencies all received children who were considered "hard to place"—older, of minority or mixed race, and disabled. Those who were successful in arranging private adoptions (both lesbians) became mothers of virtually newborn Caucasian infants with no apparent disabilities. Both of these mothers, however, were employed in health-care settings and were able to learn about impending births under conditions that facilitated the adoption process.

Among the lesbian adoptive mothers, fear that their sexual orientation might undermine the adoption surfaced under a variety of circumstances. In the most benign conditions the matter had not been discussed but, the mother surmised, was suspected. Some of these women thought the possibility had not been pursued because the adoption worker didn't want to have to stop the proceedings.

Eileen Sullivan adopted two children privately and encountered no difficulties negotiating the bureaucratic aspects of the adoption process. At the same time, she feared situations in which she might be forced to answer a lot of personal questions:

I was afraid the issue of my being gay would come up and on the basis of that they would refuse the adoption. That was the real issue. They never asked, or never had evidence enough to ask.

Janet Goldman, who also adopted privately, worked at the hospital where her daughter was born. The social worker who set up the adoption learned that she was a lesbian only after the adoption was final. She has kept in touch with Janet and her daughter, and she says now that she would not knowingly have offered a baby to a lesbian, but now that she sees how well the situation has worked out, she's glad she didn't know.

Most single women who try to adopt a child are faced with a battery of personal questions and may not be spared direct inquiries about their sexual orientation. When Emma Gibson adopted the first of two disabled minority children through an agency, she was living with a partner. The social worker asked her if the other women was her lover and she denied it. Nothing further was asked and the adoption went through. Although several years have passed, during which she adopted a second child and broke up with her lover, she continues to be extremely anxious about the possibility of being exposed. Because she lied in answer to a direct question, she fears that she has committed the equivalent of perjury and that she will lose her children if the truth is discovered. Emma's preoccupation with secrecy is reinforced by her certainty that she would be fired from her job if her lesbianism were ever revealed. For financial reasons, she recently moved to a working-class suburb far from her old neighborhood and lacks a close circle of lesbian friends. Most of her friends from the years before the adoptions are not parents, and she finds that she is out of step with their social world now.

Intentional Motherhood: What Is Intended?

American culture places tremendous emphasis on the powers of the individual, on the importance of achieving personal goals through action in one's own behalf. Lesbians who are not mothers share with other childless women a feeling of distance not only from the kinds of things "ordinary" women do but from the special relationship to the spiritual world women can derive from their connection to children. By becoming a mother, a woman can experience a moment of transcendent unity with mystical forces; by being a mother, she makes continuing contact with her inner goodness, a goodness that is activated by altruism and nurtured by participation in a child's growth and development.

By becoming a mother, a lesbian can negotiate the formation of her self; she can bring something good into her life without having to sacrifice autonomy or control. Thus the intentional single mother (whether she is lesbian or heterosexual) can achieve a central personal goal—the goodness that comes from putting the needs of a dependent being first. By becoming a mother through her own agency, she avoids the central paradox that motherhood represents to married women—a loss of autonomy and therefore of basic personhood in a culture that valorizes individualism and autonomy. Like ending a marriage, having a baby on her own allows a woman to meet her basic personal goals, and she may see it as a critical part of establishing a satisfying identity in a culture that often blocks women's efforts to be separate individuals.

Being a mother provides many benefits, but becoming a mother is a process that can be pursued in a variety of ways and can help women realize a variety of goals. The specific strategies they select— deliberate pregnancy with a man, artificial insemination, adoption— reflect not only the opportunities available to them, but the particular ends which they seek to enhance. Women who wish to distance themselves from such mainstream institutions as the medical establishment may find it difficult to maintain the anonymity of a sperm donor; those who fear the donor's intrusion on their lives may seek anonymity at the price of autonomy. There are many ways to go about becoming a mother, and they are as vital a part of women's objectives as their desire to be mothers.

Motherhood also appears to offer lesbians some resolution of the dilemmas inherent in membership in a stigmatized category. On the one hand, intentional motherhood demands specific action of some sort—a lesbian is, after all, unlikely to become pregnant by chance. On the other hand, to the extent that wanting to be a mother is a profoundly *natural* desire, and is perceived as having nothing to do with cultural or political choices, then achieving motherhood implies movement into a more natural or normal status than a lesbian can ordinarily hope to experience otherwise. But motherhood also requires planning and manipulation, and thus stands in contrast to one's natural—that is, unpremeditated—lesbian identity.

At the same time, however, a lesbian who becomes a mother has effectively rejected the equation of homosexuality with unnaturalness and the exclusion of the lesbian from the ranks of "women." In this sense, finding a way to become a mother constitutes a form of resistance to the gender limitations, and particularly to the constructions of sexual orientation, that prevail in the wider culture. Curiously, though, this act of resistance is achieved through compliance with conventional expectations for women, so it may also be construed as a gesture of accommodation.

The stories that lesbian and some unmarried heterosexual mothers tell of their ventures into motherhood, of the ways they formulated their aims and acted to achieve them, then, bring together behaviors that can be regarded simultaneously as rebellion and as compliance. For these women, negotiating motherhood consists of forging a path through these conflicting meanings and weaving them together into a rewarding definition of the self.

4

Ties That Endure

To many radical lesbians who have approached the question of motherhood in the popular feminist literature, the term "family" refers to past experience—the backgrounds, socialization, and limitations our particular family histories impose on us. The poet Jan Clausen puts it this way: "Besides being aware of the parenting experience of other generations of lesbians, I think that before we speak of creating a parenting community, we must examine how our individual ideas about being parents, and our daily experience of living with children, differ according to our identities and backgrounds—the specific oppression we face and the specific strengths we have that grow out of our memories of the people who raised us."[1]

Kinship is of special interest to lesbian mothers because it provides a specific instance of the patriarchal ideology from which they must separate themselves. Lesbians may see their families of origin as influential in the formation of their own families, but more often than not they construe that foundation as something to work against rather than as a source of ongoing meaning and validity. Most popular feminist work treats the family of origin as the place where children are socialized into heterosexuality and unequal gender roles—as the primary source of the "compulsory heterosexuality" to which Adrienne Rich alerted us.[2]

Most writers in this tradition assume that lesbian mothers differ significantly, and in positive ways, from other mothers: "As lesbian parents even more so than simply as lesbian women, I believe we are all fundamentally outlaws," writes Jan Clausen. "Like open, unashamed lesbian and gay sexuality, our chosen lesbian families call into question some terribly basic assumptions about who's important to whom, and why."[3] Lesbian writers who outline strategies for dealing with the stresses and strains of parenthood use "family" to connote the *chosen* families of lesbians and see "the [lesbian] community" as the potential source of support on many levels, functioning in essence as an extended family. They view lesbian families as explicitly political in that these families demand the redefinition of emotions and behaviors that patriarchy has confined to the traditional family.

Andrea Canaan asks, "How can I honor the commitment of friends, of loved ones, of my comother and others who hold me, who comfort me, who hold children dear and necessary to their own survival—they who understand that loving women means loving all the women we were, could have been, may become, and are becoming, including the mothers who bore us and the children we once were?"[4] Another lesbian mother writes: "As lesbians, who are automatically placed on the fringe of society by the choice of our lives, we can bring to parenting and to young children the positive aspects of being on that fringe—of possibility instead of control, acceptance instead of rejection, diversity instead of commercial homogeneity, and, yes, importantly, a world of many families in changing and varied forms, not limited by the term *traditional*."[5]

The tone of much lesbian feminist popular writing, then, has adopted the language of sisterhood that pervaded feminist discourse in the late 1960s and early 1970s, building on it to generate a series of assumptions about how important ties are constituted. Probably the first assumption is that lesbianism is a more central feature of the identity than any other, with the possible exception of femaleness. All women, and especially all lesbians, share basic life experiences and encounters in the domain of sexual politics; these common experiences eclipse ties based on kinship, work, social status, ethnicity, or geography. This literature rarely discusses the relationships lesbians establish or continue with their parents, though the absence of discussion of these ties suggests that parents are unlikely to be supportive of one's choice to be a lesbian (conceived as a largely political choice), and that in any case their support is unimportant because they have little to offer to one whose life centers on being a lesbian.

This perspective is characteristic as well of the small body of social science scholarship on lesbians. Susan Krieger's meticulous ethnography of a lesbian community, *The Mirror Dance,* for example, devotes a single chapter to "mothers and children." Here Krieger reports the kinds of concerns common to lesbian mothers: that their children may suffer ostracism, that they may be vulnerable to child custody litigation, that their children might not feel comfortable with their lesbian identities or with their lesbian friends. But this chapter, like later ones on "the outside world" of relations with co-workers, relatives, and "straight society," segregates these elements of lesbians' lives from what seems to be the more authentic center provided by the lesbian-feminist community. The lesbian community is thus presented as a bounded, independent social world, not unlike a small-scale tribal society.

Barbara Ponse's *Identities in the Lesbian World,* reveals the pathways women travel in the course of "becoming" lesbians and explores the issues of passing and disclosure in the contexts where secrecy produces its most elaborate configurations. Not surprisingly, the workplace and the family emerge as the sites where disclosure raises the most problems. But Ponse treats these contexts, without apparent question, as outside the "gay group," implying that the meanings lesbians construct for their identities are located only within the "lesbian subculture."

Even the early work of John Gagnon and William Simon, which exhorted readers to remember that the life experience of lesbians is fundamentally similar to that of other women, particularly with respect to patterns of sexual initiation, tends to downplay lesbians' family ties and virtually ignores the roles many lesbians play as mothers.[6]

Kath Weston's *Families We Choose* is perhaps the only significant contribution to gay/lesbian scholarship that attempts to document fully the relationships between homosexuals of both genders and their families of origin. She describes the conflicts gay men and lesbians have with their families, and responses of "straight families" to a child's homosexuality which range from general acceptance through limited toleration to outright and permanent rejection. Even though the responses vary, however, gays' and lesbians' narratives about their blood relatives tend to focus on fear, anxiety, and displacement, and on the family as the place where they are most likely to experience painful homophobia. Weston documents the formation of "families we choose" or "gay families," constructed from friendship networks and assuming many of the functions traditionally expected of relatives. Though these chosen families are not strictly substitutes for ties with blood kin and may exist even when ties with relatives have not been severed, they do serve to mark the limited power of biologically defined ties and to establish choice as an element in the maintenance of kinship links.

Interestingly, gays and lesbians still use kinship imagery when they speak of their chosen families and often compare them with their "straight families." Fundamental notions of what one expects from one's family—unconditional loyalty, for example—still prevail. That is, while chosen families appear to constitute instances of cultural creation, they may also be seen as adaptations of existing cultural forms, transported and adjusted to fit specific conditions. The assumptions that underlie them are the old assumptions about family ties; Weston's informants seem to be unwilling to abandon these expectations for totally new ones that might correspond more closely to their lived experience.

I had assumed that lesbian mothers would form and sustain such ties very differently from heterosexual single mothers—that their networks would consist of (mainly lesbian) friends and that heterosexual mothers' networks would include many more relatives. Lesbian mothers, I reasoned, would be cast out of or voluntarily exiled from their families of origin and therefore would be likely to construct innovative fictive kin relationships to replace them. As I spoke with mothers, however, it became clear that the importance of kinship ties for lesbian mothers reflected less a process of culture building than the continuity of kinship systems also available to heterosexual single mothers.

The Importance of Kinship Ties

As I questioned my informants about the practical challenges of single motherhood in an effort to learn how they form and maintain their social networks and how they solve specific kinds of problems, consistent patterns began to emerge. Both lesbian and heterosexual mothers reported that they received assistance from their families— emergency loans, money to make the down payment on a house, financial advice, car and home repairs, a place to live for little or no rent, money to pay for their children's music lessons and braces for their teeth, regular or emergency baby-sitting or child care, meals, transportation.

But the links with kin that both lesbian and heterosexual mothers described are more than just the best means to manage a variety of practical difficulties. These instrumental ties are located in a dense intersection of affective bonds. Ties with kin, especially with one's parents—the grandparents of one's child—represent a kind of well-being, a solid "family" context in which a child can develop securely. Thus the emotional bonds tend to overshadow the practical aid; the assistance that families provide serves to demonstrate the vigor of the kin connection, a benefit that not infrequently outweighs the value of the help received.

Eileen Sullivan and Wendy Gardner, adoptive mothers of two preschool children, have an arrangement with Wendy's mother— Grammy to the children—for child care and evening baby-sitting. They are affluent professionals and could easily afford to pay for high-quality day care, but they prefer to keep the regular care a family matter. Eileen, the children's legal mother, is open with her own parents about her situation, but as they live in another part of the country, their support is limited to friendly letters (with inquiries about Wendy) and gifts for the children. Eileen explained:

I think I'd like to have [my parents] closer so that there would be more intimacy. . . . I feel so good about my relationship with my family I really do wish we were closer so we could spend more time together. . . . There's something about having family around, like on holidays and stuff, that I think is real special.

Here Eileen's concern is more with the affective dimension of kinship than with financial assistance. She and Wendy have savings and investments and are unlikely to face a financial situation that they would not be able to manage on their own. But family is a positive good, in her view, something that should be nurtured and supported, and that gives form and solidity to children's development.

Lesbian mothers are no less likely than heterosexual mothers to regard their parents as the most appropriate source of financial and practical assistance in a variety of situations. Even when some strain has developed in relation to their sexual orientation, lesbian mothers still say that they look first to their families when they need basic support. In fact, mothers who do not go to their families for assistance are likely to feel that they must explain their reluctance or inability to do so. Most such explanations are financial: the parents or other family members are not able to help because of financial limitations or other critical demands made on their resources.

When Theresa Baldocchi describes her parents, who live in Detroit, she emphasizes their poverty and frequently mentions of the many difficulties they have survived over the years. Her relationship with them centers on highly emotional weekly telephone calls and occasional visits, which Theresa (a successful professional) pays for. She sees herself as sharing her most serious problems with them, but at the same time she is careful to protect them from any information she thinks might distress them—such as her lesbianism. She thinks her parents suspect, but she has not actually told them directly because she fears this is the sort of news that would upset them. At the same time, although their ability to do concrete things for her is limited by both their low income and their geographical distance, Theresa says their relationship is so solid that she can ask for "anything." Her parents enclose a $10 bill in nearly all their letters to her, "so they can feel they are sending money." Since Theresa's income far exceeds of her parents', she sees the bills as a sign of their unconditional support.

If I call them and need support, they're real good. They're real good for me. Sometimes I'm real down, and I feel like here I am, living this dual life, and it's not fair—I can't have a lover, and I really want someone to spend my life with. . . . I just want to meet that perfect woman and run off into the sunset with her. And here I am stuck with this kid and this ex-husband that hangs around all the time. And then they call. And it's like, God, how can I complain about my life? Look at them—they've been through so much and they've got so much spirit. They always say we love you so much.

Other women shrink from the looking to their parents for assistance out of a desire not to ask anyone for help; these mothers emphasize their ability to resolve unexpected crises through their own efforts, taking pride in their success in meeting their own needs and planning for the future.

Thus disputes over lifestyle very seldom change fundamental assumptions about the proper role of the family of origin as support in times of trouble. Not that lesbians have no friction with their families over their sexual orientation; such conflict can be intense and acrimonious. But fundamental understandings about the meaning of family are rarely threatened by these disputes; rather, disputes are seen as undermining family ties as they ought to be.

Lesbianism does not seem to have disrupted some family ties at all. For women in such circumstances, family provides the context for holidays and vacations and demonstrates the enduring strength family ties ought to have.

Rebecca Collins's parents, who live only a few blocks from her, care for her seven-year-old son after school and on evenings and weekends when they are needed. Rebecca's lover, Sheila Ryan, has been accepted into the family, and joins in large holiday celebrations and in summer vacations with Rebecca's brothers and their families. So does Rebecca's former husband. Rebecca and Sheila have a circle of friends, including several lesbian couples, but Rebecca emphasizes the cultural and recreational facets of these relationships—going to concerts and out to dinner, talking about common interests—rather than the need for concrete or even emotional support. She gains a sense of camaraderie from her friends, sharing feelings with them about being lesbian, but says that she rarely asks them for anything substantial.

Paula Abrams, the mother of a son and daughter, shares almost everything with her mother. As we saw in Chapter 2, Paula's first impulse when she came out was to call her mother. Her mother was generally supportive, despite her concern about the stigma Paula might suffer, but she did not share the information with her husband; she decided on the spot that Paula should not come out to her father.

It is more common for lesbianism to create great strain in the family, but lesbian mothers who value close bonds and mutual aid with relatives work hard to overcome barriers to continuing involvement with their families. The arrangements they devise may require them to avoid discussion of their sexual orientation, keep their lovers and friends out of the kin network, and make other compromises out of consideration for their parents' and siblings' sensibilities.

Evelyn Brandon, who lives in a blue-collar suburban community with her lesbian lover and her three-month-old son, has had to tread a narrow line to maintain good relations with her family. Her father and his wife are fundamentalists, so even the fact that she had a baby out of wedlock has been a shock to them. She has not told her stepmother that she is a lesbian, but when her brother asked her directly, she acknowledged that she was. His reaction was not wholly positive, but Evelyn explains that the relationship is not in danger.

So even though he [doesn't] approve and he would rather I didn't, he's still my brother. And he'll stand by me. He's pretty much taken that stand also for the baby.

Shortly after Evelyn became pregnant she was laid off from her job, and found herself in a precarious economic position during her pregnancy. She moved in with her lover, but various bureaucratic delays with her insurance carrier compelled her to borrow money from her brother to cover her obstetrical expenses. She expects the insurance to reimburse her for them eventually, but she is still waiting for the money three months after the baby's birth.

Evelyn and her brother talk on the phone about once a week and visit together once or twice a month. She says they have a special bond because both of their parents have remarried several times since their divorce. She and her brother had a rather unsettled childhood, living sometimes with one parent and sometimes with the other, and still view their relationship as the only bit of stability they had during those years. Her brother not only has loaned her money but advises her on such things as how to organize her finances and how to select insurance. Though he has accepted her lesbianism, he has not told his wife about it; he feels that Evelyn's unwed pregnancy is about as much as she should have to absorb right now. Evelyn sees their relationship as the most central family tie she has, and expects her son to have strong relations with his cousins, her brother's children. She has also cultivated a good relationship with the family of her baby's father. They have been generally supportive, accepting the baby as their grandchild even though their son has chosen to distance himself from Evelyn. Evelyn receives AFDC but has not revealed the father's name because she wants to keep their relations cordial. Her idea is that the baby will eventually get to know his father, and their coming together will be easier if the state has not hounded him for child support.

Other mothers have found the business of maintaining connections with their families complicated. Rita García, a lesbian mother who lives with her lover, Jill Hacker, and her eight-year old son, Jim, in a working-class San Francisco neighborhood, finds that her arrangements with her parents require constant diplomacy. Rita comes from a close-knit Mexican-American family, and the only shadow on her happiness at having found Jill and come out as a lesbian has been their refusal to accept the situation. Their first reaction was such outrage that they considered supporting her husband's early claim for custody of Jim on the grounds that she was no longer a fit mother. In the actual divorce proceedings, however, Rita's husband failed to show interest in custody. As more information about Rita's marriage surfaced and the family learned that her husband had frequently abused her, they dropped their plans to support him; their opposition to her lesbianism, however, has not abated.

The family's attitude was so hostile that Rita did not see her parents at all for about a year. She missed them constantly, often thinking of what they were doing at that moment. The situation was resolved when Rita's grandmother had major surgery. Rita had always been close to her grandmother and was the obvious choice when a family member was needed to handle daily nursing care. Rita's care of her grandmother after she returned home from the hospital reinstated her in the family and reestablished a basis for mutual assistance. Her ties to her mother were also solidified during this time as she resumed her longstanding role of confidante. Rita says of her mother:

She leans on me a lot for support. I'm glad that she can, that I can help her when things are getting her down. When she can't take any more, she'll lean on me.

Rita's son, Jim, attends a Catholic school in her parents' neighborhood. She drops him off at their house every day on her way to work. Her mother makes breakfast for him before he walks to school. After school he returns to his grandmother's, plays with neighborhood children or does his homework, and eats dinner before Rita picks him up on her way home. This arrangement permits Rita to put in for as much overtime as possible at her downtown clerical job. On the occasions when Rita and Jill have evening plans, Jim spends the night with his grandparents.

Rita also depends on her father for advice and for practical assistance. Whenever something is troubling her, she talks with her father, and he regularly helps her with her car, changing the oil and taking care of other routine service. She is particularly close to her sister as well, though her sister is still very uncomfortable about her lesbianism. Nevertheless, Rita talks often on the phone with her, discussing virtually any subject except her sexual orientation and her lover. Their children visit back and forth frequently, sometimes spending the weekend at Rita's house or her sister's. If Rita were going out of town and needed extended care for Jim, she says, she would ask her sister rather than her mother or lover to provide it. She feels it would be too much of a strain for her mother to take care of Jim for an extended period, and it never occurs to her that it would be suitable for her to leave him in Jill's care.

Rita's parents do not accept Jill as a family member. They have never visited her home (ostensibly because they think it's in a bad neighborhood), and Jill is never included in any sort of family occasion. On such holidays as Thanksgiving and Christmas, Jill visits her own family in Southern California while Rita and Jim celebrate with her family.

The revelation of Deborah Cohen's lesbianism precipitated an angry confrontation with her parents, and for several weeks they had no direct communication with her. But before long, her mother and father contacted her, explaining that they could not endure a sustained separation.

It's real painful for them. They don't want to hear it. So most of the time I don't talk about it. . . . But it's a very tight family and my mother says we can't disown you. We can be really sad and unhappy about what you're doing, and [feel] you are making a big mistake, but we love you and that's that.

Deborah sees her parents about once a week, sometimes for long visits, sometimes to pick up her daughter when they baby-sit for her. Though they have not reconciled themselves to her lesbianism and still argue with her about it at times, most of the time they stick to other topics of mutual interest: Judaism, the situation in the Middle East, Israel, and related political matters. They spend all Jewish holidays together and Deborah attends an Orthodox synogogue with her family. The ongoing strain over Deborah's sexual orientation reveals itself in visiting and baby-sitting patterns. Her mother feels that if they spent time in Deborah's home, they would somehow be condoning her lifestyle, so they visit Deborah only on her daughter's birthday. Besides providing child care virtually whenever Deborah needs it, her parents have provided the money to send her daughter to summer camp.

And I also do know that they're there. That's one thing that's really important. As much as they don't approve of what I'm doing, as much as they think it's a mistake, I have been real down and out, like with my past lover, my mother called one time and I was just crying. . . . She asked me what was happening, and I could really let loose and let her see all my feelings. She was right there. When I'm really down, my mother is there. She does not judge me. It's the normal everyday living she does her judging. . . . I know they're there, if I ever really need anything, they're there. And that's good.

When mothers' ties with their relatives had been tenuous or stressful before the birth of their babies, their new situations may lead to surprising reversals. Maggie Walters, a lesbian mother with an eighteen-month-old daughter conceived through artificial insemination, discovered that becoming a mother suddenly changed her relationship with her own mother.

She gave me all the razz about it before I got pregnant, and then I got pregnant and she was instantly supportive. Never gave me any shit about it . . . I think because I was actually pregnant, you know. And that's serious. You don't put somebody down.

Maggie and her mother talk on the phone frequently, and her mother has loaned her money and has even suggested moving in together so that she could help Maggie with the baby. Before the baby was born her mother never offered her any kind of financial assistance.

Even when assistance is on a small scale, lesbian mothers may find the support of a parent essential. Anita Korman and her fourteen-year-old daughter live a few blocks away from her mother, who moved there from another state to be closer to her daughter and granddaughter. Anita and her mother spend a lot of time together—shopping, going to movies, eating out—though Anita suspects that her mother is still unhappy about her lesbianism. Her mother is quite critical, for instance, of women whose dress and demeanor seem to her to be "masculine," and she complains about the appearance of some of Anita's friends.

She says they look just like truck drivers and I say, Momma, they are *truck drivers.*

At the same time Anita does not hesitate to ask her mother for small loans and for other kinds of assistance.

She's real helpful to me financially and she's loaned me money numerous times. Not that she has a lot of money, but if I need to borrow $25 or $50, she's right there. . . . She's the one person that I really feel helped me to raise [my daughter].

In recent years Anita's mother has become quite dependent on her daughter and granddaughter for social support. Years ago her mother provided support when Anita and her daughter were on their own; now the teenage daughter goes to visit her grandmother whenever she suspects she might be lonely. The grandmother moved to San Francisco only because Anita lived there, so she has few other social connections, as Anita is acutely aware.

Assistance from parents may require complicated and expensive arrangements. Margo Adler's parents fly to California from the East Coast (at their expense) for two weeks each year to take care of her developmentally disabled child so that Margo can have a vacation. They are the only people Margo trusts to care for her difficult and demanding daughter.

Michelle O'Neill, who feared that her staunchly Catholic mother would never accept a grandchild conceived by artificial insemination, is another lesbian who found that the birth of a grandchild improved her relationship with her family.

Since my son was born, my relationship with my mother has improved greatly, mostly on the level of relating to that I have a child and she's a mother and now she's a grandmother and [he] is her only grandchild and she's very interested in him and stuff. So now our relationship is quite good and also I've matured and kind of gone through my . . . radical phase.

Michelle is living on a very restricted budget while she attends nursing school, and her mother's support has been material as well as emotional. Her mother is fairly well off and has provided substantial amounts of money as well as a constant stream of baby clothes and other gifts. But probably most vital to Michelle is the fact that having a baby in this way and being a lesbian have not made her a pariah to her family; despite her mother's initial anxiety that Michelle's "freaky" way of getting pregnant would cause her to be written up in a medical journal.

But then, after [my son] was born . . . it has not made a difference at all—the way that I got pregnant or the fact that I'm a lesbian or that I'm a single mother.

She just is in love with her grandchild and it just doesn't make any difference to her anymore.

Ties to family and home are described as enduring, as characterized by both stability and continuity. Mothers emphasize that kinship connections compensate them for the uncertainties of other relationships, particularly those with lovers or husbands. We will see later that these are themes are prominent in their descriptions of their relations with their children as well, in no small measure because these relationships, like their links to other members of their families, are based on blood.

Bonnie Pereira described her family and her home town:

I know that no matter what happens in this world, I can go back to that little place and it'll be the same, and I'll draw some security out of that.

The ability of some lesbian mothers to maintain meaningful relationships with their relatives appears to signify that their lives are still anchored in a unit called "the family." For these women, depriving their children of the opportunity to be part of what they conceive of as a family is a far more serious kind of deprivation than the more immediate economic limitations they experience. Their definitions of "family" are often revealed in their descriptions of holiday celebrations."

Irene Willoughby and Gerry Curtis, working-class lesbian mothers who live together with Gerry's four children and one grandchild, define "family" in terms of generations living together. Irene, who lost her two sons in a custody battle, feels particularly strongly that their home should provide a family for their friends and for neighborhood kids who don't get along with their parents. A recent test of their family's strength was the pregnancy of Gerry's fifteen-year-old daughter. She decided to keep the baby, and Gerry and Irene have assumed most of the child care. Both Irene and Gerry expect that they will continue to live with at least some of the kids for some time into the future. Irene puts it this way:

See, I believe in generations living together. So that the young can learn from the old, and the old can learn from the young. Every day. We both believe in families.

This rather nostalgic concern with maintaining a sense of family is not always comfortably resolved. Marsha Lazarus, a lesbian mother who lives with her eight-year-old son in San Francisco, voices concern about how to provide her child with a "normal" childhood. She has only a tenuous relationship with her former husband, and the only blood relative available to her is her elderly father, who is quite involved with his grandson. She has a stormy relationship with a lover and doesn't expect it to continue for long. Most clearly because of the absence of a second parent in the household, Marsha defines herself as lacking a family, a situation she feels may be detrimental to her son's development. In her efforts to make up for this perceived deficit she has been extremely indulgent with Sean, and that strategy is now backfiring: the boy refuses to accept Marsha's lover into their household.

I guess part of it is that feeling I want him to have what I consider a normal childhood, and I don't want him to suffer because he has just a single parent in the house. . . . I think maybe I've gone overboard.

But Marsha's preoccupation with the absence of a family from her life was not shared by many of the other lesbian mothers I spoke with. Most lesbian mothers seem to be able to adapt their notions of family to fit their actual circumstances better than some heterosexual mothers whose nostalgia for the more traditional family they once expected to have may overwhelm their efforts to define their own domestic situation as a meaningful social unit.

Claudia Hopkins, a heterosexual mother with one teenage daughter, has been divorced for thirteen years. Though she sees her divorce as a positive development in her life, the source of the first "freedom" she has experienced as an adult, she often feels that she has to compensate her daughter for the inadequacy of their family. These feelings are particularly intense when she plans holiday celebrations. Her efforts to include lots of friends seem "contrived" to her.

It feels like not a family, because you don't have the other part of the family that you're supposed to have. You don't have two parents, and you don't have other kids. Part of my script was always to have more children, so I missed that. That's part of the way I feel, as if I'm missing somebody. Who knows who, but I have all these pieces missing. And [my daughter] really likes to have a lot more people around, and large families, so she gets that with her father and his family, because his wife has a huge, extended family, who often get together.

Another heterosexual mother, Alison Kahn, is overwhelmed by regret whenever she plans outings or excursions with her seven-year-old daughter:

One just has this fantasy of what families are doing together, boating together, fishing together, and playing tennis, hiking together, and I think that as a single parent there is much less of an incentive to do that in a twosome.

The implication here, of course, is that the unit headed by a single mother is only a part of a "real" family. To many lesbian mothers, in contrast, the family consists of their parents (and sometimes their siblings). By shifting the framework for assessing their family status from the nuclear family or married couple across generations, they are able to sustain a sense of being part of a family constellation.

In adopting this broader concept of family, lesbian mothers are using a strategy well documented among female-headed households in a variety of cultures. Poor African-American women, for example, manipulate the boundaries of family units to enlarge the pool of responsible adults in a world where marriage is an abstractly attractive goal but actual husbands are rare.[7] Throughout societies where most families are headed by women we find lineal kinship being mobilized both to enhance the notion that a mother and her children are connected and to provide emotional and material support as they face difficult conditions.[8] Mothers who emphasize their love for their blood kin often say there is no one else with whom they can speak frankly and that they know they can trust their relatives to keep their confidences because their love for them is real and unconditional. But as significant as the real solace and comfort mothers derive from these ties is the sense of connectedness that links with kin provide.

Margo Adler, whose parents have been willing to come from the East Coast to take care of her daughter so that she can have a vacation, are a major source of emotional support for her as well.

There's just some sense that they care about me, that to me is the most helpful. I can feel really miserable and everything, and I always feel like well, I could go to my parents' and my mother will take care of me and cook for me and be glad I'm there.

Alice Molinari, a heterosexual mother who chose her current apartment because of its proximity to her parents, describes her close ties with her mother in strikingly parallel language. Her parents help her out with small amounts of money, give her rides, and watch her kids when she has to go out in the evening. She reciprocates by doing errands for them downtown, and imagines that she will eventually move in with them. But her relationship with her parents, and especially with her mother, amounts to much more than the favors they exchange.

You know, your family can be a very safe haven for you, especially if you're loaded down with a lot of responsibilities. Lots of times, when you have responsibilities like that, a lot of demands are made on you that you can't respond to the way you want. A lot of stress results, an awful lot. [My mother] is the kind of woman that always makes me feel as though I'm just the greatest thing that's ever happened in her life. I know that I am just like everybody else . . . but she makes me feel so special. There's a lot of love that she communicates. Sometimes I just bask in it.

Nostalgia and Adaptation

There is no doubt that a woman's homosexuality can cause severe conflicts between her and her family. Most women's narratives reveal a desire, and sometimes efforts of nearly heroic dimensions, to resolve these disputes or at least to defuse the situation.

The compromises some mothers make are rather poignant; others describe their relatives as growing more flexible over time, perhaps because of a commitment to maintain ties with the grandchildren. In nearly all cases kinship offers lesbians a vital set of *ideas* about being connected, just as it does for heterosexual single mothers. As we have seen, links with "blood" relatives yield benefits: financial assistance, emotional support, and the like. But perhaps more important, ongoing viable relationships with members of the family of origin offer mothers a sense of continuity, a source of legitimacy for their own unconventional families. The efforts they make to sustain these ties are far out of proportion to the concrete value they provide; we must look elsewhere for their cultural significance.

Other anthropological accounts have also stressed the differential significance of kinship in the lives of women and men. Sylvia Yanagisako, for example, demonstrates the importance of woman-centered kin networks in the ongoing operation of interactions between households; even though both men and women may derive benefits from these networks, women are the organizers of kin-related activity, the "kin keepers" who keep track of family members' activities, implement arrangements for social events involving kin, and mobilize networks as the need arises. These instrumental activities are embedded in gender conventions, though their regularities are often obscured by their very informality.[9]

Anthropologists who have focused on the informal roles women have assumed in kinship systems, even under conditions that provide them with few avenues to direct influence, make similar observations. Margery Wolf offers perhaps the most arresting version of the pattern, appearing as it does in a culture that denies women virtually any formal recognition as social actors. Wolf shows that the behavior of Chinese villagers in Taiwan can be accounted for only if one assumes the existence of an ephemeral, but experientially authentic entity—the "uterine family," a set of linkages and expectations that mothers establish with their children and that (unlike the named representations of Chinese patriarchy) dissolve upon the death of the mother.[10] In like fashion, Micaela di Leonardo's depiction of Italian-American kinship as "the female world of cards and holidays" casts kinship as "work" that women do, even in the absence of formal recognition.[11]

These approaches all accord with Jane Collier's proposal that the family be understood as a "political arena" in which women actively pursue particular goals, goals that do not always resonate with those of men.[12] In framing women's kinship maneuvers as active strategies, however, Louise Lamphere reminds us that specific, consciously desired goals need not be demonstrated, but may be inferred from patterns of interaction as well as from the outcomes of particular kinds of behavior.[13] But although Lamphere (writing about women factory workers) proposes distinguishing between "strategies of resistance" and "strategies of accommodation," the narratives offered by lesbian mothers point to less easily dichotomized strategies. At the same time that explicit or obvious goals are pursued through the elaboration and maintenance of kinship ties, other purposes, better understood as related to the "work" of constructing identity, are also served.

Lesbian mothers' continuing reliance on their biological kin may also be viewed as a symbolic strategy in the sense identified by David Schneider in *American Kinship*. As lesbian mothers speak of their ties with their children and their expectations for relationships between the children and their fathers, they partake of a system of meaning Schneider identified as "American kinship." These meanings are pre-eminently normative rather than necessarily grounded in behavior, and while ideas about biology abound in American kinship, Schneider views them as cultural artifacts.[14] If creating a "meaningful social order" is a core problem for all participants in American (or any other) culture, then formulating a satisfactory connection to key cultural domains may be even more pressing for self-consciously marginalized lesbian mothers.

Ongoing links with kin offer mothers a representation of the legitimacy and stability of the family. The wider social system continues to legitimate the marriage-based family as the authentic unit in which motherhood should occur. But neither lesbian mothers nor heterosexual single mothers are any longer part of such units, and while some heterosexual mothers may entertain thoughts or fantasies of returning to this system through remarriage, lesbian mothers find themselves wholly outside it. Thus they seek legitimation in the family defined by blood relations. Ongoing links with kin help them in two ways: they connect the mother-child unit to a larger kinship grouping, making it more durable and resilient and offering continuity through time; and they validate consanguinity, rather than marriage, as a legitimate basis of family life. From this perspective, we can see that the importance of kin ties for mothers prefigures the anticipated importance of these ties in the future. As ties established through marriage become increasingly irrelevant—often as a result of the father's lack of commitment to the children—strong ties with the family of origin provide a model for those links the mother hopes to enhance in the long run.

5

"This Permanent Roommate"

"Do you have a family?" has become a commonplace euphemism for having children and, usually, a husband. Like others in our society, lesbians associate having a child with "starting a family." For women who had their children during marriages, continuing ties with children can come to represent the stability of the most meaningful of family links. For women who had their children outside of marriages, having a baby can represent their ability to overcome both concrete barriers and social disapproval, to demand a piece of family life that they value.

Daily Routines

Lesbian mothers' accounts of their relationships with their children tend to focus on the pace of daily life, the ongoing round of cooking, cleaning, shopping, laundry, and child-care arrangements that define the rhythm of existence. Particularly those who do not have partners may devote considerable energy to devising strategies for getting everything done; these strategies, however, are commonly fragile and may be easily undermined by small setbacks or unexpected obstacles.

The complex of strategies needed to manage child-care arrangements emerge as major themes in the narratives of mothers whose children are very young. Mothers not only must find adequate child care that they can afford but often are preoccupied with locating alternatives when the arrangements they have made break down. Transportation is likely to be a key issue. Mothers who do not own automobiles talk at length about the time required to travel by public

transportation to child-care providers and to their jobs, and the difficulties of handling such tasks as grocery shopping and laundry. Going
out in the evening may present problems so overwhelming that many
mothers decide it's easier just to stay home.

Margo Adler describes how the daily routine of her twelve-year-
old daughter dictates her own schedule. Because Amy is developmentally disabled, she cannot assume as much independence as most girls
her age, and Margo is acutely aware that this burden will not decrease
appreciably as Amy grows up.

Margo readily admits that the system of strategies she has devised
for arranging supervision of Amy is subject to breakdown at virtually
every point. So that she can get from her suburban home to her job in
San Francisco on time, she has persuaded the school bus operators to
pick up Amy at the beginning of their route; so, Amy's morning
"child care" is essentially provided by the bus driver. After-school
care—difficult to locate for a child as old as Amy—requires Margo to
pay to have her picked up at school. All of these arrangements are
workable, of course, only when school is in session.

*Every time the season changes I have to figure out a whole new thing to do with
her. Child care is definitely one of the biggest hassles and issues in my life. And
it's particularly difficult because she's old and still needs child care.*

The most recent disruption of Margo's routine came when Amy
joined a soccer team. This is Amy's first experience with team sports
and Margo is delighted when she wants to do it, but getting her to
soccer practice has forced Margo to leave work early once a week and
to rearrange her schedule to make up the time she misses. Amy's
health is poor, and Margo's routine is further disrupted by the need to
schedule medical appointments and manage her care when she is sick.

Finding baby-sitters among local teenagers has been so difficult—
apparently because the kids who live in Margo's upper-middle-class
neighborhood have no need to earn money—that she almost never
goes out at night, though as a last resort she sometimes takes Amy to
a friend's home in a nearby East Bay city. Her friend, a married

woman who does not work outside the home, is someone she has known since childhood and has a child the same age as Amy. Margo hates to ask her friend to watch Amy, though, because she has no way to reciprocate.

Margo's child-care problems are even more acute during the summer. Community activities when school is not in session are not necessarily scheduled to dovetail neatly; often there are gaps between the end of one program and the start of another. Sometimes her parents have come out from the East in the summer and have handled child care for her. At other times Margo has been forced to take Amy to work with her. This is far from an ideal arrangement, not only because her employer, a major financial institution, objects to children in the office, but because Amy's unpredictable behavior makes it difficult for Margo to concentrate on her work. The problems are even worse during school breaks at Christmas and Easter, when the school district runs no programs at all.

Margo knows that her child-care problems have affected her progress at work both because of the amount of time she misses and because she is often distracted and worried. She talks longingly of the possibility that her parents will move to the Bay Area; though she would lose some of her privacy, they would assume responsibility for much of Amy's care in a way she feels no one else ever will. Because Amy is a difficult and demanding child, Margo believes that few people but her parents can ever be expected to take a major role in her life.

I think the thing that seems the most important to me now is that I feel like . . . I will be the only person that has a certain kind of responsibility and feeling for this kid. That's sometimes very heavy to me. That even if I wind up with another person, that won't be their kid. That will be my kid. No matter how they feel, it's still going to be my kid. . . . I feel like she's only my kid, and not [my ex-husband's] at all. The only time I ever think of it as being any kind of shared thing is like I think if I died, he would have to take responsibility for her. But other than that, I really feel like that's my kid. It's sort of like I had this kid alone. I think that aspect of feeling like that will never change. It's probably the heaviest piece to me.

Some lesbian mothers find unusual solutions to their complex domestic problems. Ruth Zimmerman, a computer technician, lives in San Francisco with her five-year-old son and a male roommate. She recruited the roommate to live in her apartment in exchange for a wide range of household and child-care duties. He handles all of her baby-sitting needs, goes to the store, and takes responsibility for laundry and most of the house cleaning. Her friends think it's strange for her to be living with a man in this sort of situation, and she herself finds the arrangement a bit odd, but it meets a variety of needs and is difficult to give up. Her concern about continuing to have the roommate take this role is that she fears his becoming too attached to her and her son as his "nuclear family," something that doesn't seem appropriate in a situation she defines as temporary and justified only by its convenience.

If I could find somebody else to be maid, butler, child-care worker, and chauffeur, all the things he does for me, for the price, of course, the price is kind of high. Financially, it's not high. But emotionally, I guess it's starting to get a little higher.

Some lesbian mothers, then, shape their accounts of being mothers in terms of the practical challenges they must successfully overcome. Perhaps because becoming a mother so dramatically alters the daily pace of life, getting through routine tasks and devising solutions to persistent difficulties stand as evidence of a woman's ability to act as a mother in the world. These narratives tell us not only how the speakers cope with their responsibilities but that they define motherhood, at least in part, as a set of concrete constraints and challenges that demand innovative, practical solutions.

"Companionate" Households

Particularly when they live alone with a single child, lesbian mothers tend to view their relationships in a way I think of as "companionate": mother and child accomplish essential tasks in much the same way roommates might, with few trappings of the sort of hierarchical authority that one typically finds in two-parent families.

This is not a pattern unique to lesbian mothers. Heterosexual mothers I interviewed expressed similar sentiments.[1] Alma White, who lives alone with her sixteen-year-old son, sees her relationship with her son as exceptionally harmonious.

Basically, what we've tried to do since [my son is] older is to say we are two adults living in the same house. We share. We take care of each other. We take care of the house. We take care of meals, food, and chores and all of those kinds of things together collectively. . . . We just kind of do it together and it's worked out pretty well.

Besides managing basic household chores cooperatively, Alma says, she and her son seek out each other's company for "fun" things: bowling, eating out, going to the movies, going camping. They do not share all of their meals, largely because of Alma's busy schedule of community activities. She views the relationship as one in which each respects the autonomy of the other, so that arguments never arise. According to Alma, she and her son discuss "everything": her job, his schoolwork, household finances, and her homosexuality. They have had extended conversations about her most recent break-up, and he has expressed his hope that she will be somewhat discreet about being a lesbian. Alma says that out of respect for his wishes she has tried to make the public areas of the house "neutral" in decor so that he will feel comfortable when he brings his friends home. She keeps books on lesbian and gay subjects, posters for lesbian community events, and everything else of that sort in her bedroom.

Along similar lines, Leslie Addison views her relationship with her twelve-year-old daughter, Jennifer, as much like a marriage. A major theme in their relationship is compromise, a process whereby they work out differences and agree to accommodate each other's preferences. Leslie's admitted restlessness used to lead her to relocate herself and Jennifer to a different part of the country nearly every year. As Jennifer has grown older, however, she has become more assertive about expressing her wish to stay in the same place longer, largely because of the ties she forms in school and with neighborhood children. So they have compromised: Leslie has agreed not to move during the school year and Jennifer has agreed that they can travel in the summer and possibly not return to the same place next year.

We've worked out little compromises like that between us. . . . It took us a long time to work out our relationship. But now that's kind of hard, too—it makes it difficult for other people to break into it, because we have our set patterns. Like when we get a roommate, or I get a lover, or she gets a new friend, it's real hard. It's just like being a couple.

The analogy between mother-child ties and those of a couple arises frequently among single mothers, lesbian and heterosexual alike. The companionate model certainly recalls the equality of an ideal couple. Many lesbian mothers, as we have seen, describe women who have no children as "single".

Tanya Petroff speaks strongly of her feeling that she does not share the same fundamental concerns as people who have no children. Though she does not have a lover, she does not see herself as single precisely because she is a mother.

I don't seem to have the need to get together with someone of either sex as much as my single friends do. I have a real solid relationship [with my daughter] that provides me with a feeling that I am necessary and worthwhile . . . and all that other stuff.

Along similar lines, but with an added edge of anger, Leslie Addison also characterizes childless women as "single":

I think that the lesbian community is organized around the single lifestyle only. I've heard more than a hundred times from a woman, a lesbian—"I chose not to have kids, so don't push yours off on me."

And Tanya Petroff says:

I've had [lesbians] tell me that I had chosen a privileged position in having a child and if it was going to be difficult for me then it was too goddam bad.

Another lesbian mother, Gloria Frank, has lived on her own with her three children for most of their lives. Her experience has often been that important people in her life, including her lovers, have not wanted to make the kinds of sacrifices she sees as unavoidable for a mother, and she tends to feel that she cannot rely on anyone outside of the family—herself and her three kids. But there can be comfort in ties to children, as she makes clear.

I think what happens when you're alone with children is that you very frequently treat your oldest one almost as another adult; you know, you talk to them about things that you would normally share with an adult, and they . . . see themselves as having much more responsibility . . . and they really see themselves as the other adult in your life.

Gloria points out that this closeness can backfire, particularly when she wants to get involved with a lover. The child who has been acting as confidant does not want to relinquish this position to a stranger, and may try to sabotage the new relationship.

The theme of equality emerges as a core value in accounts given by other lesbian mothers about their lives with their children. Inez Escobar, who lives alone with her twelve-year-old daughter in an isolated suburban housing tract, describes a routine that is notable for its apparent lack of routine. Although her daughter is supposed to keep her room clean and wash the dishes after dinner, and often takes responsibility for doing the laundry or cleaning the house, Inez sees their arrangement as informal and easygoing.

We don't have anything definite set up for chores now, really. Whenever anything needs to be done, we just kind of decide to do it. Housekeeping is really not a priority, I don't think. We'd just as soon do something, or go to the movies, or play a game as clean. . . . We're so free. Kind of answerable to no one, really. All I know for sure is that I have to go to work. [My daughter] knows that her job is to go to school. The rest of our time is just real free-flowing. Like I say, if we want to do the housework, we can . . . or we can just slough it off.

Part of sharing responsibility for the daily operation of family life is being aware of the financial constraints the mother faces. If anything is a consistent theme in the lives of both lesbian mothers and heterosexual single mothers, it is the persistence of economic pressures, the nearly constant fear that they may not be able to manage. The mere fact of their survival becomes a mark of honor for some mothers; for others, the reality of an unpredictable financial situation is a source of ongoing anxiety.

As part of the kind of openness lesbian mothers seek with their children, discussions about budgets and finances are described as frank and explicit. In many instances, of course, financial strains can be traced directly to nonpayment of child support, so mothers must weigh the benefits of leveling with their children against the possible harm of attacking a fragile link to their fathers. Nonetheless, most mothers told me they take pains to explain their incomes and budgeting decisions, largely in hopes that children will appreciate the efforts they make to manage on skimpy resources. These frank discussions, however, may not assuage children's desires for the luxury items their friends have.

Most of the conflicts Doris Johnson has with her eleven- and fourteen-year-old daughters focus on clothes and on the narrow limits on the kinds of purchases they can make. Doris is a graduate student, trying to complete work on a doctorate in history. She lives with her lover, June Kepler, a medical student, and her two daughters in cramped campus housing, getting by on student loans, her earnings as a research assistant, small contributions from June, and sporadic child-support payments from her former husband, who lives in another state.

All of these sources together add up to a minimal income, and Doris must plan her budget carefully. The girls become upset when they compare their wardrobes with those of their friends. Though Doris wishes she could spare her daughters this experience, she also thinks that it builds character and that they will later come to appreciate the benefits of learning to economize.

They will never, probably, as long as they live, take for granted that you can just have whatever you want.

Similarly, Winnie Moses, who lives with her lover and her two teenage sons, has had to have frank discussions with her children about financial realities. Though her ex-husband is reliable about paying child support, he has resisted all her efforts to get the amount raised; there have been only very minor increases since they divorced twelve years ago. At one point the boys complained that she wasn't spending enough on them in view of the amount of the support payment. She took this occasion to explain the entire household budget and how she calculated the costs of raising them. This discussion apparently resolved the matter.

Anita Korman is also open about financial realities with her fourteen-year-old daughter. She discusses her plans to pursue a doctorate with her daughter, weighing the possible economic advantages of the degree against the costs they would both have to bear during the lengthy process of obtaining it. She doesn't feel that she can ask her daughter to sacrifice endlessly, but she knows that in the long run they would both benefit from an improvement in her credentials.

I don't burden her with every bill that I owe but we talk about it a lot in a realistic way. What we can afford and what we can't and particularly lately we've been talking about if our living situation should change, how we would deal with that, how we would deal with it financially as well as the other ways. . . . I mean she wants to know and she understands the situation.

Managing Stigma

Though lesbian mothers share with single heterosexual mothers a concern with child care and family finances and a preference for an egalitarian style of interaction, they alone have to manage the stigma attached to homosexuality. Coming out as lesbians intersects in important ways with the relationships mothers maintain with their relatives, and, as we shall see, with ongoing ties with their children's fathers. But mothers' lesbianism may have other layers of meaning for children. Mothers' interpretations of the impact of their sexual orientation on their children tends, therefore, to focus both on its significance for ties to relatives and fathers and on its presumed effects on their children's friendships.

Bernice Nelson, who lives alone in a North Bay suburb with her seven-year-old daughter, describes a rather positive self-image as a lesbian and has strong views about the importance of the independence she has achieved since coming out. She lived in several communal situations when she was still with her husband and her current lifestyle retains a counterculture flavor. Yet at the same time that she values nontraditional approaches to daily life and to child rearing and believes, at least in the abstract, that being "open" is good, Bernice is fearful about what would happen if her lesbianism became widely known.

It's hard for me to know exactly how to get across to her that it's important for her own sake that she be discreet about who she shares her life with and yet encourage her at the same time to be willing to share her feelings with someone. . . . For her my fear is that she'll be identified in school by her teachers . . . as something real strange and unusual, because of the way I live, and that that'll change the way they relate to her. That the kids will find out the way I live and start tormenting her. You know how mean kids are to each other—your mommy's a queer, and that kind of stuff.

To ensure that other children do not accidentally have access to compromising information, Bernice has developed a set of rules that restrict her daughter's friends to her room, denying them access to other parts of the house, especially when she is entertaining her own adult guests. Bernice is afraid that being known as the daughter of a lesbian not only would subject her daughter to discrimination at school but would restrict her "options" in the future. On another level, she takes seriously her ex-husband's occasional threats to seek custody, and sees any breach of family confidentiality as providing him with potential ammunition. These fears seem closely related to similar concerns about the impact of her sexual orientation on her future career. Bernice hopes to begin studies toward certification as a psychotherapist, but worries that being known as a lesbian might prevent her from practicing or obtaining licensure.

What is noteworthy about Bernice's fears is that they do not reflect any personal history of actual discrimination. Her daughter has never, to her knowledge, been teased by friends; her husband has not made any serious attempts to gain custody; and she has not even begun to train for a career in psychotherapy or counseling. Bernice's narrative tells us more about the meanings she attaches to being a lesbian than about her concrete experiences.

In a somewhat similar vein, Lisa Stark, who has an eleven-year-old daughter and a nine-year-old son, is concerned about the impact being "out" would have on her relationships with her neighbors. She would prefer to live in a neighborhood with more gay people, but explains that at present the only place she can afford to live is a rather bleak working-class neighborhood on the Peninsula. She doubts that her neighbors are open-minded about homosexuality, though she has never raised the subject with any of them. But her relationships with them are vital: they are her principal source of the babysitters on whom she depends. An available pool of local teenagers allows her to stay at her office in a city agency for the long hours she is often required to work, or which she chooses to work in the hopes of being promoted to a supervisory position.

Some children find that knowing other children whose mothers are lesbians helps them to normalize what might otherwise seem like a deviant situation. But even these children learn that information about their mothers' sexual orientation may have to be carefully managed. Judy Tolman's nine-year-old son knows many other children in lesbian families, but Judy has

a feeling that he senses that school is part of the world out there that doesn't like gay people. Same when he goes to be with his father—I don't think he really talks about it that much.

More commonly, mothers talk about the need to maintain secrecy as rooted in the possibility of a custody challenge. To protect their children from having to manage potentially damaging information, these mothers feel the best policy is to keep their lesbianism a secret from them.

Rita García has worked out a difficult truce with her family over her homosexuality. Her former husband has failed to make contact with her for several years, has never paid child support, and has a record of alcohol abuse and battery. All the same, she fears he might suddenly return and try to take their son away from her.

I feel that I would be laying a guilt trip on Jim if I told him that I was gay but to keep it a secret. Because if we ever had to go to court again and somebody found out, they would take him away from me.

Although virtually all of her friends are gay and she has lived with Jill for most of her son's life, Rita is convinced that he knows nothing of her sexual orientation. She elaborated on this belief several times during our conversation, despite the fact that he was in the room during the entire interview.

Theresa Baldocchi has carefully shielded her nine-year-old son, Tom, from knowledge of her lesbianism. Her former husband, John, sued her for custody at the time of their divorce, alleging (inaccurately at the time) that she was a lesbian. Despite the bitter memories of the divorce, which nearly bankrupted her, Theresa is pleased that John is willing to stay with Tom in her home every night while she is at work. But, this arrangement requires Theresa to be very careful about leaving any evidence of her lifestyle around the house; she feels certain that John examines everything while he is there. Her caution has extended to keeping her lesbianism a secret from her son.

If John weren't around, I would probably be real open with Tom. [But] I don't want him torn between having to lie to his father and having to accept me, too. That would really be hard for him. He loves his dad a whole lot.

Laura Bergeron, who had her three children outside of marriage, is also cautious about letting her children know that is a lesbian. The primary consideration she cites is her lover, Margaret Towers, who is married, determined to do nothing that would disrupt the customary rhythm of her life, and thus adamant that the nature of their relationship be kept secret. Laura also mentions a vague worry that the father of her two sons might try to get custody of them if he knew about her sexual orientation, even though he agreed to cooperate in her two pregnancies only with the understanding that he would never have any formal obligations to their children. The man who fathered her third child, a daughter, through insemination knows that Laura is gay, so she feels more comfortable having him visit and spend time with her and the children. But she has never discussed her lesbianism with her children and is sure she will never be able to do so.

My children don't know that I'm a lesbian. You see the relationship with my lover . . . We're very conventional. Our whole life is very conventional. My profession would be endangered, and her life is the neighborhood. . . . I mean there's just no way that we could ever be anything but heavily closeted. We have a lot of women's activities that go on here, but we don't mix the worlds. . . . That's why my children can't know.[2]

Though Laura was so eager to have children that she become pregnant three times on her own, she has more recently begun to see her children as a limitation on her ability to live spontaneously. She feels pulled between her obligations to them and her relationship with Margaret, and sees no way to harmonize these two parts of her life. Further, she believes that having children has wrecked her finances and that the expenses of child care for three children are the direct cause of her recent bankruptcy.

Laura has made arrangements for before- and after-school care, and her children also check in with Margaret, who lives next door, when they return home. To maximize the time she can spend with Margaret, Laura has installed an intercom system between the two houses, so she can listen to what is happening at her house while she is at her lover's. She fits shopping and other errands in on her lunch hour, or does them on her way home from work. These complicated arrangements have left Laura with virtually no time to herself.

When I'm alone, I'm usually doing something with my kids, because if anything I feel guilty that I don't spend enough quality time with them. I'm more of a caretaker a lot of the time. It seems like I'm always just hurrying them up and making them do this and that, so . . . I make myself take one evening a week, the same evening every week. This is it, this is theirs. And we either go out for pizza or go to a movie or sit around and read stories to each other. In other words, we are together as a family for sure at least one night a week.

These arrangements do little to allow Laura to enjoy the more creative aspects of motherhood that many other mothers speak of

with such deep feeling. She has convinced herself that her life with
Margaret can continue only if she separates herself from her children;
she is left with little beyond obligation to them, and intense self-
consciousness about maintaining the secrecy of her lesbianism.

*I just feel like I'm a robot sometimes. There's just not enough of me. And some-
day they're going to realize that, you know. And I want them to. I don't want
them to grow up and look back and think my mother was a robot. But I don't
know that there's much I can do about it because I've got too many things in motion now, you know.*

Laura and Margaret do have a limited social life with other lesbians,
hosting rather formal social gatherings such as bridge parties. These
parties, however, provide additional occasions when the children
must be segregated from interaction with adults and excluded from
Laura's life. She comments that the boys, in particular, are "under-
standably" not welcome at a lesbian social event, and that, in any
case, she can't risk having her children make observations on these
occasions.

*So I've set my life up so that it doesn't include my children. That's what it
amounts to. . . . [Being with a man] was so much easier. It seems like such a
hassle to be gay. . . . But still, I might always be a little closeted. . . . I don't
want to go around alienating everybody and destroying their reality and upsetting
their reality. I'm not trying to convert anybody and make any stand for lesbianism.
I told you I'm not in the least militant or radical or political or anything.*

At the same time, Laura understands that the gulf being created
between herself and her children will probably have long-term effects
on their relationship, effects that she can no longer control.

*I think at some point it's probably going to be important to me that my children
know I'm lesbian and I'm never going to be able to tell them as long as I'm in
this relationship, you know. I guess I have fantasies about maybe we could tell
[my daughter] when she's about fifteen or so or something. . . . But I guess I'm
never going to be able to tell the boys and I feel a distance between me and them
for that reason.*

Laura's situation contrasts sharply with that of most mothers I interviewed. She has chosen, in effect, to submerge her decisions as a mother to sustain a complex system of secrecy that she and her lover have established. The system is based on the assumption that terrible consequences would flow from any revelation of their lesbianism, and that secrecy can be maintained only if Laura's identities as mother and lesbian are strictly separated. It also rests on a related, but questionable, assumption that no one knows about her lesbianism if she chooses not to talk about it.

Laura is hardly the only lesbian mother to shield her children from knowledge of her sexual orientation, but she is in the minority. Far more of the mothers I spoke to feel strongly that being open is best for everyone involved. Elaine Weinstein's daughters are twelve and fourteen. Since her divorce she has been very circumspect about her lesbianism, both because her husband sued her for custody at the time of their divorce and because her job as a teacher might be compromised. She decided to be more open with her daughters when her lover moved into the household, and since then she has been able to look forward to spending time with them.

I used to live for the weekend that the kids would go away. . . . It was just so nice to have that break. Now I don't feel that way anymore, mostly because they know that I'm a lesbian. . . . It's like a big weight has been lifted. So I don't feel a need to have them gone.

Ruth Zimmerman, who had her son five years ago while she was living with a man, has been very open with him about her lesbianism. She does not think that her son's father will ever try to get custody, though he has retained some interest in the child and visits occasionally. Ruth believes that her son's understanding of her lifestyle can only be positive.

He doesn't think it's strange to see two women in bed together. I mean, I can only see it as a broadening experience. It's one less thing in the world for him to find strange or different.

In a similar vein, Gloria Frank, who had three children with three men, thinks her kids have an advantage because their mother is a lesbian.

I think it probably will just leave openings for more possibilities in their lives, I would hope. . . . I think it's incredibly valuable that my children be exposed to as many different lifestyles as possible.

Motherhood as a Central Identity

Mothers who are strongly committed to maintaining total secrecy about their sexual orientation find that segregation of their daily lives into time when they are "mothers" and time when they are "lesbians" creates constant concerns about information management. Their self-consciousness is heightened as they evaluate and analyze every episode that might breach their confidentiality. While some such mothers are motivated by fears about custody, others seem to be thinking more in terms of what they construe as broad community standards. They understand that homosexuality is generally disapproved of, and want to protect their children from being stigmatized in the way they feel themselves to be. Some of them also understand that motherhood tends to be perceived as contradictory to lesbianism, so that the mere fact of being mothers can protect them from being identified as gay. As Valerie Thompson, the mother of a twelve-year-old daughter, said, "Of course, I have the mask. I have a child. I'm accepted [as heterosexual] because I have a child and that kind of protection."

But fears about stigma are not the only reason for segregating roles. Virtually all the women I interviewed commented on the pressure they felt to do everything adequately alone. As we saw earlier, some women focus on the successes they have achieved and derive considerable self-esteem from the effort. Others tend to focus on how difficult it is to manage under the conditions that motherhood imposes in their situations, how discouraged and overwhelmed they feel, how little hope they see that their situations will become easier until their children are grown.

Both approaches revolve around a common understanding: that being a mother eclipses and overshadows all other roles. A few women, such as Laura Bergeron, in a sense keep motherhood at a distance in order to manage a particularly difficult lesbian relationship. But Laura does not find this separation easy, and as we have seen, she is haunted by the impact her segregated lifestyle has on her children.

Tanya Petroff is very much aware that being a mother overshadows being a lesbian. "The mothering thing," she says, "the thing about being a mother seems to be more important to me than my sexual orientation." She views herself and her seven-year-old daughter as an indivisible social unit, which takes first place over any other sort of relationship.

I'm definitely part of a package deal. I come with my daughter and people who can't relate to both of us are not people I want to relate to for very long.

That being the case, Tanya sees other mothers, regardless of their sexual orientation, as the people with whom she has the most in common. Since moving to the Bay Area a few years ago from the Midwest, she has tended to avoid the lesbian community in favor of socializing with other mothers. Her past experience was that the "lesbian community" put pressure on her to make her daughter a "little amazon." As a mother, she feels strongly that her daughter should be free to develop in whatever direction she chooses, not constrained by "political correctness." When Tanya speaks of "political correctness," she is referring to the standards that lesbian feminists first imposed on themselves in the 1970s. At that time, efforts to create a "lesbian nation" gave rise to often rigid expectations in such areas as dress, political activity, sexual behavior, and language. Behavior that could be construed as "straight" or oriented toward conventional standards of success and attractiveness was generally censured, as were such traditional markers of femininity as high heels and makeup.[3]

Being a mother seems to release some lesbian mothers from pressures to be a lesbian in that "correct" way. Most women who raise this issue frame it in terms of dress or other aspects of personal appearance, but the implication that other behavior is also involved is clear. Many of the women who discussed this problem were veterans of 1970s radical feminism, and their stories resonate with resentment over the limitations this ideology placed on their ability to express themselves as individuals. It seems that once a child is on the scene, one's presentation as a lesbian is inevitably altered, and this experience may be freeing in some ways. Louise Green, who came out as a lesbian while still in her teens and has had no heterosexual experience, has relaxed her earlier efforts to be as "butch" as possible in her personal style, though it seems that dress and style are only the outward manifestations of other levels of personal change.[4]

Since I had [my daughter] I felt it was OK to do these things I've been wanting to do real bad. One of them is to paint my toenails red. I haven't done it yet, but I'm going to do it. I felt really OK about wearing perfume and I just got a permanent in my hair. . . . I feel like I'm robbing myself of some of the things I want to do by trying to fit this lesbian code. I feel like by my having this child, it has already thrown me out in the sidelines.

Other mothers locate the centrality of motherhood in the sheer quantity of obligation that having a child imposes on one's life. Peggy Lawrence lives with her lover, Sue Alexander, her ten-year-old daughter, and Sue's two sons. Her comments on motherhood focus on the limitations it imposes on her personal freedom. Having a child makes her be more concerned with living in a stable environment than she thinks she would be otherwise, and it makes her cooperate with a social system, particularly in its educational dimension, that she personally disagrees with. Travel seems impossible when one is a mother. Making a living becomes the center of her existence because of her obligations to her daughter. She and Sue have chosen to live in a neighborhood convenient to the children's school, and though they would prefer to relocate to the Midwest, where both of them have lived before, they are reluctant to do so because they believe that the kids encounter less bigotry as the children of lesbian mothers in San Francisco. Peggy explains:

*Being a mother, to me—being a mother is more consuming than any other way
that I could possibly imagine identifying myself. . . . Any other way that I identify myself is an identification of some part of my being a mother. I am a lesbian
mother, I am a working mother—"mother" hardly ever modifies any other thing.
"Mother" is always the primary—it's always some kind of mother, but it's never
a mother-anything. "Mother" is—"mother," for mothers, is always the thing that
is more consuming. Because being a mother is so big, I have much more in common with all mothers than I have in common with all lesbians. It's so big. It
starts out as a twenty-four-hour-a-day job, and it just goes on and on and on.*

But still other mothers locate the meaning of motherhood in the
sheer intensity of feeling that exists uniquely between mother and
child. Lisa Stark, who is often visibly depressed by the unrelenting
obligations of single parenthood, has come to see her children as the
reason she can face the obstacles that seem to make up her daily life.
Since her life presumably would be easier without children, her celebration of their importance is somewhat paradoxical.

*I've . . . never had to live for myself. The only reason I get up in the morning is
to get them off to school. For me to trot off to work in order to earn the money to
support them. I don't know what I'd do if I didn't have them. They're everything
I've got. . . . I love them so much that it really is painful.*

Her comments echo her description of her own relationship with
her parents. She describes her parents as the only people other than
her children who care about her, the only reliable source of support in her rather bleak social world. This relationship contrasts dramatically with the minimal connection she maintains with the children's father, who has cut himself off from her and the children
nearly completely.

*He doesn't know [the kids] and doesn't want to. He signs their cards, or his wife
does, with [first names], not "Daddy" or "Your father" or anything.*

Similarly, relationships with women lovers have not proved to be
stable or supportive for Lisa. She is left with the intensity of her kin
relations, her closest ties being those with her children.

In a somewhat different vein, Ruth Zimmerman describes the process that led her to decide to have a child on her own.

One of the reasons I probably decided to have a kid was to have a certain kind of continuity. What you call a long-term relationship. I wanted that. I wanted to feel that important to somebody else, that committed to somebody else. I guess I really am a family person, in spite of the fact that I don't feel real comfortable with my own family. But being . . . committed to people is kind of important to me. . . . I wanted more continuity in my life than going through a series of roommates and having the household change with the roommates. That just seemed . . . so transient. It just didn't feel like a life. So now I've got me this permanent roommate. . . . And the closeness that's possible with a child—I mean, I don't know where else that's possible. . . . A lover relationship can approach the intensity of a parent-child relationship, but never have that same quality of how close that is.

Thus having a child anchors one socially, puts one in the world in a way that creates meaningful connections and that reinforces, and is reinforced by, continuity with other kin. At the same time, kin relations may also be seen as *representing* valued ties with children, as validating those links. The paradox here, as we see poignantly in the case of Lisa Stark, is that children are the source of considerable difficulty and hardship at the same time that their ability to generate feelings of intimacy and links to the ineffable constitute the apparent solution to the very problems they generate. By becoming mothers, lesbians are able to negotiate a more satisfactory stance with respect to traditional gender expectations. Paradoxically, however, this very process of accommodation presents them with further problems to be resolved, frequently demanding that they reorganize their identities with motherhood at the core.

As we saw earlier, having children has the added benefit of connecting lesbians and other women to forces of "good" in the world, of allowing them to participate in the creativity of childhood, and to be altruistic. The intensity of their feelings makes the experience of motherhood meaningful, rather than just burdensome. For some women, this is almost an astonishing transformation.

Christine Richmond, who had a baby on her own about three years ago, speaks with amazement about the changes he has brought into her life. She is a successful musician, and until she became a mother she spent most of her time perfecting her skills, planning performances and tours, and being caught up in the excitement of her professional world. But her son, she says,

brings out feelings in me that I have never experienced before, both love and anger. . . . He's the first thing in my life that means more to me than I do. I would do anything for him, I mean I would give my life for him. . . . If anything were to happen to him I don't know if I would want to go on living.

Inez Escobar sees her daughter not only as her closest friend and companion but as the person whose existence helped her to improve her life, particularly to overcome her early problems with alcohol and drugs.

I think being responsible for somebody, and kind of like having a stake in the future. Like wanting the world to be a better place. . . . But just kind of when I started to see her mirror me, it kind of made me want to change, and be a better person.

Lesbian mothers' narratives reveal the resilience of relatively traditional notions of family, even as their structural expression may vary tremendously. More profoundly, perhaps, lesbian mothers appear to accept motherhood eagerly as a core identity, and to be willing to allow its demands to attenuate other kinds of relationships and other sources of identity. Their narratives show that links to children, and particularly the need to engage in altruistic behavior and the opportunity to be in touch with the higher order one encounters with children, may be what family means in the shifting situation of lesbians. Here ideas about one's blood kin provide a model, albeit highly idealized, of what one can expect from one's connection to one's children.

Ties with children are anchored by the twin weights of responsibility and connectedness. Having a child on one's own, whether one started on that basis or not, locates one in the world, gives a woman a partner, a collaborator in the business of living, and takes some of the uncertainty and formlessness out of daily existence. At the same time, motherhood imposes heavy burdens and feelings of obligation and inadequacy that undermine other concerns and areas of competence, relegating them to triviality. Nothing else seems as important as one's children, and women paradoxically resent the tyranny of motherhood at the same time that they derive value from their experience of it.

6

Friends and Lovers

*According to lesbian lore, friendships, most notably those with other les-*bians, offer opportunities for the formation of surrogate kin ties. Popular lesbian literature tends to emphasize the "community" as "family." Former lovers, in particular, are expected to assume a role comparable to that of the extended family.[1] This theme is pervasive in advice manuals and other popular works; yet lesbians, as we have seen, turn for friendship to other mothers, especially other mothers in similar circumstances—unmarried women, whether lesbian or heterosexual.

This pattern lends itself to interpretation at more than one level. From one perspective, the shared status of single mother may help to strengthen a developing friendship, or even provide the motivation for its formation. Some accounts suggest that over time mothers become closer to other mothers already in their friendship networks, or that an existing friendship may become more important after the friend has divorced or come out, and thus has come to share the status of single or lesbian mother. From another perspective, it appears that friendships with married mothers and with people who have no children tend to fade over time. Both lesbians and heterosexual single mothers emphasize a view of childless people as selfish, superficial, or simply so unfamiliar with the "reality" of their lives as mothers as to make friendship impossible. Most important, lesbian mothers' narratives about friendship reinforce their view of motherhood as standing at the center of their identities.

Tanya Petroff articulates this position in offering her views about the kinds of people with whom she can form friendships. Living alone as she does with her seven-year-old daughter and holding a job that requires frequent overtime, she has to do a lot of planning to arrange childcare. Though she is on friendly terms with her upstairs neighbors, they are of no assistance in this respect because they are "single"—they have no children.

Tanya's most important friendships are with other single mothers, regardless of whether they are straight or gay. She believes that the values of childless people are so different from her own that they offer virtually no basis for interaction or trust, but that a difference in sexual orientation is a trivial matter among mothers. Tanya is convinced that no one who is not also a parent could be a consistently supportive friend.

There's a difference between people who have children and people who don't have children. People who don't have children, to my way of thinking, are very selfish. . . . They needn't consider anyone other than themselves. They can do exactly what they want to do at any given time. And though I admire that, it's not possible for me to do that and I guess for that reason most of my friends are single mothers, because it's hard for me to coordinate my needs and my time with someone who's in a completely different head set. "Why can't you get a sitter for the kid?"—that kind of thing. . . . And I don't want to get into that resentment all the time or educating other women. . . . I've spent years doing that and now I just prefer being with people who have some sense of what it's like to be me, and I understand where they are too.

But neither is Tanya interested in friendships with married women, even if they are mothers; maintaining a friendship with a married woman would demand some sort of relationship with her husband too.

I'm a person in my own right. I make my own decisions, I schedule my own time. And to talk to someone who cannot decide what to do because their husband or their lover might not allow them to do it or something—I don't want to hear it.

Tanya's feeling that she can find really supportive friends only among other women whose situations closely mirror her own does not stem only from her need to locate reliable sources of material assistance. As her comments indicate, friends are valued largely insofar as they affirm or validate her identity. She wants friends who have "some idea of what it's like to be me," people with whom she need not struggle to establish a recognizable image of herself. Her essential identity, by implication, is a mother; her motherhood supersedes her sexual orientation, her ethnicity, her job.

Another lesbian mother, Harriet Newman, reports similar problems in efforts to maintain ongoing friendships with married women, even when they have children. Harriet lives in a rural area north of San Francisco with her ten- and eleven-year-old daughters. It seems to her that married women are less committed to friendship, and that problem is particularly acute when she feels that she really needs her women friends.

One thing that's difficult is that I want a certain intensity or level of relationship that [married women] don't necessarily need, because they have a husband at home. . . . If you have somebody at home, if you just want an adult around, you don't have to go anywhere. I have to make dates, go out, all that business. Sometimes I have felt at a disadvantage. I always call, I'm always trying to see people who don't need that as much as I do.

Because she knows almost no other lesbian mothers in her community, Harriet often finds herself the only single person at parties or other social occasions. And when her straight friends "hole up with a boyfriend," she feels lonely and betrayed.

That's always a little betrayal. Or the married friends, who have a big to-do or a breakup with their husbands, and they turn to their women friends and their single friends very suddenly, and very urgently, for support. You get very involved and then that passes and they get back with the husbands, and they have to kind of reject or put some distance between this state and what they were doing three months ago.

Following a somewhat different pattern, Leslie Addison, the lesbian mother of a twelve-year-old daughter, has tried to get other lesbians she knows more interested in supporting women with children. She has belonged, on and off, to a lesbian rap group formed by a local gay community mental health agency, but has found the members to be not only less supportive that she had hoped, but actively hostile to her situation as a mother. In her view, the "lesbian community" is orientated primarily toward "single" women's needs.

I have a lot of anger . . . that they don't make a commitment to their kids—I mean, I consider them everybody's kids, because these are the ones that if they're raised by lesbians, and see that women around them can be open to having them, and to having them in their society, or whatever it is, then they're going to grow up with a much more open mind, more tolerant, more open to being capable women than most of the other kids that are going to be brought up in a heterosexual home. The women just cannot look beyond their own little needs. "Well, I'm single, I don't want any responsibility, I don't want anything to tie me down." I just have a lot of anger about that. It really turns me against the lesbian community. I do nothing in the lesbian community now whatsoever.

Leslie's decision to curtail her community activities has made a big difference in her daily life. She had been involved in women's writing groups, had worked with other lesbian mothers of daughters on an educational project, had written articles for lesbian papers, frequently attended women's concerts, and patronized local coffee shops, bars, and other establishments with a predominantly lesbian clientele.

I remember going to one group. . . . The mothers in the group were trying to get all the women to donate for child-care expenses. And a lot of the women—one in particular that I remember—got up and said, "I don't ask you to pay for baby-sitting my dog, I'm not going to pay for baby-sitting your kid."

Leslie's experiences with lovers parallels her disappointment with the lesbian community as a whole. Shortly after her divorce she began her first relationship with another woman. Her expectation was that a woman lover would naturally offer a lot of support to her as a mother and that it would be easier to manage being a single mother once she had come out as a lesbian. But that isn't what she found. She feels that, once she came out, she had to rely on herself a lot more. Ironically, when she was straight, she says, she could always get a boyfriend to baby-sit for her; as a lesbian, she finds that women usually refuse to help.

That wasn't quite what I expected. I expected there would be more sharing be-
tween women of the child. But I found it's really not, because another woman has
a role identity crisis. She can't be the mother, because you're already the mother.
She can't be the father, because she's not the father. Whereas the men sort of
played that role. It was easier for them to fall into it. They could just play daddy,
I could play momma, and everybody'd be happy.

Leslie is sure that she really is a lesbian, but jokes that she occasionally
thinks of getting involved with a man when she's desperate for child
care!

But she sees other problems besides child care with trying to maintain a relationship with a lover; in fact, she has decided, somewhat
fatalistically, that she must postpone her desire to have a lover until
her daughter is at least eighteen. Her relationship with her daughter is
very close, and it is difficult under the best of circumstances for an
outsider to try to become part of their family.

It can't not be. This is a whole other person. You can't just take the mother,
you've got to take the mother and the kid, too, in a relationship. That's two peo-
ple to get along with, and it's hard enough to get along with one. It took [my
daughter] and me six years to work out our relationship. I can't imagine anybody
else coming into it.

Leslie's skepticism about relationships extends to her feelings about
the durability of friendships. Most of her friends do not have children, and though she can give examples of favors she and one of
her friends regularly do for each other—rides to the airport, jump-
starting each other's unreliable cars, talking about their feelings—she
still feels that she must carefully ration her requests so as not to put
undue strain on these relationships. Her description of her closest
friendship reflects this hesitance.

Leslie: [There's] probably nothing I couldn't ask her, but I like to
limit my asking. I don't like to do it too much.
Interviewer: Any special reason?

Leslie: I guess I just think that people get tired if you get to asking too much. Since I have three friends, I can sort of swap them around. I feel that's easier on all of them, since all of them work.

Leslie's account of her experiences in the lesbian community is extremely negative, and is clearly influenced by her more general mistrust of the intentions or sincerity of anyone but her daughter. While the overall pessimism she reveals is perhaps idiosyncratic, she does resemble other lesbian mothers in assigning friends and lovers to a single domain. Her disappointment in the "lesbian community" seems particularly acute in view of her unspoken assumptions about how other women ought to feel about children. At the same time that her account underscores her feeling of distinctiveness as a mother, it marks her acceptance of traditional gendered expectations for women and men.

Even mothers whose experience with friends has been more positive perceive a gulf between their needs and priorities and those of their "single" friends. Michelle O'Neill talks at length about the dramatic changes her year-old son has brought to her life. She has far less time for the kinds of social activities she used to participate in, has to keep her time carefully organized to manage to complete her schoolwork (she began a nursing program shortly after having her baby), and often feels tired and overwhelmed by her responsibilities. Her concerns for her son's welfare make her feel more "conservative" as well. But along with these changes, she reports a major realignment of her friendship ties.

A big thing that has changed is my relationship with other people—with my friends. And particularly with my friends who are not mothers. . . . I feel very isolated from them. Some I know have left our friendship, some I have left the friendship because it was just too difficult to deal with them around that "I have a child" and stuff and I just got tired of getting them to understand what I had to go through to go to a movie with one hour notice or I just got tired of the way I felt when I said I have to try to find child care . . . and getting this feeling that they were annoyed that I had to do that and that I couldn't give them an answer right away.

Like many other mothers, Michelle can't imagine how she could manage the logistics of having a lover; her focus on her son, coupled with the time she needs to study, has made it hard for her to pay attention to other adults.

I've definitely become closer friends with other mothers. . . . But the thing is that I don't want to be only a mother. I don't want motherhood and children to be the only thing in my life and so I don't want to associate with only mothers because I have found that . . . what you talk about and what you do is children.

Heterosexual Mothers Speak

Like lesbian mothers, heterosexual single mothers view other mothers as the most reliable friends. Nancy Keenan, a secretary who had her two-year-old son on her own, has formed strong friendships with several women who meet regularly as a "single mothers' support group." Aside from this group and her roommate, who is also a single mother (and a group member), Nancy has found it difficult to maintain friendships with women who are not parents. One friend at her job has offered on numerous occasions to help out with baby-sitting, but Nancy has found that this friend is more likely to assume that baby-sitters can be obtained easily at the spur of the moment than to make a real contribution.

So [it's] been real hard, to make my friends understand that [it's hard to get a baby-sitter] and she's always been one to push me to get a baby-sitter to come in, or . . . she's always said, oh, I'd love to baby-sit, but when it comes down to it . . . she doesn't want to baby-sit when it's convenient for me.

Nancy attributes this insensitivity to the fact that her friend has no children of her own. In sharp contrast is her relationship with her roommate.

We don't really do things together, but we share almost every aspect of our lives with each other. Anything that goes on during the day, any problems that we're having, we bounce them off each other and provide kind of a sounding board and the other will throw back ideas, try to help in any way they can, and that has just been the most important. It's been like a marriage.

Nancy doesn't have to tell these friends what's important to her. As single mothers, these women share the same central concerns; in her view, the support they offer resembles what a marriage—something Nancy has never experienced—ought to provide.

Some heterosexual mothers are able to resume relationships they had with other mothers when they were still married after the friends end their marriages and become single mothers. Denise King, who lives with her fourteen-year-old son and her mother in Berkeley, has been on her own for five years. She recently completed a graduate program, and when her mother moved in after the breakup of her own marriage, the stress of managing the household while pursuing a demanding schedule of work and school was eased. Before then, however, her friendships were essential to her ability to manage when things were, in essence, unmanageable.

Most of her friends are women she met when their husbands were students and they were all living in married-student housing. They are all single mothers now, and have remained more or less in the same neighborhood, largely in order to keep the friendship network operating.

We do a lot for each other, in just needing somebody to get drunk on wine with, or jam with, date with, caring for the kids. Someone to jog with in the morning. They're just there. There's no ceremony involved. You can call them up any time of the day or night, doesn't matter if they're entertaining or not. We basically have open house for each other constantly. . . . They'd lie down in traffic for me, and I for them. [We] lend each other money. Help each other out with moving, or paint- ing. Share meals. Again, if you're just feeling down. . . . You say, sure, I'll be right there. I could ask any number of people to do almost anything for me. I pas- sed the licensing exam, I found it out at two in the morning, and I was phoning people up at three and four o'clock in the morning. They were delighted to hear from me. So you know that those are friends.

The rhythm of these friendships is determined largely by the fact that all the women have children and are single. Visits can be inter- rupted while children are fed ("Somebody runs off to McDonald's or says gee, I've got something in the refrigerator"); and the likelihood that there is never enough money or time to go around is understood.

If one mother is taking her kids swimming or to the park, she may call around and offer to take other children from the group.

I think we all feel like we participate in our kids' lives, because we all know that one parent really isn't enough. And we feel very comfortable disciplining each other's children, taking them on. Mom goes off and we just shuffle another few kids around the table for supper, and bed them down in their sleeping bags on the floor. They're just as comfortable in any of the houses. They all respect us all as mothers, and as parent figures.

Denise says that there is nothing she wouldn't ask of these friends, including money. None of them has much, but by sharing they are able to make what they have sustain them all. Beyond this help, though, her account stresses that the women in the group give each other consistent emotional support, as during the long periods of unemployment most of them have experienced. She describes little parties they have to celebrate things—one friend keeping a job she thought she would lose, another friend buying a filing cabinet and getting her life organized. Recently several of the women have moved into new careers and celebrations focus on passing the bar exam or getting a real estate license.

It would freak me out to not feel that I had this kind of support. What would I do if my car breaks down then? Christ, I don't have a car. Well, if my car breaks down, I just borrow Marge's. And the same is true if hers breaks down, she borrows mine. . . . None of us have everything we need, but as a group we do. We're a pretty good tribe, you know. So collectively our needs are met, but individually they wouldn't be. We would lead very deprived lives. We'd feel very deprived if we were solitary.

Other mothers must make do with less extensive support systems. Gwen Murphy has faced many problems since she became pregnant almost two years ago. Her son's foreign-born father, whom she had hoped to marry, had to leave the country and she is now uncertain whether he will ever return and whether he even wants her to join him, as he once claimed. Her family has been emotionally supportive but is unable to offer any financial assistance. And though her secretarial job has kept her off welfare, child-care expenses have put her under a crippling financial strain. Gwen can rarely afford to go out and often feels isolated and trapped in her sparsely furnished apartment. She talks at great length of every purchase she has made and hopes to make, clearly keeping meticulous account of every dollar she has or expects to receive.

In this context, her friendship with her boss, a lesbian mother with three children, has become central to her survival. Gwen uses the same child-care provider as Gloria Frank, her boss, and they meet there each morning when they drop off their kids. Gwen then gets a ride to work with Gloria, and a ride back to the child-care provider at the end of the day. Along with the financial pressures she faces, Gwen's struggles with child care and transportation (since she cannot afford a car) are the central themes of her daily life. She lives on the same bus line as the child care provider and a supermarket, but her job is some distance from both places and is difficult to reach on public transportation.

Gloria's support of Gwen goes beyond giving her a ride to work each morning. She has covered for Gwen at work when a problem with the baby has caused her to be late, tired, or distracted. She has also helped her to get advances on her salary when financial emergencies have struck. But with three children Gloria has her own money problems and cannot help Gwen personally.

We're both in such bad straits moneywise we can't ever lend each other, but I feel like if either of us at one point were ahead of the other, we would. . . . The other day I was supposed to get an overtime check. The girl in payroll really fucked up my check so . . . she said it would be on my next check. And I said to Gloria, but that's not the point, the point is that I need the money now. I had everything accounted for, and she goes well, listen, if you get hungry, I don't have any money, but I have a credit card. We'll go to Long's Drug Store and she means it. So it's just crazy. Two single mothers just faltering like you wouldn't believe.

Other heterosexual mothers report similar friendship patterns. Barbara Leary, who lives alone with her eleven-year-old son in Oakland, talks at length about the loneliness and isolation of her life as a single mother. She has only recently gotten off welfare, but her new job pays very little, and she continues to feel vulnerable and anxious much of the time. Her relationship with her parents has been strained, at least until recently, largely because of her unconventional lifestyle and out-of-wedlock child. Relationships with men have also proved to be difficult; Barbara feels that they tend to be jealous of her son and that she is caught in between, trying to mediate her son's connection with her lovers and experiencing considerable stress in the process.

But her women friends have provided a solid core of emotional support. In particular, her former next-door neighbor, also a single mother, trades child care with her and does other little favors from time to time. More important, she serves as a vital source of solace, and Barbara describes her as being like a sister. She is always there, rooted, in Barbara's view, like a tree.

I go see her when I'm really bummed out. Or lonely. And there aren't too many people you can do that to. Most people are real fair-weather friends. But she's a real cloudy-weather friend, you know. Somebody you can just lay your head on. We sympathize together, we get hysterical together when we're feeling low, we can make each other laugh. We both get depressed sometimes, and it's usually around the same times, so I feel like it's mutual.

Rosemary Herrera, a forty-year-old mother of five, has found that the maintenance of a critical friendship has, ironically, intensified her vulnerability to a custody threat. After twenty years of marriage, Rosemary is in the midst of an extremely acrimonious divorce. In an apparent effort to reduce his child-support obligations, Rosemary's husband is suing for custody, falsely alleging that she is a lesbian. Now she fears that her friendships with other mothers may be interpreted as evidence of lesbianism.

A number of friendships have helped sustain Rosemary through the difficult period that followed the collapse of her marriage, but one woman friend has had a particularly central role during this time. Every night at a prearranged time, she and her friend Charlotte Shafer (a divorced mother who lost custody of her children some years ago) have agreed to talk on the phone. They both discuss their problems, but in recent times Rosemary often cries while Charlotte listens.

Rosemary helped Charlotte go through the trauma of her divorce and the loss of her children; now Charlotte is reciprocating. But the support Rosemary receives from this friendship goes beyond these telephone conversations. On occasions when Rosemary feels that she cannot cope with her children alone, she can call Charlotte and ask her to join them for dinner. In addition, without much explicit discussion of Rosemary's serious financial difficulties, Charlotte often arrives at Rosemary's door with a turkey or other food that she "doesn't need."

Rosemary has not reduced her reliance on this friendship, even as she knows her husband may twist its meaning to fit his litigation strategy. Like lesbian mothers, she is fearful about having to defend her "fitness" as a mother in court; at the same time, she desperately needs the support of someone who has faced and survived a comparable crisis. Her friendship with Charlotte not only provides her with solace and material assistance; it affirms that her experience is valid and her identity valuable.

I had no opportunity to observe friendships in action, but I did speak with more than one member of a few networks and was able to get some perspective on their relationships. It was not uncommon for descriptions of particular friendships to vary dramatically. What is critical here, however, is not whether the networks could actually provide the kind of support mothers expected of them. Rather, what they offer is a way to reinforce an account of the self that places motherhood at the center of identity. Friendships work, in the views of both lesbians and heterosexual single mothers, because friends share the essential reality of being mothers without the economic support of husbands or the institutional respectability of marriage. A friendship fails to work when the friend's identity is not framed primarily by motherhood, whether the competing identity is lesbian, married woman, or non-mother.

Relationships with Lovers

It is difficult to disengage a discussion of mothers' ties to lovers from the broader context of friendship. Like friends who are not sexual or domestic partners, lesbians' lovers are, of course, women. With some lovers or potential lovers lesbian mothers share the reality of parenting; in other cases, though, the lack of understanding of what it takes to be a mother can contribute to problems and misunderstandings.

For some mothers, the possibility that the lover is anything less than complete in her dedication to the child and to the mother's family does not even come up. Rebecca Collins, who painted a picture of idyllic family harmony when I asked her about her ties with her parents, portrays her relationship with Sheila Ryan in the same vein.

Sheila is very much a part of the family, both in terms of my parents and [my son's] father. So there was no pulling [my son] away from a relationship with what ultimately turns out to be a second mother. And then from her end, she's very receptive to that, whereas a lot of women aren't; they really want that separation. Fine, we'll live together, but it's your child. She really doesn't feel that way at all. . . . In practice, she acts as much as a mother as I do.

Rebecca reports that her son regards Sheila as a second mother, sometimes responding to inquiries about his mother by asking, "Which one?" Sheila attends all functions for parents along with Rebecca and her former husband, handles child care when Rebecca is busy, and spends a considerable amount of time alone with the boy, playing catch and attending his athletic events, all of which interest her more than they do Rebecca.

Helen Lynch, a blue-collar worker who lives with her lover, Betty Vaughn, and her four children (aged nine to twenty), sees her situation as very much like that of any other family. They've been together for five years, and Helen feels that Betty often communicates better with the kids than she does. Helen reports a lot of family leisure-time activity—ball games, picnics, weekend trips—to which the children frequently bring their friends. They own a house together, have a joint checking account, and do not keep track of who buys things for the children. According to Helen, the real mark of their being "strictly like a family" is that Betty often makes purchases for the children without consulting Helen. They are close to Betty's mother, and in fact, it is to her that Helen and Betty would turn if they were to experience a financial emergency.

This experience contrasts sharply with that of Peggy Lawrence and Sue Alexander. Peggy has not told her parents that she is a lesbian. Her relationship with them has been stressful for years, marked, according to her, by their disapproval of everything she did, and she dreads their reaction if they were to find out. They have met Sue and spent time with her on their visits to California, but they give the couple no acknowledgment that they are a family.

They don't understand the extent to which we're living our lives together and raising our children together—the extent to which we are interrelated and depending on each other to do all the things we have to do in our daily lives. . . . They just think it's a shame that I don't make enough money so I have to have a roommate.

But for Peggy, the fact that they both have children and have formed a family is absolutely central to her relationship with Sue. They met at a lesbian mothers' meeting and their both having children was a key factor in their becoming lovers.

It's important to me that she takes our lives very seriously. It's important to me that she's committed to what we're doing. That I can trust that she'll be here. . . . That we're both involved in our lives with our children, and that it's a relatively permanent situation that we are involved in our lives with our children. That's something I can count on.

But their differing views on mothering, as well as what Peggy sees as the sharply different needs of their children, have led to conflict in their relationship. Their ideas about discipline, chores, and money have all turned out to be at odds; at the same time, the children themselves have had a variety of disputes that have shaken the household and placed considerable stress on Peggy's relationship with Sue. This situation has made Peggy aware that the time and energy she has devoted to establishing her new family has led some of her friendships to atrophy; she is determined to find new friends so that she will not be totally dependent on Sue.

I'm trying to extend my support group, because I'm really worried about how small it is. I feel isolated. I need to feel that I'm with more people, that I'm really with and that I can really count on.

Many mothers with partners report that their lovers collaborate with them in the business of parenting, and Peggy's concern that this situation can lead to stress, if not outright conflict, is not unique. Women describe a range of experience, from ambiguity in the un-specified role of the "second mother" to competition with the child for the mother's attention. It is not uncommon for conflict over the child or over maternal obligations to lead to the collapse of a relation-ship. Overriding all of these variations is the primary commitment mothers feel to their children in the event that a lover's needs actually or apparently conflict with theirs. Some mothers articulate this com-mitment as powerful enough effectively to rule out an intimate rela-tionship until the children are grown.

Doris Johnson has been involved with June Kepler for about three years. Her two daughters

sometimes see [June] as another mother, sometimes as a big sister, sometimes as a close friend. No one ever quite knows how to define anything, which is fine with me. . . . They're mutually very, very fond of each other. Which is one of the rea-sons that it works. There would be no way, at this point in my life, that I would live with someone who wasn't involved with the kids, and with whom they were not involved. I don't want to split my life up that way.

According to Doris, her daughters were instrumental in getting June to move in, not long after she and Doris became lovers. The girls are very aware of the nature of the relationship, discuss gay issues openly, and have told most of their friends that their mother is a lesbian, even though Doris has told them it's fine with her if they'd rather keep this information to themselves. Both girls have invited June to meet their teachers and to attend school events. Though June and Doris take turns cooking dinner and divide domestic respon-sibilities equally, June pays one-third (not one-half) of the rent and they have made no moves toward merging their finances.

Hannah Rosenberg, who has three children between the ages of ten and thirteen, also experiences some ambiguity in the relationship between her children and her lover, Lucy Weiss. Hannah and her former husband have joint custody of their children, so two are currently living with him, while Hannah lives with the third child and Lucy.

Sometimes Lucy's role bothers her. She says she isn't anything, because she's not really a parent. She has no legal standing, and she has no real authority. . . . As far as behavior around the house, I think she has an equal role. However, I'm not sure that in their eyes she's equal to my role, or if . . . they totally accept her. . . . [My older son] said he didn't know what to call her, if she was his step-mother or what.

For a number of lesbian mothers, however, these relatively mild concerns with ambiguity and parental duty have escalated into far more intense and combative disputes. It is not uncommon for mothers to report that the lover not only fails to act as a parent but requires mothering herself, sometimes competing with the child for the mother's attention.

Deborah Cohen, having broken up with a number of lovers in disputes over her ten-year-old daughter, now feels that the most sensible plan is not to move in with the woman she is currently involved with. While Deborah was living with her previous lover, Carolyn Fishman, her job required her to work long shifts and she often had to depend on Carolyn for baby-sitting. Carolyn was openly resentful and Deborah ended up feeling guilty. This problem did not seem to be unique to this relationship. Deborah believes that it has been a feature of most of her past relationships and can explain several earlier breakups.

I've had a lot of trouble, actually, with women lovers around [my daughter], and not being able to leave her with them because of the resentment and jealousy.

Deborah claims that her daughter has often behaved more maturely and responsibly in these situations than her lovers. All of this has come as a surprise to Deborah. When she first came out, she assumed that women, because of their socialization, would more readily assume responsibility for a child. She found instead that interest in her child was peripheral.

Women would be real interested in my child if they were trying to get it on with me, when they first met me. Oh, how wonderful, a girl child. They had all kinds of expectations about her, you know. . . . Oh, we're going to raise an Amazon, we're going to raise this little dyke. And [my daughter] wanted to be in long dresses, and didn't want to be a little dyke. . . . Then when I started feeling like . . . I wasn't going to oppress my child that way, then my lover started to freak out. It wasn't OK with her that I was letting [my daughter] be who she is. When I started supporting [my daughter], it wasn't OK with my lover at all.

This was not the only problem she faced. Deborah feels that she was put in a position in which she had to ration her time and energy, dividing her attention between her child and her lover, while her lover directed energy only toward her. She ultimately became quite resentful about this situation, as she sees her child as the only legitimate focus of a mother's care.

I was like in the middle, and being torn all the time, to where, like, at the dinner table, we'd sit down to have dinner together and they'd both talk to me at the same time.

Finally these conflicts became disputes over money. Deborah contributed more to household expenses because she had the child, though she felt this arrangement wasn't fair because her lover earned as much as she did. After she raised her complaints, they began to divide expenses evenly (though they never pooled their funds), but then her lover became resentful "because there was two of us eating and one of her. . . . There was always this two-of-us-and-one-of-her trip." Carolyn was not a mother and could not (or would not) try to be one; she could never be part of the essential constellation created by Deborah and her daughter. Deborah's unspoken assumptions about how women ought to be when they were offered an opportunity to act as mothers made her disappointment and sense of abandonment all the more acute.

Meg Jordan, a twenty-six-year-old mother of a six-year-old son, reports similar problems. She thinks her relationship with Vicky Estes is in trouble because of what she calls "the co-parent issue." Vicky has told her that she does not want to be cast in the co-parent role, but Meg feels that she cannot continue the relationship without help and an explicit commitment to her son from Vicky. They are in the process of working out some compromises: Vicky will take the child once a week overnight so that Meg can have a little time for herself. They also will begin to share child-care costs equally when they go out and take turns locating child care. At the same time, Vicky has been in the habit of picking up the boy at his after-school center almost every day, a task that is easier for her than for Meg because of her work schedule.

Meg feels strongly that these negotiations are forcing her to divide her life into three parts: her child, her lover, and her job. She imagines an ideal situation with someone who would be prepared to form a meaningful relationship with her son—

whether she be a single woman or a woman with a child, someone who is into co-parenting, so that the responsibility of a child or children is a mutual thing.

While for some mothers, another lesbian mother seems like a good bet for a person to become involved with, other mothers see this arrangement as yet another pitfall. Louise Green thinks it would be better to have a lover who doesn't have her own children. People with children, to her way of thinking, are preoccupied with their kids, and the inevitable result is a series of conflicts for the mothers and the children. Yet she cannot imagine having a relationship with anyone who doesn't want to share the care of her daughter.

If someone is going to be my lover, they're signing up to be my lover and something for [my daughter] too. You see, I don't want anyone if they're not into [her] too.

Heterosexual Mothers with Lovers

We might expect heterosexual single mothers to have similar experiences as they try to integrate male partners into the care of children, and perhaps feel equally discouraged when men fail to assume some parental duties. But heterosexual single mothers and lesbians differ dramatically in this area. Apparently, heterosexual mothers have more modest expectations for the men they find themselves involved with. Whereas lesbians tend to assume (or at least hope) that their female partners will "naturally" be predisposed to care for or make sacrifices for children, heterosexual mothers tend to doubt that their male partners will offer any sort of meaningful support. When the men do show interest in the children, such concern is welcomed with both enthusiasm and some surprise. Lesser commitments by men tend to be overlooked or seen as not worthy of notice.

Susan Beecher lives in Berkeley with her eight-year-old son and her boyfriend of six years, Steve Cramer. Steve technically lives in the in-law apartment connected to her house, but in fact they share meals and some of the household chores. But Susan is cautious; she feels it is important to keep their money separate and to establish herself as a single woman. In part this attitude seems to reflect the process she experienced when she left her husband, a "blossoming" of her sense of herself as a separate person and her first taste of independence. Although Susan and Steve have recently begun to speak tentatively of marriage, she fears that the legal tie might have a destructive effect on their relationship.

Steve and Susan's son, Daniel, get along well, and they spend some time together on their own. Daniel's contact with his father, who lives in another state, is far more limited, confined mainly to summer visits and occasional holidays. Nevertheless, Susan feels strongly that Steve should not make significant decisions about Daniel and in particular should not discipline him. She explains that though he is Daniel's "surrogate father" some of the time, he is still not his real father.

It just seems to me like the blood ties—It's really amazing, the blood-tie business. No matter how much time is spent, the real father really is the father. All that's saying that no matter what, I think [Steve] will always be second. He will not be the real father.

Some women would trade their problems with their lovers for Susan's any day. Phyllis Siegel has two children, a fifteen-year-old son and an eight-year-old daughter. She and her former husband, a physician, have been divorced for two years, and she continues to live in the spacious Berkeley home they occupied during their marriage.

Phyllis received a temporary spousal support award in addition to child support and hopes that by the time it expires, in three years, her new career in commercial art will permit her to maintain her current standard of living. Phyllis got involved with Greg Kaufman about a year ago, and is already experiencing some stress because he is unwilling to form a meaningful relationship with her children. Greg has a regular schedule of visits with his daughter from a previous marriage and is not eager to become involved with Phyllis's children. This is the major reason he has not moved in with her.

I'd like to think that ultimately I'd be in a relationship with somebody in which I would share my life. . . . We've gone through some very rocky times. . . . He's not a nurturing sort of person. He's supportive, but not in that nurturing sort of way.

Greg prefers not to plan many activities with Phyllis and the children because he doesn't like "the noise." She has been obliged to devise a complicated schedule on the weekends in an effort to spend time alone with Greg and also to spend time with each of her children. Sometimes Greg makes plans that require her to find a babysitter for her daughter.

Greg lives in San Francisco. When Phyllis's ex-husband used to take the kids for weekend visits, she was able to spend time at Greg's apartment. But her ex-husband recently stopped arranging regular visits, so Phyllis cannot plan to spend the weekends away from home. The present arrangement is that Greg stays at Phyllis's about four or five nights a week, though he rarely appears until after dinner, apparently because he's "uncomfortable about the family situation." Greg, a stockbroker, is quite well off financially. He and Phyllis share interests in music, fine restaurants, and other expensive diversions, which Greg always pays for. Phyllis wonders at times if her interest in him isn't enhanced to some extent by the financial need she has experienced since her divorce.

A recent dispute was sparked by Phyllis's recognition that she is contributing more than Greg to the stability of the relationship. She would like Greg to help her with her income tax, but is afraid to ask him because he will criticize her for not keeping adequate records. Nonetheless, she has been doing his laundry regularly for some time, a burden she only recently started to consider excessive.

What am I doing this fucker's laundry for? Here's his linen, and his blankets, and I'm washing and folding them. He's expecting me to do all the little things a wife does, and he doesn't want to take on the sorts of things, he doesn't want to fall into that kind of relationship. And it's not that it costs me any time or energy to do that, but I just thought it was a sort of symbol. So I told him that I didn't want to do his laundry anymore and he got really put out. He said, "Well, if that's how you feel about it, I think we should end the relationship!"

They compromised that she would wash the clothes he uses when he's at her house. But she feels that she can never ask him to help her with the kids, and arranges help from friends when problems arise.

Other Issues for Heterosexual Mothers

For some heterosexual mothers, how to deal with a man who doesn't collaborate in the business of parenthood is less of an issue than whether they can even establish a relationship in the first place. Alison Kahn, a successful professional woman who lives in San Francisco with her seven-year-old daughter, is acutely aware that her situation corresponds to wider historical changes affecting women. Her former husband, she claims, saw his career as more important than hers, and expected her to assume total responsibility for finding child care and other services that would enable her to resume her career. She sees the resentments this situation generated as the major impetus for their separation three years ago.

Since the end of her marriage, Alison has experienced considerable stress in her efforts to form workable relationships with men. On the one occasion when a man spent the night, her daughter became so upset that Alison now has a date stay over only if her daughter is visiting her father. More serious has been her failure to secure what she considers adequate recognition of the importance of her professional life. This problem is compounded by what she regards as virtually all men's insensitivity to women's sexual needs. In short, she regards most of the men she has dated as so self-centered that they are oblivious of both her sexual and her intellectual needs.

Paradoxically, even when she has found a man who seems to have a real interest in both her and her daughter, Alison avoids involvement, fearing that commitment would raise her daughter's expectations only to disappoint and hurt her in the end. All of these contradictions come together in Alison's expression of a very basic kind of loneliness. She wants intimacy and sharing even while she shies away from them. "I'd like the companionship and the sense of loving and caring for somebody and being cared for." But she is convinced that such wishes are futile.

I have this sense . . . of being in the cross-currents of social change. Where women of a generation of divorced backgrounds who are professional women who are quote feminists. And it is awfully hard to meet a man who is willing to accept that because men haven't undergone the kinds of changes that we all have.

This is a particularly painful conclusion for Alison because she has maintained a rather poignant nostalgia for the world of ordinary, two-parent families she left behind. She is constantly aware of being excluded from the way of life of "families," conscious of the ways in which being a single mother sets her apart and deprives her of support and intimacy.

[Being a single mother] is very different because what's missing is the family weekend structure which I think has a rhythm to it that the single parent doesn't. For one thing, a lot of my time is spent doing chores. Between doing the laundry and going to the cleaners and doing a full marketing . . . is often how I spend one day. And the other day [my daughter] is not with me. I either work or I see friends or I try and unwind or do something that I enjoy. But it feels less structured and somehow less integrated into what one thinks the real world is.

Alison has two close women friends, both professional colleagues, but single and childless. Her time with them is limited to activities they can pursue when her daughter is with her ex-husband, usually attending a concert, going out to dinner, or going to a movie. She has occasionally asked these friends for favors related to her daughter, but tries to do so as infrequently as possible. Though she works with a group of committed feminists, she feels that because none of them is a mother she cannot ask them for any kind of support. Whenever a baby-sitting emergency or other problem related to her daughter has required her to leave work early, she can see her co-workers' resentment—in striking contrast, she remarks, to their feminist ideology.

I guess what I feel is a sense of aloneness and a sense of a lack of community. I have a lot of feelings of rapport with single parents when I meet them. [But] I'm not sure that I would go to the child-care switchboard and seek out a single-parent support group.

Despite Alison's need for support from other women who share her situation, her resentment at having been deprived of a traditional family in which to raise her daughter keeps her from developing meaningful friendships with women. The ironic contrast between the nostalgia she voices and her acute understanding of its unrealistic foundation frames her struggle to formulate an acceptable identity as a mother.

Negotiating Motherhood through Friends and Lovers

Though these accounts reveal a wide range of personal styles in the formation and maintenance of friendships, some patterns can be discerned which lesbian mothers tend to share with heterosexual single mothers. On the one hand, women in both situations tend to ration their reliance on friendship, to be acutely aware of how much pressure a relationship can sustain, and to attend carefully to issues of reciprocity. Such concerns are sharper for mothers whose friends are not also single mothers. The accounts of mothers who attempt to continue relationships with women who have no children point to a strong perception that children's needs can alter or undermine the dynamics of a friendship. When the child emerges as a competitor, the friendship must be relegated to second place.

For those mothers who have been able to construct close friendship networks with other single mothers the picture is somewhat less strained. These women view friends as reliable sources of instrumental support and consider exchange to be a necessary element to ensure balance. Even when friendships provide the benefits of loans, assistance with child care, and other forms of help, concern about reciprocity may loom large.

Friends who can be called upon in this way tend to be other lesbian and/or single mothers. Because they face similar difficulties, they can be counted on to provide assistance when it is needed. More important, they can provide a kind of moral support, affirming the gravity of situations the mother faces, attesting to their genesis in the circumstances of the mother's life rather than as evidence of her ineptitude. Simply by facing a similar set of challenges, friends validate the mother's experience, confirm that departure from the norm of the two-parent family is reasonable and necessary. In short, they understand "who she is."

Beth Romano, a thirty-six-year-old lesbian who has been estranged from her parents for many years, describes what her best friend means to her.

She [is] like a lifeline for me. She's perfect, total validating, I can tell her anything. She's just my best friend, I guess. There's an understanding and an ease in communication. I don't have to explain things to her, and she's real open and accepting of me. I really trust her. I know that she cares about me and there's no doubt about that. Also that she's a lesbian. . . . There are other people in my life that are close, but I have to explain a lot.

Patricia Atkins, who has a seven-year-old son, also focuses on the unconditional quality of her friendship with another lesbian mother whom she met at a workshop for lesbians with sons. They do a lot of things with their children and help each other with child care.

I can share anything and everything with her without feeling put down or whacked out or any other thing. And she's fun. We laugh together and because we can share our children and not feel burdened with it . . . I can take hers, she can take mine, and yet there are no expectations on either part.

Another lesbian friend who is not a mother has little interest in being around Patricia's son. This friendship has become more and more limited over the years; they share interests in photography and philosophy (both are adherents of twelve-step programs), but her friend's dislike of children conflicts with Patricia's feeling that she should spend more time with her son. Nevertheless, Patricia feels that she continues to gain some basic validation from this friendship and is reluctant to let go of it completely.

One thing I found out about my relationships with my friends is that regardless of how long it is between times I see someone that it seems like yesterday in that we can continue from where we are without any hesitation.

Variations are evident when the friend is a lover. Some lovers provide much more tangible service or aid than other friends; but many women resisted placing too much reliance on them. As we have seen, expectations of male and female lovers differ largely along the lines of traditional gender roles, although the extent to which the actual behavior of male and female partners diverges may not be great.

The varied stories of friendships and partnerships which both lesbian and heterosexual mothers offer demonstrate the centrality of motherhood not only in the formation of the women's identities but in the way they characterize their friendship networks. They measure friendship by its ability to respond to the exigencies of motherhood; relationships that fail, or seem to fail, in this regard are relegated to the margins of their lives or abandoned altogether.

7

Life with Father

Fathers have long been ambiguous participants in the lives of American families. On the one hand, in the "ideal family" immortalized by television programs of the 1950s—*Ozzie and Harriet, Father Knows Best*—Father is a very important person. He provides material sustenance for the family while Mother stays home to see to the family's emotional and physical needs. But beyond his status as provider, he is the representative of the family in the world, the person whose activities define the cultural and social status of his family.

On the other hand, documentation of what actual fathers do has shown men to be marginal to the family in some ways, more occupied with their roles in the outside world of work than with the relational core of the family.[1] Many men spend little time with their children, contribute little besides money to the ongoing operation of the household, and after divorce have been known to sever relationships not only with their wives but with their children. Despite claims from some quarters[2] that a new, more engaged, postfeminist fatherhood is on the rise, along with a "daddy track" to rival women's focus on their families, research continues to confirm the familiar picture of fathers as removed from both the affective and instrumental centers of family life.

But for female-headed families, fathers are no longer even those people who perform specialized "masculine" tasks in a domestic microcosm of gender; they are almost totally absent.[3] In these conditions, motherhood cannot be constructed as complementary to fatherhood; rather, unmarried mothers manage their situations successfully to the extent that they can maintain autonomy, demonstrating that they don't need another parent to achieve their goals. These mothers self-consciously serve as both mothers and fathers, and while the strain of managing both aspects of parenting may have its price, mothers, as we saw earlier, also take pride in their ability to meet the challenges of heading a family. For lesbians, not surprisingly, maternal achievements may have an additional meaning: motherhood can be an arena in which stigmatized identity meets normality, as lesbian mothers do what most women do.

Mothers tend to separate their children's relationships with their fathers from their own connections with these men; their actions with regard to the children's fathers generally reflect their evaluation of the quality of their relationship with the children, regardless of the mothers' own preferences. Relations with ex-husbands vary with the current legal status of the union, the terms under which the relationship ended, the specific arrangements for visitation and child support that have been agreed upon or ordered by the court and the extent to which they are observed, and the status of continuing disputes. Other considerations enter the picture when the parents have not been married. Mothers whose children resulted from a significant relationship with a man may maintain ongoing ties that resemble those of formerly married women with their ex-husbands. Women whose children were conceived through donor insemination or as a result of a short-term or casual liaison have little or no basis for a personal relationship with their children's fathers. While some are pleased by this anonymity, as it insulates them from threats to their autonomy, others worry that their children have been deprived of an opportunity to know their fathers, though what they expect the children to gain from such a relationship they do not always clearly specify.

Most mothers see fathers as necessary to their children's development in a variety of ways: as sources of ongoing material and parental support, as role models for their sons, and as sources of biological connectedness to anchor the child in a world defined by the presumed resilience of kinship ties. Lesbian mothers are no less intent than heterosexual mothers in their pursuit of a continuing tie to the child's father. Those who can identify the father emphasize their efforts to encourage his relationship with the child. Achieving this goal not only demonstrates their competence in providing everything they believe a child needs to develop normally but appears to be a major factor in the way they assess their skill and success as mothers.

Circumstances, however, may make this objective elusive. Some fathers are unwilling to cooperate because of competing commitments or apparent disinterest and prove to be unreliable or erratic in meeting obligations to the children. And for some mothers, relationships with fathers are so acrimonious that they can be activated only at considerable emotional cost.

Further complications arise when mothers fear custody or other legal difficulties. All interactions with the father occasion some risk for lesbian mothers, but these women describe themselves as working hard to provide the children with a relationship with their father. High among the obligations they associate with being a "good mother" is the provision of a father, not just a "male role model."

Despite the unconventionality of their households, these mothers still conceive of fathers principally in terms of their blood connections to their children. Most of them do not seriously entertain the notion that there is something else fathers do, something that another man or a female lover might be able to provide. They seem to construe fathers' contributions as either very specific (and narrow) instrumental ones or as consisting of a connectedness that is as important to children as three square meals a day and eight hours of sleep. Lesbian mothers, no less than heterosexual single mothers, are sure that knowing one's father is a good thing but are hard put to explain why. It seems to me that their efforts to remain connected to the father (even to the sperm donor) represent the same high value they place on blood ties in general.

What Makes Fathers Important?

Lesbian mothers share with other mothers an assumption that fathers should be continuing figures in their children's lives. Though few mothers are able to be very specific about what makes this relationship important, their accounts of the kinds of problems they have faced with their children's fathers reveal underlying beliefs about the nature of father-child relationships. Mothers' efforts to maintain significant interaction between their children and the children's fathers range from the perfunctory to the heroic. The implication is that the responsible mother will encourage these ties, and indeed that one measure of the mother's commitment and selflessness is the extent to which she succeeds in this area.

Though these views sometimes seem to depend on an implicit theory that children learn different kinds of things from fathers than they do from mothers, more often they reflect a desire for children to feel wanted by the noncustodial parent. Mothers occasionally express the view that contact with fathers offers psychological or developmental benefits of some sort to the child. But more central to their reasoning seems to be the idea that ordinary children have fathers and that a lesbian mother's child should have one too. Other male family members and male friends of the mother cannot provide this sense of connectedness and normality, although they can offer children a valued opportunity to become acquainted with men or to learn skills and behaviors associated with men. In similar fashion, the consensus of women who have become mothers through donor insemination often centers on the children's presumed need to have a known social father in order to understand something vital about their origins. Unless they have access to the same knowledge of their biological roots that children in conventional families have, how will they know who they are?[4]

Never-Married Mothers

Lesbian mothers whose children were born outside of a marital situation are, as might be expected, far from uniform in their views of fathers. For some he is a social presence, a continuing part of their lives and of their children's lives, a "father" with developed paternal obligations. For others he has departed or been ejected from their social world, with various scenarios and varying degrees of continuing contact. For yet others he is not a social being at all, a "donor" rather than a father, though the specific reasons for maintaining separation vary considerably.

Social fatherhood can take many forms. Sarah Klein, who had her year-old daughter, Emily, in a relationship with a man to whom she is still close, has worked out an informal arrangement approximating joint custody. Sarah always wanted to have children and resisted identifying herself as a lesbian for some years because she thought lesbianism precluded motherhood. When she learned she was pregnant, she and her woman lover were in the midst of a temporary separation. She met Seth Barker, her child's father, through political work, and was strongly attracted to him. Once she became pregnant, though, her attraction to him dissolved. In retrospect, Sarah suspects that her attraction to Seth had more to do with her procreative urge than with anything truly special about him.

Despite his resentment about the end of their relationship, he has willingly assumed a parental role with their daughter. He lives nearby and typically sees her several times a week. Seth has very little money, so he does not make regular contributions, but sometimes he buys an item of clothing or a toy for Emily. Sarah feels that he's a good influence on Emily, insofar as he is an "atypical, nonmacho" man. Though she considers him a parent and discusses some child-rearing issues with him (as she does with her lover), she sees herself as the sole decision maker where their daughter is concerned. His willingness to accept this stance stems, in her view, from his respect for her innate good judgment as the mother.

Bonnie Pereira, who works as a licensed vocational nurse, would like her twelve-year-old Tina to have a more meaningful relationship with her father. Bonnie was already a lesbian when she got involved with Bob; when she found she was pregnant, she wanted to have the baby on her own, though Bob was eager to marry her. In the early years he visited her often and seemed to be interested in having a relationship with Tina. He was never comfortable with Bonnie's woman lover, though, and visits tended to be tense for that reason. As time went on, his visits became much less frequent, and finally ceased altogether.

Bonnie feels that she should do everything she can to keep the channels of communication open between Bob and Tina. The relationship has been painful for her daughter, mainly because his com-

mitment to her is less than firm. His pattern has been to make appointments with Tina and then fail to show up. Bonnie has had to
console Tina on the many occasions this has happened.

*I have done what I can do: I have written, you know, and I have called and I've
let him know where I've moved to and so forth and so on, and then I've made it
very clear that he's never going to be turned away from here if he wants to see his
daughter. He's made that decision himself, that he feels uncomfortable, I guess.
And I still feel that it's his loss, and it's a shame that he can't deal with it now.
But I also know that people have reasons for whatever they do, and people have
their own pace that they have to go by, and when he's ready he'll appear.*

Other lesbian mothers report relaxed, informal relationships with
their child's fathers; these relationships tend to be those in which
money is not an issue. Christine Richmond, a successful musician
who had her child after a brief affair with a man she'd known for
many years, decided against an abortion because she had always
wanted a child and knew she could provide for it herself. The father,
Ted Campbell, did not object to having his name appear on the birth
certificate and he takes an interest in their son, visiting with increasing
frequency as the child gets older. Though he makes no financial
contribution, his mother recognizes the child as her grandchild and
periodically sends him gifts. The ease with which Christine and Ted
have been able to maintain their relationship clearly has a lot to do
with the minimal demands she makes on him. Since Christine doesn't
depend on him for money (and doesn't expect to in the future), and
since they apparently have had no disputes about the frequency of his
visits or about his parents' recognition of the child, Christine has little
reason to anticipate conflict. And yet her description of her relationship with Ted can be seen more as a statement of her own ability to
incorporate motherhood into her already competent way of living
than as a literal account of their varied interactions.

Jessy Underwood, now living on AFDC, had two children with
one man and two more with another. Although she has had relationships with women for many years, she has also been involved with a
number of men. The two who fathered her children both lead rather
disorganized lives. Both are dependent on drugs and alcohol and are

in and out of jail. Neither of them has taken any responsibility for the children or offered anything in the way of financial support. All the same, her children wanted relationships with their fathers, and any solution had to come from Jessy. The father of her older daughter, now fifteen, has taken virtually no interest her.

He still doesn't care. . . . He doesn't send any money. . . . He's still doing the same thing he did . . . selling dope, working with women. I had a hard time making [my daughter] realize [when she wanted to meet her father]. . . . But after a while she understood that he didn't care, because if he did, he would write, he would call.

Though Jessy doesn't want her daughter to have a bad image of her father, neither does she like to see her glorifying a person she knows little about. All of her children have a tendency to call the man who fathered her sons "daddy," as he does visit occasionally and Jessy is still friendly with him. But she never even considered putting either father's name on the birth certificates.

I just didn't want [their names] on. I knew that wasn't going to happen, I wasn't going to marry anybody, you know. I knew they weren't going to give up no dough. . . . And then I don't run the risk of anybody taking them away from me. Because they're mine. And I consciously made this effort to have these children. So I wasn't about to have anybody be able to take them away from me. Custody cases and all that bullshit.

For Laura Bergeron, a civil servant who lives in Menlo Park with her three children, motherhood has been a solitary venture. The children know who their fathers are, but she expects little from these men other than their willingness to be identified as the children's fathers. Laura's two sons, now ten and eight, were born while she was in a long-term relationship with their father. He did not want to have children, though once she agreed not to hold him responsible for anything, he was willing to cooperate in impregnating her. Although he was not an active parent while they still lived together—he refused to change a diaper or even to watch the children—the boys' father is now quite involved with them, sometimes baby-sitting and providing

Laura with relief from total responsibility. His name is on the boys' birth certificates and they use his last name.

The circumstances surrounding the birth of her daughter five years ago were somewhat different. Laura had come out as a lesbian after the birth of her second son. She felt strongly that she wanted to have a daughter and at thirty-five had begun to worry that she would soon be too old to have another baby. She finally decided to advertise for a sperm donor, a strategy that brought many responses but none that appeared to be legitimate. Finally a man who had recently moved into her house as a roommate offered to serve as the donor. She took vinegar douches and carefully monitored her fertile periods to ensure that she would conceive a girl, and views the birth of her daughter as evidence that these methods are effective. She and the donor made a written contract relieving him of both social and financial obligations to her daughter and agreeing that his name would never be used for any official purposes. In Laura's view, he is "just" a sperm donor, though one with whom she has a limited personal relationship.

I was really grateful for that because the one thing that had bothered me about the sperm donor thing was although I didn't feel that I needed two parents, you know, I would like, wanted my child to know who the father was so she wouldn't have all this business of chasing around the world looking if she ever got it into her head that she needed to know. . . . So this way he's a friend of the family.

Laura and her daughter share a last name different from her sons'. At the time of her daughter's birth, she chose to replace her original surname with that of her lover in the hope of establishing a stronger basis for guardianship in case of emergency.

I wanted, in case anything happens to me, like if I get in an accident or something, [I] would want my lover to take my daughter. Because the father would take the boys, see, but she would be responsible for [my daughter] and I just thought it might be easier if we did something legal about it, so at first I changed our names, and then I'm working up a thing where, you know, a legal paper that would give her guardianship.

Some mothers attempt to limit their children's interactions with their fathers because they fear that the fathers may interfere with their own autonomy or make other claims. For Patricia Atkins, for instance, who lived with her son's father for many years, determining how much contact she wants with him is a major strain. The father, Edward Draper, did not cooperate at all in the care of their son while they were living together, but Patricia's financial situation has been difficult since she left him. She is struggling to keep her son in a private school and to set up a new household while earning low wages in a secretarial job. She thinks she could get some money from Edward but worries about being obligated to him. Still, she has turned to him for financial help in emergencies, most recently for the $300 she needed to move into her new apartment.

He would probably send me money monthly if I ask for it. But I prefer not to, because somehow money . . . gives the person power, or they think it gives them power and I don't want to play those games. . . .So for me, as a person, I would prefer to do as I am doing it. And that is to let him buy some clothes for [our son] every once in a while. If he wants to pay the school directly or something, let him pay the school directly. But I do not want to see the money come through me. Because I want to make sure that I am in control of what is going on in my life.

At the same time that Patricia worries that Edward may assume too great a role in their lives, she wants her son, now seven, to have an ongoing relationship with his father. She has encouraged visits and phone calls, and believes that the boy's need to interact with men is demonstrated by the way he behaves with his male teacher at school. Her view of the relationship places the entire burden for its existence on her: she must make sure it happens, but also take care that it does not happen too often.

The existence of a social father is even more elusive for still other lesbian mothers. Regina Carter lives alone in Berkeley with her six-year-old daughter. She had the baby after a short relationship with a man and never planned to become pregnant; the relationship collapsed before her daughter's birth and they have maintained minimal contact since then. Regina did not put his name on the birth certificate. She knows his address and has had occasional visits from him, perhaps once a year. He has never made a financial contribution and reacted angrily on the one occasion when she asked him to contribute $50 a month.

Not all the mothers think that having contact with a father is particularly desirable. Kathy Lindstrom, an insemination mother who lives with her lover and six-month-old son, expresses only limited interest in getting information about the donor. She thinks it would be useful to know his ethnic background, though she isn't at all sure what effect this information, or the knowledge that he was conceived by artificial insemination, will eventually have on her son. Her male friends will provide quite enough opportunity for interaction with men, she thinks: too much masculine influence might be harmful.

I think that he's better off not having a father. . . . I don't feel he'll be inhibited by a man's expectations of him showing his manhood and all.

Kathy says that there is no shortage of people from whom her son can learn "masculine" things such as sports; models in these areas need not even be men. She believes that her maturity (she is thirty-two) and the fact that she lives with a lover makes her situation different, in any case, from that of a "true single mother," and that she faces few of the difficulties that single mothers typically experience.

Similarly, Lilly Parker, who has a one-year-old daughter and is currently supported by AFDC, feels that she should conceal information about how she became pregnant from everyone in her network. She is still uncertain how to handle the situation when people ask her about her "husband," and generally allows people to think that she has one when it seems appropriate.

There's a lot of mystery around her conception, in that I don't tell everybody the same story. . . . I know who [her] father is, I know where he is, who he is, and a lot about him. . . . He doesn't know that he's the father. . . . I don't want him to be only half-assed involved. I'd rather have no involvement at all. I don't feel like he is a father. I feel like he's a donor.

Lilly complains about the possessiveness men develop toward their offspring and mocks the notion that being a father, which she sees as no more than contributing sperm, is a big achievement. She hopes to have another child in the next few years but would get an anonymous donor and use insemination the next time. Then she would have no need to resort to subterfuge to protect her family.

Although never-married mothers rarely have custody problems, some of them nonetheless are preoccupied with the fear that someone might try to take their children. Nineteen-year-old Louise Green feels threatened because she was acquainted with the gay man who donated sperm when she wanted to conceive a child. She never told him her real name and moved to the Bay Area from another state as soon as she knew she was pregnant to elude any effort he might make to trace her whereabouts. After these maneuvers, however, she no longer knows how to locate the donor should she wish to do so in the future. Louise's feeling of vulnerability stems as much from her marginal economic situation—she is on AFDC—as from her lesbianism.

Deep down, I wish [my daughter and the donor] could know each other. I kind of want to share her with someone because she's so wonderful, but I just don't trust him. . . . I feel real threatened about that. . . . I feel real threatened in general about child custody things. A little bit, by my being a lesbian I feel like it's a threat; my being young is a threat; my being poor is a threat.

Lesbians who have their babies through insemination are often quite concerned about the ethics of having a child under these circumstances. Maggie Walters, whose daughter is eighteen months old, used a clinic to obtain the sperm after failing to locate a donor among men she knew. She had many misgivings about doing so in view of her economic and career status and the problems a child might have with a lesbian mother.

But the biggest thing I worried about was . . . having this baby that was going to be artificially inseminated and wouldn't know who their biological father was, much less have a father.

Grace Garson, whose three-year-old son was conceived through insemination, also worries about being able to contact the donor. She found him through a gay male friend. Although she agreed at the time that the donor should remain anonymous, Grace now has second thoughts about these arrangements.

There's a problem . . . in that I feel a responsibility that when [my son] is a teenager that he be able to locate his biological father. But I haven't set it up so that that can happen and I feel a little bad about that because I feel like I'm asking an additional thing of the donor which he didn't promise.

Grace is not very specific about what she feels her son would gain by being acquainted with his "father." She has a generalized fear of being in touch with the donor because of her knowledge of lesbian custody cases. She doubts that her son will encounter bias because he spends a lot of time with other children who don't know who their fathers are, particularly with other children of lesbian mothers, born under circumstances similar to his. Though she believes that male role models are important, she also claims that boys can provide them for each other and that other men, such as teachers and friends, can help her son develop a positive image of himself as a man. She also thinks that traditional masculine expectations need to be contradicted in his upbringing and that contact with "swishy faggots" can help in this respect. Nevertheless, she still sees the identity of the donor/father as knowledge worth having; though she frames the potential importance of this tie in terms of a biological imperative to know one's "roots," she is clearly talking more about a kind of social entitlement that the child of an anonymous donor can never have.

The anonymity of the donor and the absence of a known social father are clearly separate issues for these mothers. At the same time, mothers who conceive in this way share with mothers who know their children's fathers a sense of responsibility for their absence. Just as a mother is obliged to provide a father, or try to provide one, she feels responsible for the anonymity of a donor.

For lesbian mothers whose children were born outside of marriage, decisions about how to deal with the child's father can be complicated by the legal intricacies of the welfare system. Evelyn Brandon, whose three-month-old baby was fathered by a man with whom she had a serious relationship, hesitates to apply for AFDC because she would have to identify him.

If I decide to . . . apply for cash from the state, one, they will go to Robert for child support and, two, I will be taking what I consider essentially to be welfare. And that's sort of against my grain, too, my pride enters in. . . . I don't feel bad about taking the medical aid and help for basics like food. But to have them give me care, essentially for no reason other than being poor, bothers me. Because I feel I should be able to find some other alternative, such as . . . [providing] child care in my home.

Evelyn interprets Robert's erratic behavior in recent months to guilt over fathering a child out of wedlock and failing to offer financial support. But Evelyn doesn't blame him, explaining that since she made the decision to have the baby, she should assume the financial obligations associated with the decision. Now that she's had the baby for three months, however, she has begun to wonder whether this was the right decision; expenses have been mounting and her health insurance, still in effect from her previous job, did not pay all the costs of prenatal and obstetrical care. Her lover is largely supporting her now, supplementing the disability payments Evelyn receives because of a problem secondary to the pregnancy and the government commodities she qualifies for because of her low income.

Formerly Married Mothers

Lesbians whose children were born during marriages vary widely in the extent of their ongoing relationships with their former husbands. Expectations related to the outcome of divorce proceedings may enter the picture, and concerns over custody emerge as significant determinants of the way mothers organize these links. Children are more likely than those whose parents were never married to know their fathers and to have expectations of their own about their behavior and commitment. Thus children's interests and desires become part of what mothers respond to, along with their own often complicated feelings about the men to whom they were once married.

Fathers as Financial Resources

Some mothers' accounts seem to frame fathers' contributions to their children's development strictly as an economic arrangement. But while reliable payment of child support and willingness to provide for their children's special needs may make the difference between continual financial stress and the ability to maintain one's accustomed living standard, financial support is rarely evaluated solely in material terms. Doris Johnson, a mother of two, makes it clear that she is concerned about more than financial imperatives.

Were it not for money and the child support thing, I probably would have really told him off a long time ago—just told him to go jump, and it would be fine if I didn't see him again, ever, or hear from him again, ever. But with the kids, I don't feel like I can do that. I know that I maintain a certain kind of pleasantness, probably with an edge to it, because he's totally capable of never paying another cent. That, in some ways, is the only tie the kids have. . . . And I don't want to be responsible for severing that line.

These comments point to a significant aspect of mothers' relationships with former husbands: their feeling that their performance, rather than the father's, is on the line with respect to his behavior toward the children. Mothers view themselves as bearing total, or nearly total, responsibility for the child's ongoing ties with the father; it is they who will be seen to have failed, rather than the fathers, should these relationships be disrupted.

Margo Adler has also come to view the minimal child support she receives as the only indication her developmentally disabled daughter has of her father's commitment to her. Although her former husband, Gene, is well off financially, he reduced her child support from $100 a week to $50 after she moved to California. Margo knows it would be difficult to get a better arrangement from the court; Gene has found ways to conceal his assets and can better afford the legal expenses that would be entailed by a return to court.

Margo has a good job now, so she puts the child support in a separate account and uses it only for child-care expenses. She has also charged some of Amy's medical bills to Gene, and she assumes that he has paid them, since she has heard nothing further from the doctor. She writes Gene regularly with news about Amy, particularly about her serious medical problems. But he does not write back to either of them.

Apart from the weekly checks, then, neither Margo nor Amy has had real contact with Gene for about eight years, since Margo moved from the East Coast to California. Now that Amy has started writing, she has tried to establish a relationship with her father, but has met with no success.

[She wrote him] this little kiddie letter, in little kiddie handwriting. I mailed it to him, and he totally ignored it. Which I thought was a really heavy thing to do, but on the other hand, if he's going to, just as well that he does it totally.

Margo knows that he has made numerous business trips to the Bay Area, as a mutual friend once ran into him on a plane, but he has never made contact with her during any of these visits.

Interviewer: So he could visit if he wanted to?
Margo: Yeah. But he chooses not to. It's kind of weird, because he always felt that his father only gave money and never really was there for him, didn't take him fishing, this and that, like the other kids. And it wound up that in this case, it's the most blatant [example] of that that you could possibly be. All he does give is money, in his case.

Fathers' financial contributions to the family, when they are in fact forthcoming and when they are more than symbolic payments, can make the difference between strict economizing and a more comfortable standard of living. Fathers who cooperate with arrangements for visits, holidays, and vacations may relieve mothers of total responsibility, allowing them to take vacations and to have more personal privacy. But as both Doris and Margo's comments indicate, material support may come to represent instead the father's continuing emotional commitment to his children, evidence that he still cares even when he rarely visits or calls.

Fathers as friends
Continued interaction with the child's father is most likely to be possible when the mother has a cordial relationship with him. Con-

tinued friendliness does not appear to be the most common result of the breakup of a marriage, yet some lesbian mothers express great affection for their former husbands.

Rebecca Collins, who enjoys extremely harmonious ties to her family, as we saw earlier, has a similarly positive story to tell about her ongoing relationship with Paul, her former husband. Rebecca and Paul have never been legally divorced, although four years have passed since, as Rebecca explains, she instigated their breakup by having an affair with another man. Her reasons for being dissatisfied with the marriage are difficult to pin down; she recalls feeling "frustrated" and not feeling that the marriage allowed her "choices."

She came out as a lesbian not long after the marriage ended when she and Sheila Ryan, then a co-worker, began their relationship. The first person she told about her new relationship was, in fact, Paul, who, she says, "was really excited and accepted it."

I'd definitely say [our relationship] is friendly. It's close in terms of how close I am right now to any man. I feel I can talk to him about almost anything.

Her decision to confide in Paul about this matter is very much in line with the friendly relationship she has maintained with him, strengthened, she believes, by their mutual concern for their son. Rebecca sees the tie to their son as essential to the maintenance of this relationship; without that motivating factor, she would have no reason to sustain it. As it is, Paul has continued to join Rebecca with her parents, her brothers, and her lover for summer vacations in the mountains.

Other lesbian mothers, too, still feel close to their former husbands. Tanya Petroff separated from Bill when their daughter was still a baby. He now lives in Denver, so that actual contact between them is not very frequent. Nevertheless, Tanya sees the link to Bill as permanent.

[Bill and I] have [a] relationship which has to do with the fact that we have a long history together. I have a longer history with him than I do with anyone outside my family. . . . He calls me when there's changes in his work, like when he gets a promotion or something. Like I'm the only person who understands the work that went into that. . . . I like the relationship we have now. I wish he

lived closer by. I'd like to have more of it than we have, although maybe then it wouldn't be as nice.

Tanya and Bill talk at length on the phone several times a month. Unlike Rebecca and Paul, whose relationship revolves around their child, Tanya and Bill spend relatively little time actually discussing their daughter. Rather, they engage in personal conversation she calls "maintenance," by which, she explains, "we reprocess our lives," discussing ongoing issues that require decisions concerning both their daughter and themselves. She also sees him at least once a year for a few days when she goes to pick up their daughter after summer and Christmas visits. In addition, Bill flies out to the Bay Area every few months to visit them.

Because they share decision making, Tanya can expect help from him when she needs it. Most recently he lent Tanya a substantial amount of money, about half of what she needed for the down payment on a modest house. This is not an isolated incident; Tanya has lent Bill money on several occasions.

So I just feel I have a real long-lasting relationship with him. We have a lot of differences, but I respect a lot of the knowledge that he has. . . . He's becoming a very responsible man and so that's taking some of the weight off me.

Friendly connections with former husbands are not always so easy to establish. When Deborah Cohen's ex-husband, Steve, found out after their divorce that she had become a lesbian, he was very upset and threatened to put their daughter in a boarding school to get her away from Deborah's influence. His concerns, however, were finally overcome. Deborah talked to him at length and somehow calmed him down. He never followed through on any of his threats.

He was a little uncomfortable, but . . . the last four years he's been very mellow about it. He keeps telling me what a great mother I am, and he's real proud of [our daughter] and says all these good things. It's incredible—I get a lot of support from him. I get Mother's Day cards from him.

Steve moved to Southern California several years ago. Their daughter, Pam, is now old enough to fly down alone, and does so about once a month, for one month in the summer, and for some holidays. Steve pays a substantial amount of child support and is extremely reliable about meeting this obligation. Although Deborah feels that Steve's present (large) income would permit him to pay more, she is basically satisfied with the arrangement.

She does have some problems with Steve's affluence, though. He lives on a rather extravagent scale, and Deborah is concerned about its effect on Pam. She worries that Pam will be "seduced" by Steve's lifestyle and that she will become dissatisfied with Deborah's more modest standard of living. She explains that Pam seems dazzled by the splendor of her father's life; when she returns from visits she talks at length about the things he bought for her.

Despite these concerns, Deborah describes her relationship with Steve in strikingly positive language. Though their ties revolve around Pam, they tend to engage in what she considers polite conversation on other topics: his job, her job, their relatives, and so forth. He has been remarried for a couple of years, and she likes his new wife. Most important, Deborah places Steve at the core of her support system, particularly with respect to financial needs.

He's there. If I ever need extra money, he is there. If I'm in trouble, he's there. That feels good.

The emotional intensity of some women's ties to their husbands carries over even after the marriages have ceased to be viable. Nora Olson, a mother of four now in a relationship with another lesbian mother, continues to see her relationship with her former husband, Sam, as close and trusting. She views the collapse of the marriage as less connected to anything specific about them than to the effects of the roles they felt they ought to play.

It began to end because we'd married each other with these ideas about roles and we were both real committed to those roles. . . . [But] my ex-husband is a really nice person. I like him a lot [and] we're still very close friends. He tried real hard to make changes with me so that I wouldn't feel so oppressed and that I wouldn't be so wifely, but it's kind of like the patterns were set from the beginning and I couldn't stop.

Despite their breakup, Nora feels that her fifteen years of marriage to Sam have laid the foundation for a continuing and caring relationship.

I really like him. . . . He's been a real close friend of mine for like twenty-five years and it's hard to give up those kinds of relationships. It's real painful. We've shared a lot of really good stuff. He's really a part of my life and it's just very painful. . . . I know I do not want to be married to him [but] it's still real painful to think of the divorce and finality.

Since they separated, Nora and Sam have continued to live in the same neighborhood and have worked out a rotating joint custody arrangement by which their children migrate daily between the two households. This system has remained viable partly because Sam's large income (he is a pediatrician) has allowed them to equip both of their homes with everything their children need and for him to manage most of the children's expenses while Nora is attending college. Sam knows that Nora is a lesbian, and though she thinks he sometimes fears she may do something to embarrass him, she has few real concerns, as "the liberal part of him really thinks it's cool having a gay wife."

More frequently, of course, interactions with fathers focus more on wresting court-ordered child support and other demonstrations of concern from unwilling men than on reaping the benefits of their assistance. Our legal system makes mothers responsible for collecting child support, for enforcing visitation arrangements, and in general, for sustaining children's relationships with their fathers. Paradoxically, then, the extent of the father's contact with the children represents a test of her commitment and devotion rather than his. This responsibility is intensified by the legal obligations she must meet as the person who has physical custody of the children.[5]

Being a Good Mother: Providing a Father

Lesbian mothers' accounts of their relationships with their children's fathers, whether they are their former husbands or not, vary dramatically. Mothers may choose to emphasize the frequency of contact fathers have with children, or the type of contact—whether the father has a meaningful parental role or is merely their children's weekend destination. Some fathers are noteworthy for their willingness to provide reliable financial support; others are important mainly as sources of irritation and failed expectations. Some mothers talk of their continuing affection for their ex-husbands while others speak of ongoing mutual antagonism.

These narratives highlight two important aspects of the way lesbians negotiate their identities as mothers. First, they point to their tendency to assume that they alone are responsible for all aspects of their children's welfare, even those that stem from the fathers' behavior. Since the fathers' actions are generally beyond the mother's control, their efforts are often doomed to frustration.

Second, they reveal mothers' continuing commitment to the belief that fathers are vital influences in their children's lives. Most mothers assume that fathers have a contribution to make to their children's development that only they can make. They tend to frame their discussions of this issue in terms of the "biological" foundation of ties between children and their fathers. But in casting these relationships as rooted in biology, and by implication as "natural," mothers demand that fathers provide children with a "normal family," something they cannot offer by themselves.

These two themes—the father's importance and the mother's responsibility for making him a part of her children's experience—emerge as central to the ways mothers define motherhood and attempt to establish a claim to the goodness they associate with it. These claims become even more elaborated when the fathers seek custody of the children and the mothers must prove their worthiness as parents in a public arena.

8

Lady Madonna in Court

At the core of the lesbian mother's predicament is her vulnerability to custody litigation. Though such threats are by no means confined to lesbian mothers, they do appear to be a more routine aspect of the lives of formerly married lesbian mothers in particular, and to shape their strategies more explicitly. Of the formerly married heterosexual women I interviewed, 24 percent had either experienced an actual custody action or been threatened by one. The proportion of lesbian mothers who reported such experiences rose to 41 percent.

Custody battles have come to be increasingly routine features of divorce negotiations. Despite the proliferation of no-fault divorce laws, the incidence of divorce-related litigation has grown in recent years, and a substantial proportion of these disputes center on child custody. Until children reach majority or the disputing parties exhaust their financial resources, nearly any change in the situation of either parent may be viewed as a "material change of circumstances" worthy of renewed legal inquiry.[1]

Although only a small percentage of men actually seek custody in court, as many as one-third of divorced women report that threats of custody litigation were raised in the course of divorce negotiations.[2] The outcome of negotiations after a demand for custody has been made (or even hinted at) shows that, fathers' stated motivations notwithstanding, the threat serves to enforce compliance with their other demands—for low child and spousal support awards, for a larger share of the marital property, for visitation arrangements that are convenient for the father.[3]

Even women who believe that they are "good mothers" tend to

capitulate to their husbands' demands when custody becomes an issue. Mothers know—or are advised by their attorneys—that the traditional judicial preference for maternal custody has been breaking down in recent years. The absolute number of fathers who actually become custodial parents is still small, but the reason is that few fathers attempt to win custody. Once a father brings a custody dispute to trial, his chances of winning are about equal to those of his former wife.[4] Women are at a disadvantage in custody litigation because their post-divorce employment may be seen as conflicting with their maternal obligations, because they have less to offer their children economically, or because their behavior may be more carefully scrutinized for evidence of immorality. Further, custody litigation is expensive, and women are more likely to agree to a compromise, or even to give up custody, because they cannot afford a long court battle. Finally, disputed custody can take a terrible toll on children, and mothers may compromise to spare their children a potentially traumatic ordeal.

Lesbian mothers are particularly vulnerable to such litigation. Judges tend to view them as unsuitable custodial parents solely because of their sexual orientation, even in the absence of any direct evidence of improper parental behavior.[5] Because they are aware of their poor chances in a court of law, lesbian mothers tend to develop careful and consciously crafted strategies aimed at protecting themselves against custody litigation. More frequently than heterosexual mothers, lesbians may perceive a threat to exist even when no direct challenge has been made.[6]

Motherhood and Gender

As we have seen, being a mother has generally been viewed as the natural, essential outcome of being a woman, as a status ascribed, not achieved, and as the "cause," in one way or another, of women's predicament in the world.[7] Threats to custody, however, compel women to define and codify the qualities that make them suitable parents, to be self-conscious and reflective in ways otherwise rarely required. Ties assumed to be based on sentiment become basic elements of strategies that will facilitate avoidance of custody litigation or, when it cannot be avoided, a successful outcome.

Courtroom battles over custody and the other legal machinations that may accompany, precede, or substitute for them can arise only when motherhood has come to be viewed as an achieved characteristic. The courts no longer assume that something essential about motherhood destines a woman for custody of her children.[8] Rather, motherhood is seen, though not always explicitly, as a set of skills, resources, and moral entitlements that ensure adequate care of minor children. Victory in a custody dispute, then, depends on one's ability to refute the notion that motherhood, and therefore gender itself, is natural; claimants to custody must display their skills, prove to others what would otherwise be assumed to emanate from biology.[9]

When lesbianism is raised in a custody dispute, other factors tend to slip into the background. It is difficult in any case to prove one's maternal capabilities, and to do so when two aspects of one's identity are considered to be inherently opposed is even more difficult. Judges and others who make decisions about family policy tend to assume that homosexuality cannot be compatible with parenthood under any conditions.[10] The assumption that homosexuality and parenthood cannot be harmoniously or morally combined emerges, of course, not only in custody determinations but in decisions about adoption and foster family policy, visitation rights for gay fathers, and even concerns about homosexuals working in such fields as teaching and child care.[11]

The growth of custody challenges seems to indicate an increase in fathers' interest in child rearing and increasing social recognition of their importance as caretaking parents, a goal that has been at the heart of some feminist recommendations.[12] Advocates of "fathers' rights" generally question what they consider to be an unwarranted preference for the mother in most custody awards, and complain about the size of divorce settlements, alimony, and child-support payments. Several guides for fathers who wish to seek custody have been published, and the theme of paternal nurturance has been popularized by such films as *Kramer vs. Kramer.*[13]

While a father's efforts to gain custody have the stated goal of

increasing his involvement in the rearing of his children, the strategies
the mother employs to protect herself against this threat and the social
organization that evolves from those strategies act instead to strength-
en the emphasis on the mother as head of her family. When the
possibility of custody litigation throws its shadow over the divorced
mother and her children, she tends to define parenthood as a solitary
maternal enterprise that has little room for paternal contributions.

Ironically, this outcome differs little from the picture of two-parent
families that continues to emerge even in "postfeminist" times.[14]
Despite much celebration of the growing importance of fathers as
primary parents and caretakers, studies reveal that mothers' employment notwithstanding, fathers spend only marginally more time caring for children and doing housework than they did in earlier times.[15]
Thus custody challenges have converged with other factors that produce family patterns in which mothers serve as primary, if not sole,
caretakers of children.

Mothers' Strategies

Central to most mothers' efforts to protect themselves against custody challenges are what we might call strategies of appeasement.
Mothers who fear such litigation typically keep a low profile (particularly if they are lesbians or are living with a lover), abandon claims
to marital property and to child and spousal support, and compromise on such issues as visitation.

No matter how respectable a woman may be and no matter how
much she really needs the economic or interactional involvement of her
former husband to manage her child-rearing obligations, she tends to
become extremely fearful when custody is raised as a point of contention, even when actual legal action is unlikely. These mothers feel that
they have to defend their very being; that their essential value
as persons is somehow under scrutiny. Custody cases thus present
the clearest instance in which mothers must explicitly and relatively
consciously negotiate their identity as mothers and by extension as
women.

Lesbians' fears of custody litigation are even more intense than those of heterosexual mothers, as most lesbian mothers are familiar with cases of women who have lost their children solely because of their sexual orientation. Accusations of lesbianism are quite common in custody litigation, however, even when there is no foundation for them. It is not unusual for a heterosexual mother to confront charges of lesbianism when her husband seeks custody, charges that can be quite difficult to disprove once they have been introduced.

As appeasement requires a mother to abandon or reduce her claims not only to the father's involvement but to financial support, she may find it difficult to maintain this stance unless she has female friends or kin who can provide emotional and material support. In the absence of a strong, effective network, particularly one that can cushion economic uncertainty, mothers may come to believe that they can depend only on themselves. As we saw earlier, self-reliance, competence, and ingenuity become key elements of their approach to adversity—a strategy of autonomy. Like many other aspects of the marriage-divorce system as it is emerging in American culture, self-reliance has paradoxical benefits. At the same time that divorce represents the breakdown of the family and the wife's personal failure, it gives her an opportunity to establish her self-reliance, to avoid the expected but morally ambiguous dependence that marriage implies for women. The woman who achieved adult status by marrying and having children advances toward the cultural ideal of autonomy when she is divorced.[16]

Mothers who face actual or potential custody challenges use strategies of appeasement, support, and autonomy in the course of protecting the integrity of their families. These three strategies sometimes intersect to produce unintended consequences for mother, father, and child. The claim to being a "good mother," a key element of feminine gender identity in American culture, is transformed from a natural attribute into the product of self-conscious achievement at the same time that the mothers' assumptions and behaviors are, in fact, drawn from elements and oppositions already in place in two-parent families.

Strategies of Appeasement

A challenge to a mother's custody of her children before or after a divorce dominates her view of the proceedings. Most mothers are aware that success in avoiding a battle during the divorce does not provide a permanent resolution of the problem, as a husband can return to court at any time in the future to seek a new custody ruling. Thus strategies for avoiding litigation must remain in operation at least until the children turn eighteen.

Even heterosexual mothers perceive themselves as being extremely vulnerable to custody challenges by their former husbands. Though Linda Friedman, a law student at the time of her divorce, is not a lesbian and has no specific reason to fear being declared "unfit," she was terrified by her husband's hints that he might be contemplating a custody battle. The issues arose during their settlement negotiations.

When I said you're not giving me enough money . . . he said, "Well, if we have to have a fight over money, we might as well have a fight over custody." So I got real panicked and real scared, and I didn't want to fight a custody battle with him. So I agreed just down the line with his financial arrangements. I was real scared. Although he didn't file a custody suit at that time, I knew it was going to come sooner or later. I hoped I could postpone it until I was out of law school and could fight back.

Linda believed that conciliatory behavior would make her husband less eager to pursue a custody challenge. But for lesbians, conciliation may not be enough. Avoidance of a custody suit frequently hinges on secrecy, maintaining strict separation of private and public lives, and, in some cases, deceiving the children. Mothers must weigh the potential damage that may result if their children "let something slip" to their father against the psychological effects on the family of keeping a secret.

Shortly before Elaine Weinstein, a suburban schoolteacher, filed for divorce, she had become the lover of another married woman. Her husband hired a private detective to observe her activities, and she soon found herself at the center of a custody trial.

That only got resolved because I lied on the stand, and said it had been a passing phase but it was over. Interestingly enough, the shrink . . . got on the stand and also said he thought it was a passing phase and he thought I was cured. So I got the kids.

Because Elaine lied at the trial, and also because her teaching position could be threatened by disclosure of her sexual orientation, she has had to be extremely cautious in the years since the divorce and has felt unable to challenge any of the financial arrangements she worked out with her former husband.

Here I am leading this double life. Publicly I'm a flaming heterosexual, when in truth I'm a lesbian and my kids don't even really know about it. To go back to court over child support would give my ex-husband the opportunity to bring in the lesbian issue again, so I just figured I'd make it. And I did make it financially. I took in boarders, rented out the garage.

Theresa Baldocchi, the mother of a nine-year-old son, went through a lengthy custody trial that left her virtually bankrupt. She was not a lesbian at the time of the trial and John, her former husband, was unable to substantiate his accusations that she was. Since the custody dispute, however, she has come out and now feels that she must carefully separate her lives as a mother and as a lesbian in order to protect herself against more litigation. She does not perceive her husband's history of psychiatric illness and her own record of social stability and professional accomplishment as improving her chances in any way.

Now that I'm gay, I'd lose. There's just no way in the world I would win, after having had my fitness questioned when I was Lady Madonna, let alone now. So I would just simply tell him no, I won't go to court, if you want custody, take it. . . . I've done everything to keep my ex-husband or my son from finding out.

The precautions Theresa has taken include living in a middle-class suburban neighborhood and arranging her house in a way she considers unimpeachably "bourgeois." The Bay Bridge, which separates her home from San Francisco, where she works and meets her lesbian friends, has become a symbol to her of her divided life. She undergoes a transformation as she crosses the bridge back and forth, experiencing the commute as an opportunity to prepare herself for the requirements of her destination. The most vital factor in her strategy is her resolve to prevent her son from discovering her lesbianism, to keep him from bearing the burden of her secret.

Ironically, avoidance of her former husband, which would enable Theresa to relax her vigilance a bit, is the very thing that she refuses to consider. She describes John, who has a disability that keeps him from regular employment, as a model father, and has accepted his offer to care for Tom in her home while she works. On one level, this arrangement saves her a great deal of money and ensures that Tom has regular contact with his father, something she sees as desirable. On another level, the arrangement has eliminated any possibility of privacy for Theresa. She must not only restrict the kinds of friends who visit her home but make sure that no compromising material of any sort can be found in the house.

Many husbands only indirectly threaten to use lesbianism as a weapon. Jean Jacobs, a lesbian mother of two daughters, describes the negotiations surrounding her divorce, which ended only when she sacrificed nearly all of the money she had contributed to the purchase of a house.

He never brought it into the negotiations directly. But he would like call me and harass me, and by innuendo suggest that there were many issues that he could bring up if he wanted to. . . . So basically, I traded my equity in the house for that issue not being raised at that time.

Besides losing her share of the house, Jean was unable to get Richard to agree to contribute to the children's education or their medical expenses. She has considered returning to court to change the agreement, but the possibility that Richard would raise the issue of her lesbianism has discouraged her from doing so. Richard nearly always sends his child-support payments late and has refused to contribute to the costs of the children's orthodontia. In an effort to improve relations with him, Jean offered to send him a monthly written report of the children's activities. He said that he would like her to do so, but refused to consider doing the same for her when the children are with him in the summer.

Rita García reports that she has no way to enforce the child-support and visitation agreement made at the time of her divorce because of her fear that a custody challenge might arise. Although Tony was supposed to pay her $100 a month and see their son every other weekend, he has never made a single payment and has almost never visited the child, failing even to remember his birthday. Despite this history, Rita still thinks that Tony might become interested in custody, perhaps if he were to remarry.

Rita believes, though, that the longer Tony fails to pay child support, the stronger her position in a possible custody case becomes. In a further effort to protect herself, Rita has not directly discussed her lesbianism with Jim, her son. She lives openly with her lover, sharing a bedroom with her, and nearly all of their friends are gay. Nevertheless, as we saw earlier, she feels sure that Jim is unaware of the situation and thus is protected from having to keep a secret. Rita has no faith that Tony's record of violence toward her (which once resulted in an arrest for battery) would help her in a custody battle.

Some custody threats are even less explicit, but still serve to affect the way mothers manage their relations with their former husbands. Judy Tolman, the mother of a nine-year-old son, left her marriage after she got involved in the women's movement and began a relationship with a woman. Judy works part-time in an office and is active in local feminist organizations.

I figured I should tell the lawyer I was gay, since he was really pushing to get a lot of money out of my husband . . . [but] I was saying no, don't push it, to the lawyer, because I'm gay and I don't want a custody hassle.

Judy's son, Michael, spends each summer with Patrick, and each summer Patrick raises the possibility of having the boy live with him year round. Judy has given some thought to this request, seeing it as evidence of Patrick's commitment to their son. A lawyer she recently consulted, however, has advised her that such an arrangement, even on a temporary basis, would open the door to a permanent transfer of custody. Judy also perceives any challenge to the existing financial arrangement as too provocative to consider. Since the divorce, Judy's husband has remarried and is doing very well financially. He has never increased his small financial contribution, and has refused to help pay for any unusual expenses, such as music lessons, claiming that this stance is in line with Judy's feminist principles.

He's said that since I made this feminist decision to live on my own and not be dependent on a man, why should he give me more money? Which I sort of agree with in a lot of ways. I don't really want to be dependent on him financially.

Patrick knows that Michael will not be deprived of anything he really needs, because Judy's parents, who are well-to-do, are willing to help her with expenses beyond her means.

The effect of Patrick's custody threat, subtle though it has been, is to limit the amount of contact he has with his son and to make quite unlikely any sort of authentically joint custody arrangement.[17] Were Judy not fearful that Patrick might launch a custody battle once he had "possession" of Michael during the school year, she might be willing to allow an arrangement that would give her son longer and more meaningful exposure to his father. She also might be more aggressive in seeking child-support payments that would reflect the actual cost of raising her son and correspond more accurately to Patrick's income. Judy's knowledge that she can depend on her parents for assistance, however, mitigates her need to make further financial claims on him. Rita and Jean have no such help, yet Rita makes no effort to obtain a more significant financial and personal commitment from Tony while Jean accepts the asymmetrical arrangement she has worked out with Richard.

The Effect on Fathers

The effect of these strategies is to reinforce the mother's role as the sole support of the household, to limit contact between father and child, and to accentuate differences between the cultural and economic climates of her home and his. The need to keep distance from her former husband makes him the last person with whom she discusses issues affecting the child; to share real problems with him would be to admit to weakness or error, and the mothers whose custody claims are in doubt cannot risk such exposure. Thus, while the father's interest in custody implies an interest in raising the child, the actual effect of his custody bid is to exclude him from most aspects of parenting.

Carol Martin lost custody of her son and daughter for several months but finally regained it after a lengthy trial. Although her children visit their father regularly, she never discusses any of their problems with him.

I do not want to talk with him about any of that kind of stuff because I think he would use it against me. I don't trust him still and I do feel that he would like custody of our son for sure.

Similarly, Linda Friedman, the heterosexual law student, is conscious of not being able to rely on her ex-husband for any level of material or emotional support. She characterizes him as a "spectator" in his approach to fatherhood. He sees himself as doing a good job if he takes the children on excursions, but is unable to manage any of the problems that arise when they make their weekly visits.

If he has a headache, the kids come home. If one of the children has the sniffles, the kids come home. He puts up with the fun, but he doesn't quite know how to handle the inconveniences. In fact, at times he's just dropped them off on the doorstep and pulled away.

Because of the continuing history of custody threats since the end of the marriage, Linda does not feel that she can discuss any parental matters with him.

When I do present problems to him, he points out what I'm doing wrong. And it makes me feel that he's gathering evidence for another custody suit. He will reveal nothing of what he perceives as problems to me. So we don't communicate at all. Luckily, I have friends that I can talk to about my concerns about the kids. The man that I'm involved with I talk to about them. My happiness I want to share as much as the problems, and it makes me sad that I can't share that with him. But there's too much of a wall of bitterness to talk about us sharing the good things about our kids. And there's not trust enough to share the problems, so there's just no communication around that.

Even expressions of interest in spending more time with the children can cause mothers to become fearful. Mothers often suspect that custody threats are made cynically to reduce the amount of child support paid, to negotiate a more favorable property settlement, or otherwise to influence mothers to accept less than adequate economic arrangements. Yet because custody decisions are never final, even fathers who have a sincere interest in their children may find themselves distanced from them as mothers avoid any kind of contact that might generate evidence usable in a custody challenge.

Strategies of Support

We have seen that support from relatives and women friends can enhance a mother's ability to maintain the separateness of her family unit and so to withstand pressure from the children's father. Both Rita García and Judy Tolman, for example, rely on their parents' support—in the form of child care in the first instance and financial assistance in the second—to enable them to do without the elusive benefits they might be able to obtain from their former husbands. In both cases, the threat of custody litigation seems remote, though both mothers are preoccupied with the possibility of such a challenge in the future.

Strategies of appeasement and strategies of support can dovetail neatly, with support systems enhancing mothers' efforts to appease ex-husbands. But sometimes the two strategies conflict, as when the way to appease a litigious father appears to be to include him in the day-to-day family routine. Arrangements of this sort create particularly stressful situations for mothers, as it's difficult to keep a "low profile" when one's former husband is constantly on the scene.

Theresa Baldocchi's situation, which gives her little choice but to involve her husband as her son's regular caretaker, undermines her efforts to incorporate friends into her support system. The result is a fragmented, highly specialized network. She gets her main emotional support from her friends at work, who accept her as a lesbian and respect her as a skilled professional. But these friends do not cross the bridge into her personal life.

Theresa's lover also provides some needed emotional support, but it is compromised by the secrecy that shrouds their relationship; the relationship itself is a source of as much stress as support, since it is the most likely point at which secrecy might be breached. Nor can Theresa look for concrete support from her family, in view of their own financial difficulties. She is protective toward them, and hesitates to share with them any information that might alarm them.

Similarly, the price of the extensive emotional and economic support Rita García receives from her family has been the peripheralization of her tie with Jill Hacker. At the same time that her parents refuse to visit her home or to include Jill in family events, however, their assistance makes it easier for Rita to maintain a relationship that could discredit her in a custody action.

Maximizing Autonomy

Some mothers' ability to insulate themselves from threats to custody depends on self-reliance; these women find it difficult to form supportive networks, particularly when caution restricts their contacts with relatives and with their ex-husbands. As one lesbian mother said:

I feel like I'm some kind of a spy-agent or something like that with a secret assignment that I have to be protecting. Like the state secrets or something. It's a pressure on me.

Similarly, Theresa's inability to maintain enough distance from her ex-husband to bring supportive friends into her life has essentially pushed her toward a strategy of autonomy. Other women describe disappointments in their efforts to sustain supportive networks because their friends have no children and seem not to understand the problems that mothers face.

It is not uncommon for a mother who describes herself as her child's only parent to see this condition as having begun while she was still married. Martha Kennedy, the lesbian mother of an eleven-year-old son, maintains a tense relationship with her ex-husband. Though he tends to send the child-support check late (he usually makes sure it reaches her by the end rather than the beginning of the month) she tries to keep on somewhat friendly terms with him so that their son will be able to visit him. Yet she feels that her life as a parent has changed little since she split up with her husband.

In terms of responsibility, I don't think there's been any change at all. The things that I am responsible for in terms of [my son] now are exactly the same responsibilities I had when I was married. I very much always felt like [he] was my child and that in the responsibility realm [my husband] was not there.

Rita García, in contrast, views the end of her marriage as a significant step toward autonomy.

I feel I'm not tied down to a baby. I always had to make the decisions—Tony's decisions for him, even if they didn't involve me. . . . The older Jim gets, the better I like it, because he's more independent, you know. I don't want people to lean on me and I feel stifled by it. . . . I like freedom.

While for some women self-reliance implies the absence of an effective, reliable support system, for others it reveals competence and skill they were never able to display before, or couldn't acknowledge. As we saw in Chapter 2, Carol Martin, the lesbian mother of two who won her children back from their father in a lengthy custody suit, described becoming a single mother in terms of personal growth and development. In her account, becoming a lesbian, ending her marriage, and managing on her own with her children merge into a unified struggle for autonomous personhood.

The fact of being a mother is not enough for women involved in custody disputes; they come self-consciously to break down their roles into specific components and skills that fathers cannot or will not perform. Instead of looking to nature to legitimate her claim to motherhood, a woman must both demonstrate her competence and invalidate the father's claims, either in the formal legal system or through informal negotiation.

Women are perhaps most self-conscious about this process when they are forced to respond to accusations that have no foundation. Rosemary Herrera, a forty-year-old heterosexual mother of five, is now going through an extremely bitter divorce after twenty years of marriage. Although Rosemary has never had a lesbian relationship, her husband is gathering evidence about her friendships with other women to allege that she is a lesbian, apparently in an effort to get a more favorable financial settlement. So Rosemary is forced to do as lesbians do and prepare to defend her "fitness" in court.

Intellectually, I realize that [my children] are not going to be taken from me. But emotionally, I feel like I'm in a panic, because how the hell do I go around and prove I'm a good parent? You can find a hell of a lot of proof to find you're bad. But you can't find proof that says you're good.

A further irony in Rosemary's situation stems from the conflict between her need to quell the rumors of her lesbianism and the vital support she gets from her friendships with women. As we saw in Chapter 6, her friendship with Charlotte Shafer in particular has helped to sustain her during the emotional and financial ruin that followed the collapse of her marriage, and it is this close tie to another woman that may finally compromise her in the courtroom.

These mothers have lost the financial support once available to them from their children's fathers but few suggest that divorce has deprived them of a collaborator in the business of parenting. When a woman faces or fears a custody battle, the need to defend the central-ity of her position as a parent adds a bitter irony to her situation: she usually knows that the custody challenge is a strategy for providing less rather than more care for her children. Even when the father's interest in the children is sincere, the mother understands that she will gain nothing if she offers what her husband ostensibly wants—more involvement in the daily business of parenting—as she will then be vulnerable to more litigation.

In this situation a competent mother is one who accedes to enough of her husband's demands to discourage a custody challenge but not so much that her concessions can be turned against her. Being a "good mother" is thus transformed from a state of being, a natural attribute, into evidence of skill, rewarded by the father's failure to gain custody or, better yet, by his failure to pursue it at all.

At the same time, then, that custody threats exacerbate the pressures on single mothers, they provide a context within which women can demonstrate their competence and achieve not only the status of "good mother" but that of autonomous adult. In establishing their claims to motherhood, women who face custody disputes also explicitly negotiate gender, deriving pride from their struggles and defining motherhood as achievement and strength.

Negotiating Motherhood in Custody Disputes

Lesbian and heterosexual mothers construct maternal obligations with respect to fathers along similar lines. These similarities are more clearly defined when custody disputes enter the picture: both lesbians and heterosexual women must demonstrate their goodness, and a major way of doing so is to enhance the children's ties with their fathers. At the same time, all of these women have a stake in preserving the autonomy and integrity of their families. They emphasize biological links in the course of a general emphasis on blood relationships, but must at the same time limit the father's ability to intrude on the female-headed household.

The more cordial the relations between a mother and her former husband, the greater their mutual regard, the less she needs to view his involvement with their children as a threat to her autonomy. But if their relationship is acrimonious, she may find it necessary to limit his connections with the children at the same time that she feels obligated to provide them with a father. These are the situations in which the most poignant conflicts present themselves.

Mothers' accounts of disputes with their children's fathers provide particularly clear evidence of the ongoing process of negotiation between gender categories and one's performance as a mother. More than other domains of interaction, ongoing ties with fathers may require mothers to forgo their personal preferences in favor of what they take to be the best interests of their children. The perpetuation of these ties also gives rise to instances, particularly when disputes accelerate and litigation is threatened, in which taken-for-granted assumptions about motherhood must be made explicit and in which self-conscious strategies aimed at averting the threat to custody are apt to be implemented. Custody disputes provide a platform for the performance of gender, a platform on which claims to goodness and value are dramatized and in the process reinforced. They also constitute arenas in which the mother's motivations conflict with each other, for enhancement of the children's ties with their father, valued as an element of their kin network, may threaten her ability to sustain her position as the head of the family. Though this process can affect both lesbian and heterosexual mothers, lesbian mothers perceive themselves, accurately, as facing the greater risk when such situations arise. Their manipulations of behavior and demeanor are perhaps even more self-conscious, revealing the ways in which motherhood, like womanhood, must be constantly negotiated.

9

Natural Achievements: Lesbian Mothers in American Culture

In the years since I began my interviews, the study of lesbian and gay people and communities has grown, in anthropology as well as in history, sociology, and literature. Much of this new scholarship has been carried on by researchers who do not hesitate to identify themselves as gay or lesbian, or whose sympathetic stance is clear. Certainly little of this new work is informed by older models of deviance and abnormality, and virtually none of it is built around the questions central to earlier approaches which aimed at "explaining" homosexuality.[1] Though these writings are quite diverse in both subject matter and theoretical perspective, they are unified by their concern to define the multitude of worlds that can be called, on some basis, lesbian or gay.

While the new lesbian and gay scholarship has tried to avoid the kind of determinism and orientation toward pathology that distorted earlier work, and has offered views that contradict the facile essentialism of much popular writing, I think it nonetheless has failed to take full account of the ambiguities, areas of overlap, and occasional blurring of boundaries between gay/lesbian and heterosexual experience. If a study of lesbian mothers does anything, it forces us to confront the issue of boundaries, to understand definitively that most of the categories that shape our work should be treated with skepticism. Despite the efforts of E. R. Leach and Fredrik Barth years ago to see social and cultural categories as ephemeral and negotiated,[2] anthropologists still suffer from a tendency to want to locate people in defined tribes or other bounded units; despite the critiques of essentialism that have become standard fare in academic circles and that are particularly insistent in feminist theory, many feminist scholars concerned with "difference" traffic in the same notions of deterministic boundaries that they seek to overturn.[3]

At first glance, the accounts of the lesbian mothers I interviewed reveal little about how lesbian mothers fit into the framework called for in the new research. I had hoped to show that lesbian mothers could be "normal," but I had not expected them to look quite so ordinary as they did as I listened to their accounts of day-to-day struggles in the world. I had looked for evidence that would help lesbian mothers facing persecution in the courts, and I had expected to find that they had devised uniquely adaptive cultural forms, something that I could perhaps call "lesbian-mother culture." What I found instead was creativity directed toward the complexities of negotiating identity rather than toward delineating bounded behavior or institutions particular to lesbian mothers.

Despite the many concrete differences that separate the experiences of lesbians and heterosexual women, whether they are mothers or not—most notably their vulnerability to the effects of heterosexism[4] and stigma—I noted striking similarities in the language and imagery women of both groups chose to frame their experience, to explain themselves, to tell me what it felt like to live their lives. At first I viewed these similarities as deriving from fundamental, concrete areas of convergence in the lives of lesbian and heterosexual mothers. I considered the financial difficulties both groups face; I thought about their common struggles to keep their children's fathers in their lives, to find adequate housing, to locate reliable and affordable child care, to deal with their own loneliness, to manage conflicts between the demands of friends and children. But the similarities I listened to in the narratives of 135 mothers were not just about concrete realities; they were about meaning, and most specifically about the meaning of motherhood.

My findings show, I think, not that lesbian mothers resemble heterosexual mothers in a way that minimizes the importance of their lesbianism[5] but that lesbian mothers, like other mothers, share in the system of meaning that envelops motherhood in our culture. I had asked all the mothers I interviewed to tell me about themselves, to tell me what being a mother meant to them, how they organized the activities mothers must undertake, what a mother is. And they did just that: they told me what a mother is in American culture.

These narratives did not, in the final analysis, describe accurately (or inaccurately) what women do on a day-by-day basis, how they actually spend their time, or what their relations with various categories of people—family, friends, children, ex-husbands, lovers—are "really" like. They told me what these relationships mean in the culture, and that lesbians, like other people, draw their meanings from the same repertoire of cultural possibilities.

Kath Weston's research on "families we choose"—the self-consciously created kinship systems she learned about from gay men and lesbians in the San Francisco Bay Area—shows much the same process.[6] Her informants, by casting their friendship ties in the mold of "family," by always contrasting the comfort they found in their "gay families" with the problems they encountered in their "blood families," highlighted the continuing centrality of kinship as the model of intimacy, as the label appropriately applied to relationships that are permanent, reliable, unconditional, and accepting. Gay people she interviewed didn't reject the framework of family; they drew analogies from it, they created an understanding of the intimacy they had achieved with their friends from the meanings that surround kinship in our culture. Rather than build a new culture, they re-modeled existing culture to fit their immediate needs.

Similarly, although the pro-choice and antiabortion activists whom Faye Ginsburg studied in Fargo, North Dakota, espoused antithetical political ideologies and were engaged in bitter struggle with each other, both groups of women claimed nurturance "as a central feature marking feminine identity in this culture" and construed it as an achievement.[7] Their political stances, antagonistic though they were, were explained and made meaningful by a shared system of belief and identity.

So too with lesbian mothers. Lesbian mothers, like other mothers, select elements of their narratives from a circumscribed repertoire, a language of caring and nurturance, a language that makes motherhood supersede and engulf other aspects of identity. Unlike most people who subscribe to biologically derived gender ideologies, however, to whom motherhood is a *natural* attribute of all authentic women, lesbian mothers must consciously craft themselves into mothers. When motherhood is an *achievement*, it permits a woman to claim characteristics that are valued in American culture—independence and adulthood.

Highly elaborated and celebratory beliefs about motherhood and an emphasis on the ongoing structural significance of consanguineal ties are key elements of these mothers' long-term strategies, as they are for many women in poor American communities and in other situations that foster matrifocality.[8] Kinship systems, for women in these circumstances, are arrayed around sets of lineal connections; elaboration of relationships with parents can serve to highlight the ongoing importance of ties to children. Just as kinship links one to one's parents, it establishes the continuing utility of ties to one's child. The central place of kinship in mothers' ideas about how to manage under adverse material conditions helps us to understand the seemingly contradictory stress they place on strengthening children's ties with their fathers. The fathers are the blood kin of children who are likely to need such connections in the future.

Though lesbians are still outsiders in American culture, the fact that they are mothers pulls them, however ambiguously, into a central position in the gender system. Resistance to the relegation of lesbians to the nonprocreative and hence nonwomanly domain thus constitutes a kind of accommodation to this gender distinction. At the same time, lesbians are perhaps more conscious of the need to craft their identities under these conditions; the "option" to become mothers that heterosexual women are expected to exercise is rarely readily available to lesbians.

The Changing Climate

Some political and social trends indicate that my initial concern with lesbian mothers' rights in custody disputes continues to be relevant. The New Right in its various guises has continued to oppose what its proponents perceive as challenges to gender and family forms they claim as "traditional."[9] They have been joined, in some unlikely coalitions, by liberals who also trace problems in American society to the "breakdown" of the family. An article in the *New York Times* of May 1, 1991, reported, for example, on a coalition being formed by such figures as Phyllis Schlafly and Pat Schroeder, based on agreement that "strengthening the family is the best way to make progress on a number of domestic ills from drug abuse to poor achievements in education."[10] Coalition members seek, among other goals, to institute tax incentives and revisions in the divorce laws which would discourage couples with children from divorcing. Representative Dave McCurdy, one of the Democrats seeking to strengthen "profamily, moral values," is quoted as criticizing the platform on which the Democratic party has stood since the 1960s as "the agenda of narrow and special interests. You had the formation of women's groups, and organizations like the Gay and Lesbian Alliance, and the pro-abortion and anti-abortion debate. The interests got so narrow, and the agenda got dictated by those narrow interests, and we lost sight of the broader principals and objectives."

Efforts of this sort assume that ongoing controversies over abortion, over child care and women's place in the labor force, and over the organization of families are basically moral debates. As Anna Tsing has hauntingly shown in her account of the public response to women accused of infanticide, they depend on underlying images of "good" (that is, altruistic, not sexual) and "bad" (that is, selfish, sexual) women and mothers, just as they do on shared concepts of what "good" and "bad" families are.[11]

As we have seen, they are also played out in custody disputes, a domain in which assumptions about the "good mother" are most dramatically deployed. No-fault divorce and gestures toward mechanical gender equity in adjudication of divorces have been institutionalized.[12] Thus increasingly frequent custody disputes become the most accessible arena for public recitation of the attributes of good mothers and chastisement of "bad" mothers before the wider community.

But varying manifestations of the normalization of high-technology reproductive interventions are perhaps most revealing of the continuing conservatism of the popular construction of motherhood. Public discussions appear with deadly regularity over presumed conflicts between mothers' desires to protect their own welfare on the one hand and the well-being of their fetuses or children on the other. Drug cases, disputes over presumed reproductive hazards in the workplace, discussions of alcohol use during pregnancy, disputes about obstetrical interventions and consent to medical procedures, debates about surrogacy, all point to the assumption that motherhood is a special state that appropriately consumes all of a woman, obliterating her ability to make choices on behalf of her offspring, framing her interests and those of her offspring as inherently antithetical.[13]

The interplay between culture and technology in the domain of "heroic" or improbable pregnancies is most telling. I am thinking particularly of the possibilities of extending childbearing even into old age. On October 25, 1990, the *New York Times* headlined an article on the use of donated eggs in experimental pregnancies "Menopause Is Found No Bar to Pregnancy."[14] Some less futuristic scenarios are already in place as a range of other issues surrounding surrogacy and other extreme methods for "becoming" mothers move into ordinary discourse. The increasing routinization of these techniques, their leap out of the world of science fiction into daily life, and even into the reproductive repertoire of lesbians, tells us that even homosexuality offers no explanation for failure to achieve motherhood. Motherhood, it seems, takes up the slack as gender and sexuality no longer institutionalize each other.

But a number of other things also have happened since I began this work in the 1970s. Whereas the existence of lesbian mothers then had barely penetrated public consciousness, these women have joined members of a wide range of other nontraditional family or household configurations in gaining a public face. While I was trying to make lesbian mothers visible, the rest of the world was already discovering them.

This was the period that witnessed not only the "lesbian baby boom" but the rise of a vocal movement for gay and lesbian rights. During these years the nation saw a proliferation of gay and lesbian parades and demonstrations (including the national march on Washington in 1987, which drew several hundred thousand participants); the "coming out" of several gay political figures, as well as campaigns for public office by open lesbians and gay men; debates over gay rights ordinances, domestic partners legislation, and other official policies; the growth of gay-oriented civil rights organizations and public-interest law firms such as Gay Rights Advocates and the National Center for Lesbian Rights; and extensive discussion in several religious denominations over the place of lesbians and gay men in congregations and among the clergy. These were also the years during which the AIDS epidemic forever changed the tone of all discussions of gay life, both intensifying the stigma already attached to homosexuality and humanizing the image of gay people to a wide and previously uninvolved audience. [15]

So-called postfeminism seems also to be characterized by an acceptance of many previously unacceptable forms and behaviors at the same time that feminism appears to have abandoned its earlier critical position vis-à-vis the family and marriage. Judith Stacey, for example, has described the dizzying complexity of "postmodern" families in California's Silicon Valley. [16] While some structural features of these families are nothing like those of the typical suburban family configurations of their parents' generation, their emotional bonds and the expectations that frame them are strikingly familiar. Colleen Johnson has documented much the same sort of functional resilience among families after divorce. [17]

Despite the efforts of activists on the right, then, some populations defined as outside the "traditional" forms have come to redefine themselves and to achieve some acceptance as insiders. Many gay men and lesbians have developed a new sense of entitlement to the same kinds of privileges and legitimacy heterosexuals enjoy. [18] No longer seeking mere tolerance, some lesbians and gay men are demanding that their relationships be recognized as morally and even legally equivalent to more conventional forms: they want to be able to marry. [19]

The issues that surround these shifts are not clearly either cultural or economic; it is difficult to tease apart the extent to which marriage and family are valued primarily because of the cultural legitimacy they entail or because of the financial advantages they confer. Philosophical arguments about "legitimacy" and "equality" become particularly strained when the stakes involve significant benefits such as health insurance. It appears, then, that we may be witnessing less the burgeoning of new family forms that Stacey has proposed than a shift in the ways comparatively marginal groups stake their claims to existing cultural and material resources, a particularly vital strategy as resources become increasingly scarce.

These developments involve parallel and apparently contradictory constructions of gender. While it appears that we are experiencing an *expansion* of our view of what kinds of people can reproduce or constitute a family, we are also witnessing a *contraction* of popular notions about how families live their lives.

Consider some newspaper headlines, all from 1990: "New Spin on the American Family: Gay, Straight Parents Share Joys, Chores" (*Oakland Tribune*, June 20); "Lesbian Custody Fights Test Family Law Frontier" (*New York Times*, July 4); "Suit Over Death Benefits Asks: What Is a Family?" (*New York Times*, September 21). Most simply, these headlines tell us that something called the "lesbian and gay family" has captured the popular imagination, adding a new element to the longstanding discussion (or lamentation, depending on your point of view) of how traditional family forms may be changing. The language of these and similar articles that appear periodically in the mainstream press reminds us that unusual sorts of people are claiming legitimacy for their "families," but that the standard of comparison in all of these situations remains the "normal" heterosexual two-parent family, or at least what most people imagine it to be.

If the discussions of these "new" kinds of families in the media indicate that their status has been somewhat normalized, it is also true that little new is actually described. Formidable symbols of conventional (read "natural") family life are presented to back up claims that families headed by lesbian or gay parents are, in fact, families like any others. A woman who is suing her deceased lover's employer for death benefits tells the reporter that their life together was "as much a marriage as any heterosexual union," citing a ceremony they held to formalize the union and the fact that they had purchased a home and raised the children of the surviving partner together.[20] An article about a lesbian mother, her sperm donor–co-parent, and their young son begins with an image of the child playing with wooden trains and a stuffed dog. In describing the co-parenting arrangement the lesbian mother has made with a heterosexual man, the article further evokes normality by describing their joint participation in Jewish holiday celebrations, family vacations, and the boy's trips to visit his paternal grandparents. Because the father is in the picture as an active parent, this family seems less deviant than those created with anonymous donors, and much is made of this difference in the article. The director of a local sperm bank is quoted as saying, "There is a real shift in how lesbians are defining family. Ten years ago, it would have been lesbians raising a child, preferably a female child. Now that preference doesn't seem to be stated as strongly. More and more lesbians are seeking out men who want to play some role in their child's life. At that point, I'm not so sure we can still call the person a donor."[21]

At the same time, "traditional" images of family and kinship are revived in articles about visitation disputes between lesbian biological mothers and their former partners. The biological mothers are apt to retreat into conventional notions of kinship and parenthood to invalidate the former lover's claims to continuing involvement with the children. The former lover's claims, while based on the assertion that biological ties are not the only kind that forge parental bonds, finally depend on images of behaviors that conventionally constitute parenthood.

In a case described in the *New York Times* of July 4, 1990, Michele G, who is suing her former partner, Nancy S, for the right to visit the two children she calls her son and daughter, says, "These judges don't understand what it is to be a mother. To sit there and say with a straight face that someone who has stayed up all night nursing a child, swabbing her chicken pox, taking joy in her every advancement, picking her up every time she's skinned her knee, or singing her to sleep is not a 'mother' is an absurdity." But the lawyer for the biological mother says, "These children were produced by Nancy, and Michele is not the legal or biological anything to them."[22]

The final decision in this case was reported in the *New York Times* of March 24, 1991. The state appeals court denied all custody and visitation rights to Michele because "her status was not the same as a biological or adoptive parent." A decision to expand "the definition of a 'parent' in the manner advocated" could expose "other natural parents to litigation brought by child-care providers of long standing, relatives, successive sets of step-parents, or other close friends of the family."[23] So while the legitimacy of the family formed by a lesbian mother through artificial insemination is affirmed, the former partner is not seen as the noncustodial parent in the way that a former husband would be.

Motherhood and Womanhood

What do these developments suggest about my efforts to show that lesbian mothers are "as good as" heterosexual single mothers, or at least not definably different? When my interviews consistently yielded familiar domestic scenarios, I first thought my job was essentially over. It seemed that I had found pervasive similarities between lesbian mothers' and heterosexual mothers' accounts of their lives, and could thus substantiate my claims that lesbian mothers deserved social recognition and legal protection.

As my analysis progressed, I found that these similarities could be explained less readily as the products of adaptation to similar circumstances than as aspects of a common cultural process. It became clear that lesbian mothers' stories focused on establishing claims to motherhood and on affirming motherhood as a central identity, whether they were describing how they became mothers, their relationships with their children, or how they organized their ties with their relatives. They thus showed how achieving motherhood can enable them to share in its meanings without submitting to implications of biological inevitability. By being lesbians *and* being mothers, the women I interviewed revealed a complicated strategy that moved between resistance and accommodation.

But lesbian (and heterosexual) mothers' narratives tell us something even more interesting, and more significant in terms of some of the directions the politics of reproduction are taking in the last years of the twentieth century. What these narratives tell us, over and over again, is that motherhood and womanhood continue to be conflated and mutually defined. At the same time that the emergence of all sorts of nontraditional family forms suggests that something is changing and that conventional limitations on sexuality seem to be retreating, the continuing location of motherhood at the defining edge of gender necessarily sabotages those changes.[24] Lesbians are no longer automatically denied access to the system of meanings we call "motherhood"; rather, they now have the possibility of *choosing* motherhood (whether the choice is to become a mother or to derive one's identity from being a mother), and thereby gaining access to "womanhood" through negotiation. While the category of "woman" thus expands, the definitions associated with it do not. "Women" are still mothers (or potential mothers). Non-mothers are still not quite women, though heterosexual women without children are more easily perceived as on the way to becoming mothers. To the extent that (presumed) heterosexuality is linked, at least in the imagination, to reproduction, heterosexual childless women are less likely to find their claims to womanhood in question, at least while their fertility remains intact. In fact, if developments in popular culture can be said to offer a reflection of social mores, even the lack of a husband is no longer viewed as an impediment to achieving motherhood. An article in the *New York Times* of October 16, 1991, enumerated television programs that featured "older" (in their thirties or forties) single women. In just one season no fewer than seven of these shows developed plot lines in which their heroines contemplated or carried out insemination in defiance of the "biological clock," generating a veritable epidemic of out-of-wedlock pregnancy.[25] The message conveyed by these story lines is complex, to be sure, but can probably to taken to suggest not only that singleness and advancing age need not impede motherhood but that they provide no excuse for failing to do so.

Neither, it seems, does the fact that one is a lesbian. Whereas I had assumed that the very existence of lesbian mothers posed an implicit challenge to the hegemonic family criticized by Second Wave feminism, the revelation of similarities between lesbian and heterosexual mothers can threaten to nourish a trend that accords more value to mothers than to women who have no children, regardless of their sexual orientation.

Certainly by becoming mothers lesbians can gain access to the same intrinsic rewards motherhood offers other women. But motherhood also allows lesbians to claim membership in the group known as "women" on the same basis as heterosexual single mothers, rather than because of the stigma they share as women in the workplace and on the streets. The otherness of childless lesbians may be intensified not because they are lesbians but because they are not mothers. Like gay and lesbian marriage, the new access to traditional womanhood can divide lesbians and gays on the basis of respectability. At the same time, motherhood continues to divide women into two groups with different economic opportunities, different social status, and possibly conflicting political interests.

But perhaps a deeper question to be addressed is why we hear more about lesbian mothers today than we used to. On one level, their emergence into mainstream visibility points to the growing pride and sense of entitlement and legitimacy that lesbian and gay people in America have gained, as demonstrated by decreasing levels of secrecy and new symbols of acceptance. But on another level, this change may reflect the further calcification of the old construction of gender in terms of motherhood and the simultaneous defusing of the threat to traditional gender categories the lesbian and gay movement and feminism seem to have achieved. For this reason, it suggests some rather ominous scenarios for reproductive politics. We may, in fact, be moving into an era in which class will be based not on the means of production, but on the means of reproduction, with mothers and nonmothers poised against each other in conflict not only over diminishing resources but over contested meanings of gender.

Appendix

The findings reported in this volume are based on interviews with 135 women, 73 lesbian mothers and 62 heterosexual single mothers. To be eligible for inclusion in the study, the women had to have at least half-time physical custody of one child under the age of eighteen. Both natural and adoptive mothers were included, all of whom lived apart from their child's father.

The criteria used to select women for interviews were dictated by the theoretical sampling design developed for the research proposal. Theoretical sampling is an approach usually used when a random sample is impossible to obtain. Instead of selecting participants who can be assumed statistically to represent the wider population with which the research is concerned, the researcher uses categories generated by the research questions to define the criteria by which selections will be made. By holding these factors constant, the researcher can hope to isolate the influence of the primary variable under investigation: in this case, the sexual orientation of the mother.

In the situation I faced when I first constructed a research design, lesbian mothers had to be selected from a larger population or universe whose characteristics remain unknown. Since I hypothesized that I could best understand lesbian mothers' resemblance to heterosexual single mothers in terms of a number of easily defined factors, I used these factors to generate independent variables that would organize my sampling strategy. Informants were stratified according to these variables; that is, they were selected to fill specific slots in the research design.

First, I reasoned that lesbian and heterosexual single mothers would face similar economic problems and that women's ways of managing their lives might differ according to their socioeconomic status. But a woman's socioeconomic status is notoriously hard to pin down; women tend to draw their status from the men in their lives—their husbands and fathers. Women's incomes also vary less than men's even when education and occupation are taken into account. I decided to create a tripartite category called "socioeconomic status" (SES) based on how each woman currently supported herself and her family. The "professional" group was composed of women who received most of their income from professional work in such fields as law, medicine, nursing, teaching, and business administration. My idea was that these occupations might offer women more flexibility (and possibly more money) than less prestigious work, but that they would also be more demanding and require more commitment. The "nonprofessional" group was composed of women who received most of their income from white-collar, blue-collar, and pink-collar occupations such as secretary, nurses' aide, or skilled tradesperson. Finally, I decided to locate women whom I called "dependent" because they obtained most of their income from child support and/or such state support as AFDC. Although the incomes of these women varied widely, they had in common a lack of direct control over the source of their support.

A second independent variable was the ages of the women's children. Here I was concerned with the amount of supervision children need, and with the likelihood that mothers would incur significant child-care expenses. I used age ten as a rough indicator of relative maturity, and I divided mothers into those with at least one child under the age of ten and those with no children younger than ten.

A third independent variable was household composition. My concern in this case was adequately to match lesbian and heterosexual mothers. Because most previous studies of lesbian mothers focused on the issue of "father absence," they used single heterosexual mothers who lived alone with their children as controls, whether or not the lesbian mothers had partners or lovers with whom they lived. Since I was interested in social support systems rather than in the psychological impact on children of growing up without a man in the household, such a comparison would not have been useful. I thus matched lesbian mothers of each SES and age-of-child group with heterosexual mothers according to whether or not the household included a co-residential partner. For the heterosexual mothers, the male partner could not be the biological father of any of the woman's children.

This design was applied to both phases of the study. First, from 1977 to 1979 I interviewed women whose children were born, conceived, or adopted in a marital context (a group I called "formerly married"). Later, from 1979 to 1981, after I obtained additional funding, I interviewed women who became mothers outside of marriage, whether by conventional means, donor insemination, or adoption (a group I called "never married"). I decided whether to categorize women as lesbian or heterosexual by directly asking prospective informants to designate their sexual orientation. Women who did not describe themselves as either lesbian or heterosexual were not selected for interviews.

I located women primarily through personal referrals. As I interviewed each new informant, I asked her if she knew other women who might be appropriate participants. In order to include women who were relatively socially isolated, and thus less likely to be located through referrals, I also placed some announcements in local newspapers and at child-care referral agencies and other organizations likely to reach single mothers. Women to whom I was referred, or who contacted me, were screened on the telephone. When a woman met the basic criteria and qualified to fill one of the cells in the design, I explained the study to her and invited her to participate. In explaining the study to potential participants, I devoted special attention to a discussion of the procedures to be followed to ensure complete confidentiality and anonymity. All participants were referred to by a code number, and records containing their real names and other identifying information were kept in a location away from the university. Even so, some women agreed to be interviewed with the stipulation that even the research staff not know their real names. No fees were paid to informants.

Because of the complexity of this design and the large sample size it required, I decided not to develop race or ethnicity into additional independent variables. If I included race, I reasoned at the time, I would have either to settle for small or token numbers of minority participants or to expand the total size of the study population far beyond anything I realistically could manage on the grant I expected to receive. Thus I decided to let a category I thought of as "race/ethnicity" freely vary; that is, not to try for representative samples of women on the basis of race, but to include women of any race whenever they met the other criteria. Since personal referrals were the main source of participants and since my initial contacts were with white women, the final population reflected the composition of women's social networks. Out of the final group of seventy-three lesbian and sixty-two heterosexual mothers, four lesbians were African-American and two Latina. The remaining "white" women, however, were highly varied with respect not only to their current socioeconomic status and their class origins but to their religion, ethnicity, and regional origins. Despite these differences, they displayed little variation with respect to education, income, and family size.

The women's ages ranged from 19 to 47, with a mean age of 34.8 for the formerly married and 33.5 for the never married. Families were generally small; nearly all of the women (88 percent) had one or two children. The children of the never-married women were younger and most of these women had only one child. The women were relatively well educated; more than four out of five had attended college and about two-thirds had graduated. More than three-quarters of the women lived in San Francisco or Alameda County; others were scattered throughout the wider San Francisco Bay Area, some in relatively isolated rural and dispersed suburban settings.

Interviews lasted between three and seven hours, nearly all conducted in the women's homes, usually in two or more sessions. In a few cases, usually for reasons of confidentiality, informants arranged to be interviewed away from their homes. Although the same basic topics were covered in all the interviews, I used an open-ended, semi-structured interview guide, so the order of topics and specific issues covered in any segment of the interview varied from woman to woman. The interviews were recorded on tape in their entirety and transcribed verbatim. To protect informants' privacy, all tapes were erased after they were transcribed. All interviews were carried out either by me or by my research associate Terrie A. Lyons.

Once these procedures had been completed, two members of the research staff coded the transcripts, which averaged 100 pages in length. (In addition to Ms. Lyons, two graduate student assistants worked on the project and participated in data analysis.) We discussed and resolved discrepancies in coding, and used SPSS to analyze the correlations between the key independent variables and the dependent variables that emerged from the interviews. We found virtually no statistically significant relationships, though the descriptive statistics yielded by these procedures greatly facilitated data management. Final analysis of the interviews depended on repeated readings and content analyses of the complete transcripts and of shorter summaries I later generated. Once analysis and writing were done, I donated the interview transcripts to the archive of the Gay and Lesbian Historical Society of Northern California.

Notes

Prologue

1. See, for example, Reiter 1975 and Rosaldo & Lamphere 1974 for examples of formative statements of what would become feminist anthropology.

2. Support for this kind of research might be viewed as a surviving element of the policies of the 1960s and 1970s which also brought us the war on poverty, Project Headstart, and a host of other social programs stimulated, in part, by Michael Harrington's influential book *The Other America* (1962). These research priorities suffered the same fate as housing subsidies, food programs for the poor, and other programs eliminated or weakened after the 1980 election of Ronald Reagan (Ehrenreich 1989; Harrison & Bluestone 1988).

1. Looking for Lesbian Motherhood

1. Judges hearing custody cases involving lesbians tend to make the same assumptions. Because they implicitly define lesbianism as purely sexual, they conclude that lesbians cannot be adequate mothers. The pursuit of sexual gratification, according to this reasoning, is antithetical to the kind of altruism expected of mothers. This view also can affect the outcome of custody cases of nonlesbians who are sexually active (Lewin 1981).

2. Escoffier 1990.

3. Rapp 1988; Stacey 1990.

4. Ehrenreich 1989. As I completed final revisions of this manuscript, the "family values" debate erupted as the centerpiece of the 1992 Republican presidential campaign.

5. Herman n.d.

6. The term "cultural feminism" refers to a body of theory that emphasizes differences between men and women and holds that these differences

have given rise to a "female culture" with desirable attributes. Some writers who espouse this position have concerned themselves with theories about matriarchal origins, using speculations about the benevolent qualities of hypothetical matriarchies to support claims that rule by women would be beneficial for all (see Davis 1971). Proponents of this stance disagree as to the degree to which this culture reflects inherent biological differences or is socially created. Early examples of this position include Alpert 1973 and Burris 1973; varied elaborations include Brownmiller 1975, Daly 1978, Dworkin 1974, and Griffin 1978. See also Eisenstein 1983 for an overview of cultural feminist thought as it developed during the Second Wave and Echols 1989:243–286 for an account of the rise of cultural feminism as a response to contradictions that developed in radical feminism.

7. The term "community" has often been used with relatively little precision in studies of gay men and lesbians. Deborah Wolf's (1979) usage, for example, rests on the implicit assumption that the "lesbian feminist community" of San Francisco, which she studied in the early 1970s, is a closed and self-sustaining collectivity, whose boundaries are not only firm but mutually agreed upon by "community" members. Though I already was critical of the monolithic fiction that this usage tends to encourage when I began my investigation, I still retained some notion that there was such a thing as a lesbian "community." I know better now. All the same, I shall continue to use the term occasionally, for want of a better one.

8. See, for example, Rich 1976.

9. *Newsweek,* March 12, 1990, cited in Faderman 1991.

10. Bozett 1987; Faderman 1991; Hanscombe & Forster 1981; Pollack & Vaughn 1987.

11. Lefkowitz & Withorn 1986; Sidel 1986.

12. Beauvoir 1952; Cassell 1977; Millett 1970; Mitchell 1971; Morgan 1970; Rosaldo & Lamphere 1974.

13. Gibson 1977; Hitchens 1979; Lewin 1981; Rivera 1979.

14. Farrell, Hill & Bruce 1973.

15. Vida 1978.

16. Stevens 1978.

17. Berzon 1978.

18. Brown 1970; D'Andrade 1966.

19. Ortner 1974.

20. Chodorow 1974, 1978; Dinnerstein 1976.

21. Collier 1974; Lamphere 1974; Rosaldo 1974; Wolf 1972.

22. Shulamith Firestone's cybernetic vision was far more dramatic than

most of these early critiques of women's role in reproduction, if not vastly different in underlying philosophy.

23. See, for example, Gilligan 1982; Griffin 1978; Ruddick 1989; and Snitow 1991, who offers a useful overview of changing ideas about motherhood in feminist theory.

24. Lewin 1974. Wolf 1972 takes a similar approach to mothers in rural Taiwan. See also Collier 1974; Stack 1974; and Whitten & Whitten 1972 on strategies. Browner & Lewin 1982 apply this approach to two populations of Latin American women.

25. Goodman 1973; Osman 1972; Weeks, Derdeyn & Langman 1975.

26. Green 1978; Hoeffer 1981; Hotvedt & Mandel 1982; Kirkpatrick, Smith & Roy 1981.

27. Typical of these narratives are Jullion 1977 and Oddone 1977. More recent examples of this genre are Hanscombe & Forster 1981 and Jullion 1985.

28. Armanno 1973; Basile 1974; Boggan 1975; Gibson 1977; Hitchens 1979; Hunter & Polikoff 1976; Riley 1975; Van Gelder 1976.

29. Alice, Gordon, Debbie & Mary 1988; Johnston 1973.

30. Brandwein, Brown & Fox 1974; Clarke 1957; Clayton 1971; Gonzalez 1969; Goode 1956; Herzog & Sudia 1970; Klein 1973; Kriesberg 1970; Ross & Sawhill 1975; Stack 1974; Vincent 1962; Weiss 1975.

31. Abbott & Love 1972; Caprio 1967; Cory 1965; Martin & Lyon 1972; Miller 1966; Rosen 1974; Swanson et al. 1972; Thompson, McCandless & Strickland 1971; Wolff 1971.

32. Gagnon & Simon 1973.

33. Rapp 1987:128.

34. Similar problems arise in the study of multiple sources of oppression in other contexts, e.g., when race is added to gender in investigations of the situation of black women (King 1988).

35. While this finding seems to contrast dramatically with Weston's (1991) discussion of the "families we choose," which gay men and lesbians tend to oppose to their biological kin, elements of choice were also critical to the descriptions lesbian mothers offered. Weston's data, while pointing to the rise of innovative social forms, also emphasize the continuing vitality of kinship language as the framework gay men and lesbians use to describe significant or committed relationships.

36. Mascia-Lees, Sharpe & Cohen 1989.

37. Barth 1969; Boissevain 1974; Firth 1951; Leach 1954.

38. Ortner 1984; Reiter 1975; Rosaldo & Lamphere 1974.

39. Goodale 1971; Weiner 1976; Wolf 1972.
40. Nelson 1974; Rogers 1975.
41. DuBois et al. 1987; Eichler 1982; Harding 1987; Roberts 1981.
42. Echols 1989; Koedt, Levine & Rapone 1973.
43. Boissevain 1974; Bott 1971.
44. Anzaldúa 1990.
45. Jones 1991.
46. Anzaldúa 1990; Trinh 1989.
47. Cruikshank 1980; Lewin 1991; Stanley & Wolfe 1980.
48. Personal Narratives Group 1989.
49. Steedman 1987.
50. Rosaldo 1989:129.
51. Ginsburg 1989.
52. Hoffman 1968; Weston 1991:156.

2. Becoming a Lesbian Mother

1. Faderman 1991; Riley 1988; Weston 1991.
2. Because of the methods I used to gather information and particularly because of the necessity of restricting my interviews to mothers who were no longer living as married women, there can be no discussion of the situations of lesbian mothers who remained in heterosexual marriages even after they began lesbian relationships or took on lesbian identity.
3. Bellah et al. 1985; Tocqueville 1956.
4. Echols 1989.
5. All names and some biographical details have been changed to preserve the anonymity of women I interviewed.
6. Bellah et al. 1985; Perin 1988; Varenne 1977.
7. Clark & Anderson 1967:425 (italics in original).
8. Bellah et al. 1985:146, 65, 82–83.
9. Cohen & Katzenstein 1988.
10. Hartmann 1987; Kuhn & Bluestone 1987.
11. Susan Faludi's *Backlash* (1991) deals extensively with both the varied cultural representations of women as more eager to marry than men and research by social psychologists and others whose findings show the reverse. Particularly compelling are numerous studies she cites which indicate that the mental health of single women is better than that of married women, and that the opposite pattern obtains for single and married men.

12. Cherlin 1981.
13. Riley 1991.
14. Weston 1991.
15. Gerson 1985; Margolis 1984.

3. *"This Wonderful Decision"*

1. Arendell 1986; Weiss 1979; Weitzman 1985.
2. Pies 1985; Robinson & Pizer 1985.
3. Chasnoff & Klausner 1986; Zheutlin, Reid & Stevens 1977.
4. Shah with Walters 1979; Stern 1979.
5. Hanmer 1983:184.
6. Corea 1985.
7. Langer 1969.
8. Curie-Cohen, Luttrell & Shapiro 1979:588.
9. Corea 1985:36.
10. Hanmer 1983; Muller 1961.
11. Lasker & Borg 1987.
12. Curie-Cohen, Luttrell & Shapiro 1979; McGuire & Alexander 1985; Strong & Schinfeld 1984.
13. Smart 1990.
14. Achilles 1989; Hornstein 1984; Ruzek 1978.
15. Editors of the *Harvard Law Review* 1989:135.
16. Ricketts & Achtenberg 1987.
17. Pies 1985; Ricketts & Achtenberg 1987; Zuckerman 1986.
18. D'Emilio 1983; Fuss 1989; Kitzinger 1987. The public reaction to the discovery by the neuroscientist Simon LeVay that the hypothalamus, an area of the brain that possibly controls sexual desire, is smaller in homosexual men than in heterosexual men demonstrates the continuing intensity of the debate over this issue. Perhaps more interesting than the experiment itself, which many scientists point out is questionable on numerous methodological grounds, has been the immediate interest of the media in its possible implications for the meaning of homosexuality. *Newsweek*, for example, ran a story on the research as its lead article on February 24, 1992, picturing an infant's face on the front page with the headline "Is This Child Gay? Born or Bred: The Origins of Homosexuality." The story quotes a number of gay community leaders who claim that the research proves that being gay is no more blameworthy than being lefthanded. But some gay activists, far from welcoming evidence of a genetic basis for homosexuality, worry that such infor-

mation may lead to eugenic campaigns to abort fetuses identified as carrying the "homosexual gene" (Gelman et al. 1992).

19. Although some types of prenatal testing, such as amniocentesis, were already in use when these women had their children in the late 1970s and early 1980s, the proliferation of prenatal diagnostic techniques that had characterized standard obstetrical care by the early 1990s was not yet fully in place (Browner & Press 1991; Rapp 1990; Rothman 1986; Sargent & Stark 1989).

20. See Fabe & Wikler 1979.

21. Carole Browner's (1979) study of abortion decision making among lower-class women in Cali, Colombia, reveals much the same process of evaluating economic resources.

22. Ricketts & Achtenberg 1987.

23. Some mothers omit the father's name from the birth certificate to simplify their claims to AFDC or other benefits or to protect the father from harassment.

24. See Lewin 1985.

4. Ties That Endure

1. Clausen 1987:336.
2. Rich 1980.
3. Clausen 1987:341; see also Vaughn 1987.
4. Canaan 1987:285.
5. Gambill 1987:300.
6. Gagnon & Simon 1973.
7. Stack 1974.
8. Clarke 1957; Gonzalez 1969.
9. Yanagisako 1977, 1985.
10. Wolf 1972.
11. Di Leonardo 1987.
12. Collier 1974.
13. Lamphere 1987.
14. Schneider 1968; Schneider & Smith 1973.

5. "This Permanent Roommate"

1. See Weiss 1979 for similar findings in a study of postdivorce families.
2. Lillian Faderman (1991:218–219) notes that lesbian feminists frequently use "woman" as a euphemism for "lesbian," particularly when they

refer to the cultural developments—women's books, women centers, women's music, and the like—that emerged in the 1970s.

3. Faderman 1991 and Echols 1989 discuss the pressure to be "p.c." and its effects on feminists in the 1970s.

4. Some commentators claim that "butch/femme" roles are both historically and economically situated and no longer are key dimensions of lesbian communities, but evidence points to the continuing salience of these roles and in some cases to renewed enthusiasm for their symbols. See Kennedy & Davis 1989, 1993; Nestle 1987, 1992; Newton 1984; Newton & Walton 1984; Weston 1990.

6. Friends and Lovers

1. See, for example, Lesbian Mothers' Group 1987.

7. Life with Father

1. Hartmann 1981; Hochschild with Machung 1989.

2. Faludi 1991.

3. Arendell 1986.

4. Controversies about donor insemination in the gay press have focused in large part on presumed parallels between the situations of children conceived through insemination and adopted children. The conventional wisdom is that adopted children have a "natural" desire to locate their birth parents, to find out who they "really" are; it is assumed that the children of sperm donors have the same sort of biologically determined urges.

5. Because their practical situations are quite similar, I include here both mothers who have sole legal custody and those with joint legal custody but primary physical custody.

8. Lady Madonna in Court

1. Chesler 1986; Polikoff 1983; Weitzman 1985.

2. Weitzman 1985:310.

3. Arendell 1986. Single-mother families already derive little income from child and spousal awards, as numerous studies have shown. About 40% of divorced fathers are not required to make payments, and of the 60% who receive support orders, about half do not comply. See Bergmann & Roberts 1987.

4. Polikoff 1983:184.

5. Hunter & Polikoff 1976; Lewin 1981; Rivera 1987.

6. Lyons 1983.

7. Brown 1970; Browner & Lewin 1982; Chodorow 1978; Ortner 1974; Rosaldo 1974.

8. Since the nineteenth century custody law has shifted from a primary concern with parental rights (associated with the notion that children are the property of the father) first to a maternal preference (so that mothers could lose custody, particularly of children of "tender years," only if they were deemed "unfit") and then to the current standard of the "best interests of the child," purported to be gender-neutral. See Committee on the Family 1980; Weitzman 1985:36.

9. The culture increasingly views reproduction itself in this light. The interests of pregnant women and fetuses, for example, are increasingly supposed to be separate and antithetical. See Rothman 1986 and Annas 1987:13–15 for discussions of technological interventions during pregnancy and birth and recent approaches to such matters as surrogate motherhood. Michelle Stanworth (1987) has pointed to the ongoing development of guidelines to ensure that women who avail themselves of new conceptive technology are heterosexual and married. Not coincidentally, the law has come increasingly to resolve custody disputes by making mothers demonstrate their qualifications. Womanhood, as well as motherhood, must be achieved in all of these contexts.

10. Lewin 1981:7.

11. Ricketts & Achtenberg 1987; Rivera 1979.

12. E.g., Chodorow 1978:211–219; Dinnerstein 1976.

13. E.g., Roman & Haddad 1978; Silver & Silver 1981. See also the critique of these views in Polikoff 1983:183–197.

14. Rapp 1988; Stacey 1990.

15. Hartmann 1981; Hochschild with Machung 1989.

16. Hoffman 1978; Bellah et al. 1985.

17. See Roman & Haddad 1978; Ware 1982; Weitzman & Dixon 1979.

9. *Natural Achievements: Lesbian Mothers in American Culture*

1. See, for example, Bérubé 1990; Duberman, Vicinus & Chauncey 1989; Faderman 1991; Greenberg 1988; Herdt 1987; Kennedy & Davis 1993; Newton in press; Roscoe 1991; Sedgwick 1990; Weston 1991; Williams 1986; Zimmerman 1990.

2. Barth 1969; Leach 1954.

3. See Anzaldúa 1990; Butler 1990; Fuss 1989; Phelan 1989; Trinh 1989.

4. Weston 1991:223n argues, following Nungesser 1983, that "heterosexism" is a better term than "homophobia" because it avoids the implication of pathology along with related notions that antigay practices are individual quirks displayed under exceptional circumstances. "Heterosexism" emphasizes the systematic and structured oppression of lesbians and gays.

5. Pollack 1987.

6. Weston 1991.

7. Ginsburg 1989:144.

8. Clarke 1957; Gónzalez 1969; Stack 1974.

9. Ehrenreich 1989.

10. Holmes 1991.

11. Tsing 1990.

12. Weitzman 1985.

13. Petchesky 1987; Rothman 1986.

14. Kolata 1990.

15. Altman 1986; Faderman 1991; Miller 1989; Shilts 1987.

16. Stacey 1990.

17. Johnson 1988.

18. The dilemma of rights and entitlements has figured prominently in the struggles of most disadvantaged groups. See, e.g., Williams 1991.

19. See Herman n.d. This issue has stimulated considerable debate in the gay and lesbian community. In 1989 a lesbian and gay quarterly magazine ran two articles on gay marriage, one supporting and one opposing it (Ettelbrick 1989; Stoddard 1989).

20. T. Lewin 1990.

21. Ghent 1990.

22. Margolick 1990.

23. Sack 1991.

24. Feminist theory has long relied on just such a conflation to "explain" gender asymmetry. See Chodorow 1978; Dinnerstein 1976; Gilligan 1982; Ruddick 1989; Yanagisako & Collier 1987.

25. James 1991.

Works Cited

Abbott, Sidney, and Barbara Love. 1972. *Sappho Was a Right-On Woman.* New York: Stein & Day.

Achilles, Rona. 1989. Donor Insemination: The Future of a Public Secret. In *The Future of Human Reproduction*, ed. Christine Overall, pp. 105–119. Toronto: Women's Press.

Alice, Gordon, Debbie, and Mary. 1988. Lesbian Mothers. (1973.) In *For Lesbians Only: A Lesbian Separatist Anthology*, ed. Sarah Lucia Hoagland and Julia Penelope, pp. 304–306. London: Onlywomen Press.

Alpert, Jane. 1973. Mother Right: A New Feminist Theory. *Ms.*, August, pp. 52–55, 88–94.

Altman, Dennis. 1986. *AIDS in the Mind of America*. Garden City, N.Y.: Doubleday.

Annas, George. 1987. Baby M: Babies (and Justice) for Sale. *Hastings Center Report* 17(3):13–15.

Anzaldúa, Gloria. 1990. Haciendo Caras, una Entrada. In *Making Face, Making Soul: Haciendo Caras*, ed. Gloria Anzaldúa, pp. xv-xxviii. San Francisco: Aunt Lute Foundation.

Arendell, Terry. 1986. *Mothers and Divorce: Legal, Economic, and Social Dilemmas*. Berkeley: University of California Press.

Armanno, Benna F. 1973. The Lesbian Mother: Her Right to Child Custody. *Golden Gate Law Review* 4(1):1–18.

Barth, Fredrik, ed. 1969. *Ethnic Groups and Boundaries*. Boston: Little, Brown.

Basile, R.A. 1974. Lesbian Mothers. *Women's Rights Law Reporter* 2(3).

Beauvoir, Simone de. 1952. *The Second Sex*. New York: Knopf.

Bellah, Robert N., Richard Madsen, William M. Sullivan, Ann Swidler, and Steven M. Tipton. 1985. *Habits of the Heart: Individualism and Commitment in American Life*. Berkeley: University of California Press.

Bergmann, B. R., and M. D. Roberts. 1987. Income for the Single Parent: Child Support, Work, and Welfare. In *Gender in the Workplace*, ed. Clair

Brown and Joseph A. Pechman, pp. 247–270. Washington, D.C.: Brookings Institution.

Bérubé, Allan. 1990. *Coming Out under Fire: The History of Gay Men and Women in World War II.* New York: Free Press.

Berzon, B. 1978. Sharing Your Lesbian Identity with Your Children. In *Our Right to Love: A Lesbian Resource Book*, ed. Ginny Vida, pp. 69–77. Englewood Cliffs, N.J.: Prentice Hall.

Boggan, E. C., et al. 1975. *The Rights of Gay People.* New York: Avon.

Boissevain, Jeremy. 1974. *Friends of Friends.* New York: St. Martin's Press.

Bott, Elizabeth 1971. *Family and Social Network: Roles, Norms, and External Relationships in Ordinary Urban Families.* New York: Free Press.

Bozett, Frederick W., ed. 1987. *Gay and Lesbian Parents.* New York: Praeger.

Brandwein, R. A., C. A. Brown, and E. M. Fox. 1974. Women and Children Last: The Situation of Divorced Mothers and Their Families. *Journal of Marriage and the Family* 36:498–514.

Brown, Judith K. 1970. A Note on the Division of Labor by Sex. *American Anthropologist* 72:1073–1078.

Browner, Carole. 1979. Abortion Decision Making: Some Findings from Colombia. *Studies in Family Planning* 10:96–106.

Browner, Carole, and Ellen Lewin. 1982. Female Altruism Reconsidered: The Virgin Mary as Economic Woman. *American Ethnologist* 9(1):61–75.

Browner, Carole H., and Nancy Ann Press. 1991. The Normalization of Prenatal Screening: Women's Acquiescence to the Alpha-Fetoprotein Blood Test. Paper prepared for Wenner-Gren Foundation for Anthropological Research Symposium no. 113, Teresopolis, Brazil.

Brownmiller, Susan. 1975. *Against Our Will: Men, Women, and Rape.* New York: Simon & Schuster.

Burris, Barbara. 1973. The Fourth World Manifesto. In *Radical Feminism.* ed. Anne Koedt, Ellen Levine, and Anita Rapone, pp. 322–357. New York: Quadrangle.

Butler, Judith. 1990. *Gender Trouble: Feminism and the Subversion of Identity.* New York: Routledge.

Canaan, Andrea. 1987. God Bless the Child. In *Politics of the Heart: A Lesbian Parenting Anthology*, ed. Sandra J. Pollack and Jeanne Vaughn, pp. 279–285. Ithaca, N.Y.: Firebrand Books.

Caprio, Frank S. 1967. *Female Homosexuality.* New York: Citadel Press.

Cassell, Joan. 1977. *A Group Called Women: Sisterhood and Symbolism in the Feminist Movement.* New York: David McKay.

Chasnoff, Deborah, and Kim Klausner. 1986. *Choosing Children*. Film distributed by Cambridge Documentary Films, Cambridge, Mass.

Cherlin, Andrew. 1981. *Marriage, Divorce, Remarriage*. Cambridge: Harvard University Press.

Chesler, Phyllis. 1986. *Mothers on Trial*. New York: McGraw-Hill.

Chodorow, Nancy. 1974. Family Structure and Feminine Personality. In *Woman, Culture, and Society*, ed. Michelle Z. Rosaldo and Louise Lamphere, pp. 43–66. Stanford: Stanford University Press.

——. 1978. *The Reproduction of Mothering*. Berkeley: University of California Press.

Clark, Margaret, and Barbara Gallatin Anderson. 1967. *Culture and Aging: An Anthropological Study of Older Americans*. Springfield, Ill.: Charles C Thomas.

Clarke, Edith. 1957. *My Mother Who Fathered Me*. London: George Allen & Unwin.

Clausen, Jan. 1987. To Live Outside the Law You Must Be Honest: A Flommy Looks at Lesbian Parenting. In *Politics of the Heart: A Lesbian Parenting Anthology*, ed. Sandra J. Pollack and Jeanne Vaughn, pp. 333–342. Ithaca, N.Y.: Firebrand Books.

Clayton, Patricia N. 1971. Meeting the Needs of the Single-Parent Family. *Family Coordinator* 20:327–36.

Cohen, Susan, and Mary Fainsod Katzenstein. 1988. "The War over the Family Is Not over the Family." In *Feminism, Children, and the New Families*, ed. Sanford M. Dornbursch and Myra H. Strober, pp. 25–46. New York: The Guilford Press.

Collier, Jane F. 1974. Women in Politics. In *Woman, Culture, and Society*. ed. Michelle Z. Rosaldo and Louise Lamphere, pp. 67–88. Stanford: Stanford University Press.

Committee on the Family, Group for the Advancement of Psychiatry. 1980. *Divorce, Child Custody, and the Family*. San Francisco: Jossey-Bass.

Corea, Gena. 1985. *The Mother Machine: Reproductive Technologies from Artificial Insemination to Artificial Wombs*. New York: Harper & Row.

Cory, Donald Webster. 1965. *The Lesbian in America*. New York: McFadden-Bartel.

Cruikshank, Margaret. 1980. *The Lesbian Path*. Monterey, Calif.: Angel Press.

Curie-Cohen, Martin, Lesleigh Luttrell, and Sander Shapiro. 1979. Current Practice of Artificial Insemination by Donor in the United States. *New England Journal of Medicine* 300(11):585–590.

Daly, Mary. 1978. *Gyn/Ecology: The Metaethics of Radical Feminism*. Boston: Beacon.

D'Andrade, Roy. 1966. Sex Differences and Cultural Institutions. In *The Development of Sex Differences*. ed. Eleanor E. Maccoby, pp. 173–204. Stanford: Stanford University Press.

Davis, Elizabeth Gould. 1971. *The First Sex*. Baltimore: Penguin.

D'Emilio, John. 1983. *Sexual Politics, Sexual Communities: The Making of a Homosexual Minority in the United States, 1940–1970*. Chicago: University of Chicago Press.

di Leonardo, Micaela. 1987. The Female World of Cards and Holidays: Women, Families, and the Work of Kinship. *Signs* 12(3):440–454.

Dinnerstein, Dorothy. 1976. *The Mermaid and the Minotaur: Sexual Arrangements and Human Malaise*. New York: Harper & Row.

Duberman, Martin Bauml, Martha Vicinus, and George Chauncey, Jr., eds. 1989. *Hidden from History: Reclaiming the Gay and Lesbian Past*. New York: New American Library.

DuBois, Ellen Carol, et al. 1987. *Feminist Scholarship: Kindling in the Groves of Academe*. Urbana: University of Illinois Press.

Dworkin, Andrea. 1974. *Woman Hating*. New York: Dutton.

Echols, Alice. 1989. *Daring to Be Bad: Radical Feminism in America, 1967–1975*. Minneapolis: University of Minnesota Press.

Editors of the Harvard Law Review. 1989. *Sexual Orientation and the Law*. Cambridge: Harvard University Press.

Ehrenreich, Barbara. 1989. *Fear of Falling: The Inner Life of the Middle Class*. New York: Pantheon.

Eichler, Margrit. 1982. *Nonsexist Research Methods: A Practical Guide*. Boston: Allen & Unwin.

Eisenstein, Hester. 1983. *Contemporary Feminist Thought*. Boston: G. K. Hall.

Escoffier, Jeffrey. 1990. Inside the Ivory Closet. *Out/Look* 10:40–48.

Ettelbrick, Paula L. 1989. Since When Is Marriage a Path to Liberation? *Out/Look*, Fall, pp. 8–17.

Fabe, Marilyn, and Norma Wikler. 1979. *Up Against the Clock*. New York: Random House.

Faderman, Lillian. 1991. *Odd Girls and Twilight Lovers: A History of Lesbian Life in Twentieth-Century America*. New York: Columbia University Press.

Faludi, Susan. 1991. *Backlash: The Undeclared War against American Women*. New York: Crown.

Farrell, Sherrie, John Gordon Hill, and Peter M. Bruce. 1973. *Sandy and Madeleine's Family* (film). San Francisco: Multi Media Resource Center.

Firestone, Shulamith. 1970. *The Dialectic of Sex: The Case for Feminist Revolution*. New York: William Morrow.

Firth, Raymond. 1951. *Elements of Social Organization*. London: Watts.

Fuss, Diana. 1989. *Essentially Speaking: Feminism, Nature, and Difference*. New York: Routledge.

Gagnon, John J., and William Simon. 1973. A Conformity Greater than Deviance: The Lesbian. In *Sexual Conduct*, pp. 176–216. Chicago: Aldine.

Gambill, Sue. 1987. Love in Motion. In *Politics of the Heart: A Lesbian Parenting Anthology*, ed. Sandra J. Pollack and Jeanne Vaughn, pp. 296–300. Ithaca, N.Y.: Firebrand Books.

Gelman, David, et al. 1992. Born or Bred? *Newsweek* February 24:46–53.

Gerson, Kathleen. 1985. *Hard Choices: How Women Decide about Work, Career, and Motherhood*. Berkeley: University of California Press.

Ghent, Janet Silver. 1990. New Spin on the American Family: Gay, Straight Parents Share Joys, Chores. *Oakland Tribune*, June 20, pp. D1–2.

Gibson, Gifford Guy. 1977. *By Her Own Admission: A Lesbian Mother's Fight to Keep Her Son*. Garden City, N.Y.: Doubleday.

Gilligan, Carol. 1982. *In a Different Voice*. Cambridge: Harvard University Press.

Ginsburg, Faye D. 1989. *Contested Lives: The Abortion Debate in an American Community*. Berkeley: University of California Press.

Gonzalez, Nancie L. Solien. 1969. *Black Carib Household Structure*. Seattle: University of Washington Press.

Goodale, Jane C. 1971. *Tiwi Wives: A Study of the Women of Melville Island, North Australia*. Seattle: University of Washington Press.

Goode, William J. 1956. *Women in Divorce*. New York: Free Press.

Goodman, Bernice. 1973. The Lesbian Mother. *American Journal of Orthopsychiatry* 43:283–284.

Green, Richard. 1978. Sexual Identity of 37 Children Raised by Homosexual or Transsexual Parents. *American Journal of Psychiatry* 135(6):692–697.

Greenberg, David F. 1988. *The Construction of Homosexuality*. Chicago: University of Chicago Press.

Griffin, Susan. 1978. *Woman and Nature: The Roaring Inside Her*. New York: Harper & Row.

Hanmer, Jalna. 1983. Reproductive Technology: The Future for Women? In *Machina Ex Dea: Feminist Perspectives on Technology*, ed. Joan Rothschild, pp. 183–197. New York: Pergamon.

Hanscombe, Gillian E., and Jackie Forster. 1981. *Rocking the Cradle: Lesbian Mothers, a Challenge in Family Living*. London: Peter Owen.

Harding, Sandra, ed. 1987. *Feminism and Methodology*. Bloomington: Indiana University Press.

Harrington, Michael. 1962. *The Other America: Poverty in the United States*. New York: Macmillan.

Harrison, Bennett, and Barry Bluestone. 1988. *The Great U-Turn: Corporate Restructuring and the Polarizing of America*. New York: Basic Books.

Hartmann, Heidi I. 1981. The Family as the Locus of Gender, Class, and Political Struggle: The Example of Housework. *Signs* 6(3):366–394.

———. 1987. Changes in Women's Economic and Family Roles in Post–World War II United States. In *Women, Households, and the Economy*, ed. Lourdes Beneria and Catharine R. Stimpson, pp. 33–64. New Brunswick, N.J.: Rutgers University Press.

Herdt, Gilbert H. 1987. *Guardians of the Flutes: Idioms of Masculinity*. New York: Columbia University Press.

Herman, Ellen. N.d. It's All in the Family: Lesbian Motherhood Meets Popular Psychology. Unpublished paper.

Herzog, Elizabeth, and Cecilia E. Sudia. 1970. *Boys in Fatherless Families*. For Office of Child Development, Children's Bureau, Department of Health, Education, and Welfare. Washington, D.C.: U.S. Government Printing Office.

Hitchens, Donna. 1979. Social Attitudes, Legal Standards, and Personal Trauma in Child Custody Cases. *Journal of Homosexuality* 5:89–95.

Hochschild, Arlie, with Anne Machung. 1989. *The Second Shift*. New York: Viking.

Hoeffer, Beverly. 1981. Children's Acquisition of Sex-Role Behavior in Lesbian-Mother Families. *American Journal of Orthopsychiatry* 51(3):536–543.

Hoffman, Lois W. 1978. Effects of the First Child on the Woman's Role. In *The First Child and Family Formation*, ed. Warren B. Miller and Lucile F. Newman, pp. 340–367. Chapel Hill: Carolina Population Center.

Hoffman, Martin. 1968. *The Gay World: Male Homosexuality and the Social Creation of Evil*. New York: Basic Books.

Holmes, Steven A. 1991. Unlikely Union Arises to Press Family Issues. *New York Times*, May 1, p. A12.

Hornstein, Francie. 1984. Children by Donor Insemination: A New Choice for Lesbians. In *Test-Tube Women: What Future for Motherhood?* ed. Rita Arditti, Renate Duelli Klein, and Shelley Monden, pp. 373–381. London: Pandora.

Hotvedt, Mary, and Jane Mandel. 1982. Children of Lesbian Mothers. In *Homosexuality: Social, Psychological, and Biological Issues*, ed. W. Paul, J. Weinrich, J.Gonsiorek, and M. Hotvedt, pp. 275–285. Beverly Hills, Calif.: Sage.

Hunter, Nan, and Nancy D. Polikoff. 1976. Custody Rights of Lesbian Mothers: Legal Theory and Litigation Strategy. *Buffalo Law Review* 25(691).

James, Caryn. 1991. A Baby Boom on TV as Biological Clocks Cruelly Tick Away. *New York Times*, October 16, pp. B1, B7.

Johnson, Colleen Leahy. 1988. *Ex Familia: Grandparents, Parents, and Children Adjust to Divorce*. New Brunswick, N.J.: Rutgers University Press.

Johnston, Jill. 1973. *Lesbian Nation: The Feminist Solution*. New York: Simon & Schuster.

Jones, Kathleen B. 1991. The Trouble with Authority. *Differences* 3(1):104–127.

Jullion, Jeanne. 1977. Lesbian Custody Case. *Plexus* 4(3):1.

——. 1985. *Long Way Home: The Odyssey of a Lesbian Mother and Her Children*. San Francisco: Cleis.

Kennedy, Elizabeth Lapovsky, and Madeline Davis. 1989. The Reproduction of Butch-Fem Roles: A Social Constructionist Approach. In *Passion and Power: Sexuality in History*, ed. Kathy Peiss and Christina Simmons with Robert Padgug, pp. 241–256. Philadelphia: Temple University Press.

——. 1993. *Boots of Leather, Slippers of Gold: The History of a Lesbian Community*. New York: Routledge.

King, Deborah. 1988. Multiple Jeopardy, Multiple Consciousness: The Context of a Black Feminist Ideology. *Signs* 14(1):42–72.

Kirkpatrick, Martha, Katherine Smith, and Ron Roy. 1981. Lesbian Mothers and Their Children: A Comparative Study. *American Journal of Orthopsychiatry* 51(3):545–551.

Kitzinger, Celia. 1987. *The Social Construction of Lesbianism*. London: Sage.

Klein, Carole. 1973. *The Single-Parent Experience*. New York: Avon.

Koedt, Anne, Ellen Levine, and Anita Rapone, eds. 1973.*Radical Feminism*. New York: Quadrangle.

Kolata, Gina. 1990. Menopause Is Found No Bar to Pregnancy. *New York Times* October 25:A1,A13.

Krieger, Susan. 1983. *The Mirror Dance: Identity in a Women's Community*. Philadelphia: Temple University Press.

Kriesberg, Louis. 1970. *Mothers in Poverty*. Chicago: Aldine.

Kuhn, Sarah, and Barry Bluestone. 1987. Economic Restructuring and the

Female Labor Market: The Impact of Industrial Change on Women. In *Women, Households, and the Economy*, ed. Lourdes Beneria and Catharine R. Stimpson, pp. 3–32. New Brunswick, N.J.: Rutgers University Press.

Lamphere, Louise. 1974. Strategies, Cooperation, and Conflict among Women in Domestic Groups. In *Woman, Culture, and Society*, ed. Michelle Z. Rosaldo and Louise Lamphere, pp. 97–112. Stanford: Stanford University Press.

———. 1987. *From Working Daughters to Working Mothers: Immigrant Women in a New England Industrial Community*. Ithaca: Cornell University Press.

Langer, G., et al. 1969. Artificial Insemination: A Study of 156 Successful Cases. *International Journal of Fertility* 14(3):232–240.

Lasker, Judith N., and Susan Borg. 1987. *In Search of Parenthood: Coping with Infertility and High-Tech Conception*. Boston: Beacon.

Leach, E. R. 1954. *Political Systems of Highland Burma*. Boston: Beacon.

Lefkowitz, Rochelle, and Ann Withorn, eds. 1986. *For Crying Out Loud: Women and Poverty in the United States*. New York: Pilgrim Press.

Lesbian Mothers' Group. 1987. Our Lovers Will Never Be Fathers, but Our Community Can Be Our Family. In *Politics of the Heart: A Lesbian Parenting Anthology*, ed. Sandra Pollack and Jeanne Vaughn, pp. 289–295. Ithaca, N.Y.: Firebrand Books.

Lewin, Ellen. 1974. Mothers and Children: Latin American Immigrants in San Francisco. Ph.D. dissertation, Stanford University.

———. 1981. Lesbianism and Motherhood: Implications for Child Custody. *Human Organization* 40(1):6–14.

———. 1985. By Design: Reproductive Strategies and the Meaning of Motherhood. In *The Sexual Politics of Reproduction*, ed. Hilary Homans, pp. 123–138. London: Gower.

———. 1991. Writing Lesbian and Gay Culture: What the Natives Have to Say for Themselves. *American Ethnologist* 18(4):786–792.

Lewin, Tamar. 1990. Suit over Death Benefits Asks, What Is a Family? *New York Times*, September 21, pp. B1, B9.

Lyons, Terrie A. 1983. Lesbian Mothers' Custody Fears. In *Women Changing Therapy*, ed. Joan H. Robbins and Rachel J. Siegel, pp. 231–240. New York: Haworth.

McGuire, Maureen, and Nancy Alexander. 1985. Artificial Insemination of Single Women. *Fertility and Sterility* 43:182–184.

Margolick, David. 1990. Lesbians' Custody Fights Test Family Law Frontier. *New York Times*, July 4, pp. 1, 10.

Margolis, Maxine L. 1984. *Mothers and Such: Views of American Women and Why They Changed*. Berkeley: University of California Press.

Martin, Del, and Phyllis Lyon. 1972. *Lesbian/Woman*. New York: Bantam.

Mascia-Lees, Frances E., Patricia Sharpe, and Colleen Ballerino Cohen. 1989. The Postmodernist Turn in Anthropology: Cautions from a Feminist Perspective. *Signs* 15(1):7–33.

Miller, Neil. 1989. *In Search of Gay America: Women and Men in a Time of Change*. New York: Atlantic Monthly Press.

Miller, W. G. 1966. Characteristics of Homosexually Involved Incarcerated Females. *Journal of Consulting Psychology* 30:193–198.

Millett, Kate. 1970. *Sexual Politics*. Garden City, N.Y.: Doubleday.

Mitchell, Juliet. 1971. *Woman's Estate*. New York: Pantheon.

Morgan, Robin, ed. 1970. *Sisterhood Is Powerful: An Anthology of Writings from the Women's Liberation Movement*. New York: Vintage.

Muller, Herman J. 1961. Human Evolution by Voluntary Choice of Germ Plasm. *Science* 134(3480):643–649.

Nelson, Cynthia. 1974. Public and Private Politics: Women in the Middle Eastern World. *American Ethnologist* 1(3):551–563.

Nestle, Joan. 1987. *A Restricted Country*. Ithaca, N.Y.: Firebrand Books.

——, ed. 1992. *The Persistent Desire: A Femme-Butch Reader*. Boston: Alyson.

Newsweek. 1990. The Future of Gay America. March 12, p. 21 (cited in Faderman 1991:309,n.3).

Newton, Esther. 1984. The Mythic Mannish Lesbian: Radclyffe Hall and the New Woman. *Signs* 9(4):557–575.

——. In press. *Cherry Grove, Fire Island: Sixty Years in America's First Gay and Lesbian Town*. Boston: Beacon.

Newton, Esther, and Shirley Walton. 1984. The Misunderstanding: Toward a More Precise Sexual Vocabulary. In *Pleasure and Danger: Exploring Female Sexuality*, ed. Carole S. Vance, pp. 242–250. Boston: Routledge & Kegan Paul.

Nungesser, Lon G. 1983. *Homosexual Acts, Actors, and Identities*. New York: Praeger.

Oddone, Maureen. 1977. Going Public with a Private Hell: One Lesbian Mother's Custody Battle. *Advocate* 224:34–35.

Ortner, Sherry B. 1974. Is Female to Male as Nature Is to Culture? In *Woman, Culture, and Society*, ed. Michelle Z. Rosaldo and Louise Lamphere, pp. 67–88. Stanford: Stanford University Press.

——. 1984. Theory in Anthropology since the Sixties. *Comparative Studies in Society and History* 26(1):126–166.

Osman, Shelomo. 1972. My Stepfather Is a She. *Family Process* 11:209–218.

Perin, Constance. 1988. *Belonging in America: Reading between the Lines.* Madison: University of Wisconsin Press.

Personal Narratives Group, eds. 1989. *Interpreting Women's Lives: Feminist Theory and Personal Narratives.* Bloomington: Indiana University Press.

Petchesky, Rosalind Pollack. 1987. Foetal Images: The Power of Visual Culture in the Politics of Reproduction. In *Reproductive Technologies: Gender, Motherhood, and Medicine,* ed. Michelle Stanworth, pp. 57–80. Minneapolis: University of Minnesota Press.

Phelan, Shane. 1989. *Identity Politics: Lesbian Feminism and the Limits of Community.* Philadelphia: Temple University Press.

Pies, Cheri. 1985. *Considering Parenthood: A Workbook for Lesbians.* San Francisco: Spinsters Ink.

Polikoff, Nancy D. 1983. Gender and Child-Custody Determinations: Exploding the Myths. In *Families, Politics, and Public Policy: A Feminist Dialogue on Women and the State,* ed. Irene Diamond, pp. 183–202. New York: Longman.

Pollack, Sandra. 1987. Lesbian Mothers: A Lesbian-Feminist Perspective on Research. In *Politics of the Heart: A Lesbian Parenting Anthology,* ed. Sandra Pollack and Jeanne Vaughn, pp. 316–324. Ithaca, N.Y.: Firebrand Books.

Pollack, Sandra, and Jeanne Vaughn, eds. 1987. *Politics of the Heart: A Lesbian Parenting Anthology.* Ithaca, N.Y.: Firebrand Books.

Ponse, Barbara. 1978. *Identities in the Lesbian World: The Social Construction of Self.* Westport, Conn.: Greenwood.

Rapp, Rayna. 1987. Toward a Nuclear Freeze? The Gender Politics of Euro-American Kinship Analysis. In *Gender and Kinship: Essays toward a Unified Analysis,* ed. Jane Fishburne Collier and Sylvia Junko Yanagisako, pp. 119–131. Stanford: Stanford University Press.

———. 1988. Is the Legacy of Second-Wave Feminism Postfeminism? *Socialist Review* 97:31–37.

———. 1990. Constructing Amniocentesis: Maternal and Medical Discourses. In *Uncertain Terms: Negotiating Gender in American Culture,* ed. Faye Ginsburg and Anna Lowenhaupt Tsing, pp. 28–42. Boston: Beacon.

Reiter, Rayna R., ed. 1975. *Toward an Anthropology of Women.* New York: Monthly Review.

Rich, Adrienne. 1976. *Of Woman Born: Motherhood as Experience and Institution.* New York: Norton.

——. 1980. Compulsory Heterosexuality and Lesbian Existence. *Signs* 5(4): 631–660.

Ricketts, Wendell, and Roberta Achtenberg. 1987. The Adoptive and Foster Gay and Lesbian Parent. In *Gay and Lesbian Parents*, ed. Frederick W. Bozett, pp. 89–111. New York: Praeger.

Riley, Claire. 1988. American Kinship: A Lesbian Account. *Feminist Issues* 8(2):75–94.

Riley, Glenda. 1991. *Divorce: An American Tradition*. New York: Oxford University Press.

Riley, Marilyn. 1975. The Avowed Lesbian Mother and Her Right to Child Custody: A Constitutional Challenge That Can No Longer Be Denied. *San Diego Law Review* 12:799.

Rivera, Rhonda R. 1979. Our Straight-Laced Judges: The Legal Position of Homosexual Persons in the United States. *Hastings Law Journal* 30: 799.

——. 1987. Legal Issues in Gay and Lesbian Parenting. In *Gay and Lesbian Parents*, ed. Frederick W. Bozett, pp. 199–227. New York: Praeger.

Roberts, Helen, ed. 1981. *Doing Feminist Research*. London: Routledge & Kegan Paul.

Robinson, Susan, and H.F. Pizer. 1985. *How to Have a Baby without a Man*. New York: Simon & Schuster.

Rogers, Susan Carol. 1975. Female Forms of Power and the Myth of Male Dominance: A Model of Female/Male Interaction in Peasant Society. *American Ethnologist* 2(4):727–756.

Roman, Mel, and William Haddad. 1978. *The Disposable Parent*. New York: Holt, Rinehart & Winston.

Rosaldo, Michelle Z. 1974. Woman, Culture, and Society: A Theoretical Overview. In *Woman, Culture, and Society*, ed. Michelle Z. Rosaldo and Louise Lamphere, pp. 17–42. Stanford: Stanford University Press.

Rosaldo, Michelle Z., and Louise Lamphere, eds. 1974. *Woman, Culture and Society*. Stanford: Stanford University Press.

Rosaldo, Renato. 1989. *Culture and Truth: The Remaking of Social Analysis*. Boston: Beacon.

Roscoe, Will. 1991. *The Zuni Man-Woman*. Albuquerque: University of New Mexico Press.

Rosen, David H. 1974. *Lesbianism: A Study of Female Homosexuality*. Springfield, Ill.: Charles C Thomas.

Ross, Heather L., and Isabel V. Sawhill. 1975. *Time of Transition: The Growth of Families Headed by Women*. Washington, D.C.: Urban Institute.

Rothman, Barbara Katz. 1986. *The Tentative Pregnancy: Prenatal Diagnosis and the Future of Motherhood.* New York: Viking.

Ruddick, Sara. 1989. *Maternal Thinking: Toward a Politics of Peace.* Boston: Beacon.

Ruzek, Sheryl Burt. 1978. *The Women's Health Movement: Feminist Alternatives to Medical Control.* New York: Praeger.

Sack, Kevin. 1991. Crux of Visitation Case: Definition of Parenthood. *New York Times,* March 24, pp. 20.

Sargent, Carolyn, and Nancy Stark. 1989. Childbirth Education and Childbirth Models: Parental Perspectives on Control, Anesthesia, and Technological Intervention in the Birth Process. *Medical Anthropology Quarterly* n.s. 3:36–51.

Schneider, David M. 1968. *American Kinship: A Cultural Account.* Englewood Cliffs, N.J.: Prentice Hall.

Schneider, David M., and Raymond T. Smith. 1973. *Class Differences and Sex Roles in American Kinship and Family Structure.* Englewood Cliffs, N.J.: Prentice Hall.

Sedgwick, Eve Kosofsky. 1990. *Epistemology of the Closet.* Berkeley: University of California Press.

Shah, Diane K., with Linda Walters. 1979. Lesbian Mothers. *Newsweek,* February 12, pp. 1.

Shilts, Randy. 1987. *And the Band Played On: Politics, People, and the AIDS Epidemic.* New York: St. Martin's Press.

Sidel, Ruth. 1986. *Women and Children Last: The Plight of Poor Women in Affluent America.* New York: Viking.

Silver, Gerald A., and Myrna Silver. 1981. *Weekend Fathers.* Los Angeles: Stratford.

Smart, Carol. 1990. "There Is of Course the Distinction Dictated by Nature": Law and the Problem of Paternity. In *Ethical Issues in the New Reproductive Technologies,* ed. Richard T. Hull, pp. 69–86. Belmont, Calif.: Wadsworth.

Snitow, Ann. 1991. Motherhood: Reclaiming the Demon Texts. *Ms.,* May/June, pp. 34–37.

Stacey, Judith. 1990. *Brave New Families: Stories of Domestic Upheaval in Late-Twentieth Century America.* New York: Basic Books.

Stack, Carol. 1974. *All Our Kin: Strategies for Survival in a Black Community.* New York: Harper & Row.

Stanley, Julia Penelope, and Susan J. Wolfe. 1980. *The Coming Out Stories.* Watertown, Mass.: Persephone Press.

Stanworth, Michelle. 1987. Reproductive Technologies and the Deconstruction of Motherhood. In *Reproductive Technologies: Gender, Motherhood, and Medicine*, ed. Michelle Stanworth, pp. 10–35. Minneapolis: University of Minnesota Press.

Steedman, Carolyn Kay. 1987. *Landscape for a Good Woman: A Story of Two Lives*. New Brunswick, N.J.: Rutgers University Press.

Stern, Susan. 1979. A Different Type of Baby Boom in S.F.: Artificial Insemination for Lesbians. *Synapse*, December 6, pp. 1, 4–5.

Stevens, Mary L. 1978. Lesbian Mothers in Transition. In *Our Right to Love: A Lesbian Resource Book*, ed. Ginny Vida, pp. 207–211. Englewood Cliffs, N.J.: Prentice Hall.

Stoddard, Thomas B. 1989. Why Gay People Should Seek the Right to Marry. *Out/Look*, Fall, pp. 8–17.

Strong, Carson, and Jay Schinfeld. 1984. The Single Woman and Artificial Insemination by Donor. *Journal of Reproductive Medicine* 29:293–99.

Swanson, D. W., S. D. Loomis, R. Lukesh, R. Cronin, and J. Smith. 1972. Clinical Features of the Female Homosexual Patient: A Comparison with the Heterosexual Patient. *Journal of Nervous and Mental Disease*. 155:119–124.

Thompson, C., B. R. McCandless, and B. P. Strickland. 1971. Personal Adjustment of Male and Female Homosexuals and Heterosexuals. *Journal of Abnormal Psychology* 78:237–240.

Tocqueville, Alexis de. 1956. *Democracy in America*. New York: New American Library.

Trinh T. Minh-ha. 1989. *Woman, Native, Other*. Bloomington: Indiana University Press.

Tsing, Anna Lowenhaupt. 1990. Monster Stories: Women Charged with Perinatal Endangerment. In *Uncertain Terms: Negotiating Gender in American Culture*, ed. Faye Ginsburg and Anna Lowenhaupt Tsing, pp. 282–299. Boston: Beacon.

Van Gelder, Lindsay. 1976. Lesbian Custody: A Tragic Day in Court. *Ms.*, September, pp. 72–73.

Varenne, Henri. 1977. *Americans Together: Structured Diversity in a Midwestern Town*. New York: Teachers College Press.

Vaughn, Jeanne. 1987. A Question of Survival. In *Politics of the Heart: A Lesbian Parenting Anthology*, ed. Sandra J. Pollack and Jeanne Vaughn, pp. 20–28. Ithaca, N.Y.: Firebrand Books.

Vida, Ginny, ed. 1978. *Our Right to Love: A Lesbian Resource Book*. Englewood Cliffs, N.J.: Prentice Hall.

Vincent, Clark E. 1962. *Unmarried Mothers*. New York: Free Press.

Ware, C. 1982. *Sharing Parenthood after Divorce*. New York: Viking.

Weeks, R. B., A. Derdeyn, and M. Langman. 1975. Two Cases of Children of Homosexuals. *Child Psychology and Human Development* 6: 26–32.

Weiner, Annette B. 1976. *Women of Value, Men of Renown: New Perspectives in Trobriand Exchange*. Austin: University of Texas Press.

Weiss, Robert S. 1975. *Marital Separation*. New York: Basic Books.

——. 1979. *Going It Alone*. New York: Basic Books.

Weitzman, Lenore. 1985. *The Divorce Revolution: The Unexpected Social and Economic Consequences for Women and Children in America*. New York: Free Press.

Weitzman, Lenore, and Ruth Dixon. 1979. Child Custody Awards: Legal Standards and Empirical Patterns for Child Custody, Support, and Visitation after Divorce. *UC Davis Law Review* 12:473–521.

Weston, Kath. 1990. Do Clothes Make the Woman?: Butch/Fem and Gendered Transformation. Paper presented at annual meetings of American Anthropological Association, New Orleans.

——. 1991. *Families We Choose: Lesbians, Gays, Kinship*. New York: Columbia University Press.

Whitten, Norman E., Jr., and Dorothea S. Whitten. 1972. Social Strategies and Social Relationships. *Annual Review of Anthropology* 1:247–270.

Williams, Patricia J. 1991. *The Alchemy of Race and Rights*. Cambridge: Harvard University Press.

Williams, Walter L. 1986. *The Spirit and the Flesh: Sexual Diversity in American Indian Culture*. Boston: Beacon.

Wolf, Deborah Goleman. 1979. *The Lesbian Community*. Berkeley: University of California Press.

Wolf, Margery. 1972. *Women and the Family in Rural Taiwan*. Stanford: Stanford University Press.

Wolff, Charlotte. 1971. *Love between Women*. New York: Harper & Row.

Yanagisako, Sylvia Junko. 1977. Women-Centered Kin Networks in Urban Bilateral Kinship. *American Ethnologist* 4(2):207–226.

——. 1985. *Transforming the Past: Tradition and Kinship among Japanese Americans*. Stanford: Stanford University Press.

Yanagisako, Sylvia Junko, and Jane Fishburne Collier. 1987. Toward a Unified Analysis of Gender and Kinship. In *Gender and Kinship: Essays toward a Unified Analysis*, ed. Jane Fishburne Collier and Sylvia Junko Yanagisako, pp. 14–50. Stanford: Stanford University Press.

Zheutlin, Cathy, Frances Reid, and Elizabeth Stevens. 1977. *In the Best Interests of the Children*. Film distributed by Iris Films, Berkeley, Calif.

Zimmerman, Bonnie. 1990. *The Safe Sea of Women: Lesbian Fiction, 1969–1989*. Boston: Beacon.

Zuckerman, E. 1986. Second Parent Adoption for Lesbian-Parented Families: Legal Recognition of the Other Mother. *UC Davis Law Review* 19:729, 731.

Index

Library of Congress Cataloging-in-Publication Data

Lewin, Ellen.
  Lesbian mothers : accounts of gender in American culture / Ellen
Lewin.
        p. cm. — (Anthropology of contemporary issues)
  Includes bibliographical references and index.
  ISBN 0-8014-2857-2 (cloth). — ISBN 0-8014-8099-X (paper)
    1. Lesbian mothers—United States.   2. Single mothers—United
States. I. Title. II. Series.
HQ75.53.L49 1993
306.874'3'086643—dc20   92-54977
                                                                CIP

Anthropology of Contemporary Issues

A SERIES EDITED BY

ROGER SANJEK

Sunbelt Working Mothers: Reconciling Family and Factory
  BY LOUISE LAMPHERE, PATRICIA ZAVELLA, AND FELIPE GONZALES, WITH
  PETER B. EVANS
Creativity/Anthropology
  EDITED BY SMADAR LAVIE, KIRIN NARAYAN, AND RENATO ROSALDO
Lesbian Mothers: Accounts of Gender in American Culture
  BY ELLEN LEWIN
Civilized Women: Gender and Prestige in Southeastern Liberia
  BY MARY H. MORAN
The Magic City: Unemployment in a Working-Class Community
  BY GREGORY PAPPAS
State and Family in Singapore: Restructuring an Industrial Society
  BY JANET W. SALAFF
Uneasy Endings: Daily Life in an American Nursing Home
  BY RENÉE ROSE SHIELD
Children of Circumstances: Israeli Emigrants in New York
  BY MOSHE SHOKEID
History and Power in the Study of Law: New Directions in Legal Anthropology
  EDITED BY JUNE STARR AND JANE F. COLLIER
"Getting Paid": Youth Crime and Work in the Inner City
  BY MERCER L. SULLIVAN
City of Green Benches: Growing Old in a New Downtown
  BY MARIA D. VESPERI
Renunciation and Reformulation: A Study of Conversion in an American Sect
  BY HARRIET WHITEHEAD
Upscaling Downtown: Stalled Gentrification in Washington, D.C.
  BY BRETT WILLIAMS
Women's Work and Chicano Families: Cannery Workers of the Santa Clara Valley
  BY PATRICIA ZAVELLA